D0944824

Solar Building Architecture

Solar Heat Technologies: Fundamentals and Applications
Charles A. Bankston, editor-in-chief

1. *History and Overview of Solar Heat Technologies*
Donald A. Beattie, editor

2. *Solar Resources*
Roland L. Hulstrom, editor

3. *Economic Analysis of Solar Thermal Energy Systems*
Ronald E. West and Frank Kreith, editors

4. *Fundamentals of Building Energy Dynamics*
Bruce Hunn, editor

5. *Solar Collectors, Energy Storage, and Materials*
Francis de Winter, editor

6. *Active Solar Systems*
George Löf, editor

7. *Passive Solar Buildings*
J. Douglas Balcomb and Bruce Wilcox, editors

8. *Passive Cooling*
Jeffrey Cook, editor

9. *Solar Building Architecture*
Bruce Anderson, editor

10. *Fundamentals of Concentrating Systems*
Lorin Vant-Hull, editor

11. *Distributed and Central Receiver Systems*
Lorin Vant-Hull, editor

12. *Implementation of Solar Thermal Technology*
Ronal Larson and Ronald E. West, editors

Solar Building Architecture

edited by Bruce Anderson

The MIT Press
Cambridge, Massachusetts
London, England

© 1990 Massachusetts Institute of Technology

This book was set in Times Roman by Asco Trade Typesetting Ltd., Hong Kong and was printed and bound in the United States of America.

Library of Congress Cataloging-in-Publication Data

Solar building architecture / edited by Bruce Anderson.
    p. cm.—(Solar heat technologies ; 9)
  Includes index.
  ISBN 0-263-01111-5
  1. Solar buildings—United States—Design and construction—History. 2. Solar energy—Research—United States—History.
I. Anderson, Bruce, 1947– . II. Series.
TJ809.95.S68   1988 vol. 9
[TH7413]
697'.78 s—dc20
[720'.472]   89-33602
                                                   CIP

Contents

Series Foreword

Charles A. Bankston

This series of twelve volumes summarizes research, development, and implementation of solar thermal energy conversion technologies carried out under federal sponsorship during the last eleven years of the National Solar Energy Program. During the period from 1975 to 1986 the U.S. Department of Energy's Office of Solar Heat Technologies spent more than $1.1 billion on research, development, demonstration, and technology support projects, and the National Technical Information Center added more than 30,000 titles on solar heat technologies to its holdings. So much work was done in such a short period of time that little attention could be paid to the orderly review, evaluation, and archival reporting of the significant results.

It was in response to the concern that the results of the national program might be lost that this documentation project was conceived. It was initiated in 1982 by Frederick H. Morse, director of the Office of Solar Heat Technologies, Department of Energy, who had served as technical coordinator of the 1972 NSF/NASA study "Solar Energy as a National Resource" that helped start the National Solar Energy Program. The purpose of the project has been to conduct a thorough, objective technical assessment of the findings of the federal program using leading experts from both the public and private sectors, and to document the most significant advances and findings. The resulting volumes are neither handbooks nor textbooks, but benchmark assessments of the state of technology and compendia of important results. There is a historical flavor to many of the chapters, and volume 1 of the series will offer a comprehensive overview of the programs, but the emphasis throughout is on results rather than history.

The goal of the series is to provide both a starting point for the new researcher and a reference tool for the experienced worker. It should also serve the needs of government and private-sector officials who want to see what programs have already been tried and what impact they have had. And it should be a resource for entrepreneurs whose talents lie in translating research results into practical products.

The scope of the series is broad but not universal. It is limited to solar technologies that convert sunlight to heat in order to provide energy for application in the building, industrial, and power sectors. Thus it explicitly excludes photovoltaic and biological energy conversion and such thermally driven processes as wind, hydro, and ocean thermal power. Even with this limitation, though, the series assembles a daunting amount of information. It represents the collective efforts of more than 200 authors and editors. The volumes are logically divided into those dealing with general topics such as the availability, collection, storage, and economic analysis of solar energy and those dealing with applications.

The present volume covers the role of solar energy in present-day architecture and planning. Beginning in 1973, the federal government supported most areas of solar research. The emphasis was on solar technology and on the performance of that technology when it is deployed in buildings. This technology and knowledge base is essential, but ultimately what matters most is whether and to what extent buildings actually make use of them. This requires design and planning skills and experience. In the beginning, architects and planners found it difficult to integrate solar concepts effectively into their designs, and a research program evolved to determine the "best" solar building design solutions. The emphasis of this volume, then, is on the evolution of the integration of solar concepts into overall architectural design and planning nationally, that is, on the changing nature of what has been considered the best available solutions to the use of solar energy. For further specific information on solar technologies and concepts, such as passive and active systems, readers should consult other volumes in this series.

Acknowledgments

Bruce Anderson

This series of volumes was initiated by Frederick H. Morse, director of the Office of Solar Heat Technologies, Department of Energy, and his clear vision and unwavering support kept the project moving forward through a long time schedule. In addition to his initiative to document progress that was clearly based on research in the traditional sense of that term and was funded with federal dollars, Dr. Morse also insisted that this project document progress in the area the ultimately matters most, namely, how and to what extent buildings actually make use of solar technology. This volume on solar architecture and planning is the result of his vision, and we are most grateful to him for it.

Editor-in-chief Charles Bankston, CBY Associates, Inc., provided the perfect combination of unflappable patience, tenacious persistence, organizational mastery, and sage advice. Lynda McGovern-Orr, his assistant, always made the extra offer of help, effectively clearing away barriers, keeping us organized, and doing whatever needed doing, and always cheerfully.

Paul Notari, Charles Berberich, and Nancy Reece used the fullest measure of their skills to bring the resources of the Solar Energy Research Institute to bear in processing the manuscripts in preparation for the publisher. In particular, Nancy and others with her superbly and efficiently edited each chapter.

Jack Roberts and Oscar Hillig of ETEC simplified the process of contracting with and being paid by the federal government and were very cooperative with editors and authors. The extent of their efforts, in fact, set an example for their peers in similar government positions.

There are no doubt many, many other people who worked with those who are mentioned above and who contributed to this volume. We are grateful to them all.

I thank Ellen Ruggles, Marilyn Werbinski, and Karen Cloutier for their clerical support.

Many professionals gave of their time and expertise to review drafts of the chapters. Their comments were used by the authors to improve the final material for the book. I am grateful to the following reviewers: J. M. Ayres, Ayres Associates; Mark Bohn, Solar Energy Research Institute; Frank Bridgers, Bridgers & Paxton Construction Eng.; Harvey Bryan, Massachussets Institute of Technology (MIT); Jeffrey Cook; Michael Corbett;

John Crowley, Ryan Homes, Inc.; Fred S. Dubin, Dubin-Bloome Associates; Greg Franta; Drew A. Gillett, R. G. Vanderweil Eng.; Michael Holtz, Architectural Energy Corporation; Bruce Hunn, University of Texas at Austin; Chris Johnson; Ralph Johnson, NAHB Research Foundation; Ralph Jones; Doug Kelbaugh, Kelbaugh & Lee Architects; Jan F. Kreider, University of Colorado; Frank Kreith; Ted Kurkowski, U.S. Department of Energy (DOE); George Löf, Colorado State University; Vivian Loftness, V.L.H. Associates; Peter Lunde; Michael Maybaum, Coesantini Associates; Edward Mazria, Mazria, Schiff and Associates; Allan Michaels, Argonne National Laboratory; Don Neeper, Los Alamos National Laboratory; Dave Pellish, U.S. Department of Energy (DOE); Peter Pfister, Pfister Architects; Richard Rittelman, Burt Hill Kosar Rittelmann; Richard T. Rush, American Institute of Architects; Larry Spielvogel, L. C. Spielvogel, Inc.; Bob Stromberg, Sandia National Laboratory; C. J. Swet; Didier Thomas; John Tomlinson, Oak Ridge National Laboratory; Donald Watson; Tom Vonier; Steven Weinstein, Ehrankrantz Group; Eric M. Wormser, Wormser Scientific Corp.; Bill Wright, Bill Wright and Associates; John Yellott, deceased, Arizona State University.

Finally, I thank the authors, who through their chapters share with the rest of us their most valuable possession—their knowledge and expertise.

Solar Building Architecture

1 Introduction

Bruce Anderson

1.1 Summary

The functions of buildings have evolved over centuries to meet the changing needs of society. At one time, buildings needed only to keep weather and enemies out. Today, they usually perform dozens of functions. With the advent of concern about energy resources in the 1970s, substantial research advanced the performance of a major set of these functions. The functions of buildings now include the utilization of the solar energy that strikes the exterior of buildings, use of other naturally occurring energy phenomena (such as sky radiational cooling and daylighting), and more efficient use of energy.

To design buildings that perform these functions as economically and as effectively as possible requires professional building design and engineering. This involves the careful integration of energy components, subcomponents, and systems with architectural techniques that perform the above set of functions in a way that best satisfies the program needs of the building and recognizes the myriad of other considerations that determine the final design.

This volume recognizes that most solar research focuses on solar energy components and systems as though they were "furnaces" or "air conditioning systems." Just as conventional furnaces and air conditioners (HVAC systems) are integrated into buildings and have repercussions on their design, solar energy applications also affect the way buildings and groups of buildings are planned, designed, and engineered.

Although the integration of HVAC systems with buildings is so commonplace that its impact on the building is well understood and all but taken for granted, the integration of solar applications is relatively new. For more than a decade, beginning in 1973, considerable research and development (R&D), both federal and private, was conducted on this subject. This volume summarizes that work.

1.2 Introduction

When the oil embargo began in late 1973, the word "solar" was nearly nonexistent in the construction industry. Most of the 20 or so solar buildings in existence were houses designed and built by or under the direction of inventors or engineers—not architects or builders.

As the federal government subsequently evolved its solar program, this dominance by engineers and, to a lesser extent, inventors, continued. This was natural because of the traditional role of engineers in designing HVAC systems, the emphasis on systems that could be retrofitted to existing buildings, and the bureaucratic nature of Washington, D.C., was easier for engineers to deal with than it was for architects or builders.

In fact, the natural reluctance of the construction industry to participate in federal programs was recognized early on by most government agencies involved in solar work, and they made an effort to reduce the problem. Although some programs succeeded commendably, most federal solar research programs focused on the development of high-performance technology. For the most part, the construction industry was left with the task of integrating this technology into market-acceptable buildings. Here the emphasis was on ease of construction, low first cost, operational dependability, appearance, marketability, and owner/user satisfaction—not high performance.

It was natural then, that both the efforts and the results of the national effort—in and out of government—to bring about solar architecture and planning would be two-pronged.

The technology prong was spearheaded by the federal government. Space and weapons scientists and engineers from national laboratories such as Brookhaven and Los Alamos worked with private sector research engineers and manufacturing firms to develop materials, components, and systems that could be used on new and existing buildings. The report of those efforts dominates most of the other books in this series.

This volume is dominated by the second prong—the one driven by the realities faced by the construction industry in satisfying the demands of the marketplace. Sometimes these demands required trying products and systems developed through federal research programs, and sometimes it required use of an idea that had no federal support whatsoever.

Coming on the heels of the rebelliousness of the 1960s that challenged almost every convention in society, the energy crisis in combination with rampant inflation made the 1970s the most innovative decade in the history of American construction.

In the early 1980s, energy prices softened and inflation subsided, calming the turbulent waters of crisis. The energy efficiency and solar energy techniques that have become standard practice in building design represent the enduring legacy of that creative era.

This volume is an effort to look back over that period of robust activity, to reconstruct, at least in part, how today's standard practice in solar architecture and planning is based on the research and experimentation that has occurred since 1973.

1.3   Historical Perspective—pre-1973

Contemporary architecture and urban planning are the beneficiaries of a long history in which solar energy was often considered an important design feature. Buildings and town plans constructed in ancient times by the Egyptians, Greeks, and Romans were sensitive to the benefits of solar energy. A few examples illustrate this.

The ancient cities of Priene in Asia Minor and Olynthus in Northern Greece were laid out to enable all buildings to face south to capture heat of the winter sun, despite a difficult sloping terrain. The Romans were taught, through the writings of Vitrivius and the Greeks, that buildings should be designed to benefit from the sun's thermal radiation. Recent excavations at Herculaneum, long-buried in the ashes of Mount Vesuvius, indicate that the homes had "sun rooms" facing south. There is evidence that bathing rooms were enclosed with *double glazed* windows.

The history of windows also reflects the evolution of solar buildings. For example, the Egyptian Temple of Amman at Karnak, built in 2466 BC, admitted light through a clerestory running along the central aisle of the building core. The roof covering that clerestory rested on 70-foot columns, which rose 27 feet above columns running along the sides. The Roman baths of Caracalla were designed to take advantage of solar energy to transmit heat and daylighting through large windows deep into the interior spaces.

The medieval cathedrals throughout Europe refined the early clerestory daylighting concepts to a fine art. Gothic construction enabled those impressive structures to exploit the benefits of diffused sunlight through large stained glass windows. The great Renaissance architect Palladio employed the "thermal window," to use his own expression, to transmit the sun's rays into the building interior as a key feature of his designs.

American solar architecture can trace its roots to the Southwest Indian culture. Their villages were constructed to permit each dwelling unit to enjoy full exposure to the winter sun. While the doors and windows faced south, roof construction insulated interior rooms from the long hot summer sun. The early New England "salt box" houses faced the sun and the long roof sloped steeply from front to back to provide protection from the cold winter winds.

At the beginning of this century, well before the current generation of "solar architects," a Boston architect, William Atkinson, designed a "sun house" based upon his own experiments with solar energy. He published a book entitled *The Orientation of Buildings, or Planning of Sunlight*. In the 1930s and 1940s, "solar homes" made their appearance as result of pioneering designs efforts by such well-known architects as George Fred Keck and the appearance of double pane glazings in the market.

In the 1950s the typical office building used 1,400 MJ/m^2 yr (115,000 Btu/ft^2 yr). By the early 1970s, this had more than doubled to 3,000 MJ/m^2 yr (250,000 Btu/ft^2 yr). This phenomenon was due in large part to the significant increase during the previous 20 years of the total wattage of electrical lighting used in office buildings and to ventilation requirements. To a lesser extent, it was due to greater use of glass and an increase in the number of office machines. Also, larger sized buildings, coupled with the rising air quality and comfort demands of occupants, required ever larger energy consuming mechanical systems. Again, historically low prices made energy an inconsequential consideration in the design of lighting and mechanical systems.

Solar architecture's modern scientific and research base was initiated at the Massachusetts Institute of Technology (MIT), shortly before World War II. The project used funds contributed by Dr. Godfrey L. Cabot that were designated strictly for the advancement of the use of solar energy. MIT's first three solar houses were built as test structures. A fourth, located in a Boston suburb, was designed for resale.

The architectural appearance of most pre-oil-embargo solar houses (that shaped the public perception of solar buildings) was driven by the need to accommodate solar technology rather than by the need to make solar buildings acceptable to the public. The importance of the technology to the design is evidenced by the professions of the designers and builders. Dr. Maria Telkes, who was responsible for the 1949 Dover House, in Dover, MA, was a research scientist. Ray Bliss and Mary Donovan were engineers (the Desert Grassland station, 1954, Amado, AZ, and the Tucson Laboratory, 1959, Tucson, AZ). So was Dr. George Löf (the Boulder Bungalow, 1944, Boulder, CO, and the Denver House, 1956, Denver, CO). Harry Thomason, who built several homes in Washington, DC, beginning in 1959, was an inventor and entrepreneur. Norm Saunders (the Saunders House, 1960, Weston, MA) was an eclectic inventor, as was Steve Baer (the Zome House, 1972, Corrales, NM). Bridgers and Paxton (the Bridgers and Paxton Office Building, 1956, Albuquerque, NM) was an engineering firm, the Centre Nationale de la Recherche Scientifique (the Odeillo Houses, 1956, Odeillo, France) an energy laboratory.

These buildings produced much of the basic and most valuable information about solar building performance prior to 1973. For detail and further references, see Löf, 1971; Anderson, 1973, 1976; Butti and Perlin, 1980; and Shurcliff, 1978.

1.4 State of the Art—1973–1975

In 1973, the limited data on 20–30 solar buildings around the world represented the state of the art in "solar architecture and planning" as it is ordinarily described. But, in addition—perhaps even more stimulating to the imaginations of the energy innovators and building designers in the 1970s and early 1980s—there was a staggering array of traditional climate-responsive architecture. The absence of actual performance figures of these buildings (or of their individual energy-related subsystems and components) and the lack of analytical techniques and tools made it difficult to adapt traditional ideas to contemporary buildings with much confidence in their energy performance or in their ability to provide acceptable levels of human comfort.

Simplistic analysis and considerable finger crossing, therefore, dominated the design of most of the first generation of solar buildings following the energy crisis.

In addition, the energy crisis, together with skyrocketing inflation, which was particularly acute in building construction, created a fertile ground for down-home American ingenuity. People were willing to try almost anything to save energy and to cut construction costs. The renaissance of ideas that flourished in this historically unique environment produced an astounding array of products and building designs.

1.5   Federal Involvement in Solar Architecture and Planning

The federal government responded. The preembargo federal solar research budget at the National Science Foundation (NSF) in 1973 was $13 million. The federal government spent more than half a billion dollars in the next decade on solar building-related research.

The scientific and engineering research community, not planners, architects, building engineers, builders, inventors, and do-it-yourselfers, tended to be the recipients of those dollars.

As a result, the federal priority in the early to mid-1970s was to promote high-performance technology that often was at odds with the market's need for simplicity, cost-effectiveness, and appearance. As an example of this priority, the Department of Housing and Urban Development (HUD) Solar Demonstration Program funded 11,915 housing units through its first four cycles of federally funded solar projects, but only 86 of them had passive features, according to the Government Accounting Office (GAO). In later cycles, more passive homes were included because of the success of those earlier passive projects. Energy efficiency received to financial (or other) support in the HUD program.

In the second half of the decade, as experience was gained from numerous mistakes and successes, energy building design research evolved into three predominant areas: the so-called "active" system approach; "passive" building design; and energy efficiency and conservation. The engineering and manufacturing communities, together with federal government officials, tended to rally behind active systems. Architects and other building design professionals favored passive approaches. The construction trades and the general public favored energy efficiency.

"Passive" design, in the purest sense of the word, was used to describe systems that operated only with sources of energy that strike the buildings. Invariably, however, human comfort is increased by using mechanical energy produced by sources off-site to control the performance of passive systems. The most common method is to include a fan to circulate air from a solar-heated room through the rest of a building or through thermal energy storage for later use. Many combinations of passive techniques, active systems, and mechanical power proliferated.

The phrase "hybrid systems" was coined as a catch-all term for the ideas and techniques that were not easily described by "active" and "passive."

This middle ground tended increasingly to become the norm in good building design.

The ground swell of successful, nonfederally funded grassroots work in passive design, hybrid systems, and energy efficiency eventually precipitated R&D programs at DOE that were better suited to the construction industry. From the standpoint of the building designer, this was an important step. However, research activities in active and passive each had its own DOE program manager. And each technology tended to become an end in itself, instead of a means of achieving affordable, low-energy building design. Some types of hybrid systems eventually became the responsibility of the DOE program manager for passive systems.

Energy efficiency and conservation in buildings was managed by yet another group at DOE under a different assistant secretary. Despite the compelling logic for substantial coordination and, preferably, for common program management of active, passive, energy efficient, and hybrid technologies, this approach never came to pass to any significant extent. Research that managed to cross technologies was usually a combination of passive and active or of passive and conservation. Also, these combinations usually were done because of the enlightened efforts of a program manager —without overt fanfare but with subtle game playing to avoid conflict within federal agencies. Ultimately, most of the prodigious task of architectural integration was left to the private sector, and most of this volume is about that effort.

1.6   Building Design as "Research"

The major objective in the design of buildings is to provide an environment that supports and enhances the ability of people to do whatever it is that the building is designed for. The good designer will remain true to the major objective. Energy conservation and solar energy can enhance this major objective by providing comfortable conditions for people. For the designer, then, heating and cooling and related techniques and systems are not viewed as providing heating, cooling, humidity control, and clean air, but rather are viewed as producing conditions that provide the "human comfort" levels that people need in order to accomplish whatever it is that a building is designed for. In some buildings and for some designers, the energy techniques and systems seem to have an unusually large effect on the overall design. In others, the integration is subtle and little noticed.

Given this major objective of building designers, is it fair or realistic to suggest that, like the scientist, research engineer and product developer, the building designer also perform "research" per se? In a compendium such as this, which documents research progress in the field of solar energy, should a volume that strives to document the research progress in the field of architecture and planning be included?

These are appropriate questions, and important ones. They are appropriate because the work of building designers is not thought, typically, to include "research," and they are fair questions from people who do not design buildings. Also, this compendium is about research, so what is included certainly should represent research.

The questions are important because the answer helps to explain, for nonbuilding designers, the design process and the role that research plays in it. The answer also helps to explain the rather unique and exciting role that building designers played in advancing the state of the art of energy conservation and solar energy in buildings.

Research, as it is frequently defined, involves defining a problem for the purpose of solving it. It invariably requires that a method or approach be established to solve it. It requires that information be gathered and analyzed—either new information produced by the researcher or information that exists elsewhere. In any event, the information is rearranged, manipulated, and analyzed, sometimes using numerical formulas and sometimes using the verbal or oral cognitive and integration functions of our minds. Sometimes a single pass through the various steps of the process produces a satisfactory answer, but usually it is an iterative process, requiring many passes, each building on the results of previous ones.

Building designers apply a variation of this process to the design of buildings. Designers begin with a "program" that defines in considerable detail what the final building must achieve if it is to prove satisfactory. If alternative energy techniques are to be included, substantial amounts of information must be gathered about weather, the performance of various energy techniques, the costs of constructing and operating them, and the projected energy performance of the building. The designer analyzes this information, making trade-offs among them and also between energy considerations and the enormous number of other program requirements.

Many, many iterations are typical in the design of a building before a final solution is selected.

But the research process does not end with a building's construction. The information on which a building designer bases decisions rarely is complete. Invariably questions, often important ones, remain unanswered. This was particularly true of solar related techniques in the 1970s. These were included in buildings oftentimes without accurate knowledge about how they would perform, how durable they were, or whether and to what extent the public would accept them. Therefore, follow-up research and data collection often is a necessary component in the design.

This volume, then, does cover research. It is research that, for the most part, is performed by building designers in the private sector.

1.7   Social Forces That Influence Solar Architecture and Planning

As the economic issues surrounding energy policy began to receive public attention, many people also came to believe that solar (and conservation and other renewable energy sources) offered social benefits. Resulting social pressures influenced the development of solar architecture. For example, energy self-sufficiency—a return to the land, independence from electric utilities—was a dominant theme. Solar buildings and communities that offered this hope ignited a dream in the hearts and minds of many Americans.

Energy conservation and solar energy, along with other forms of renewable energy, have the distinct advantage of being environmentally clean. Even for the nonenvironmentalist, this gives solar buildings an edge when compared with other methods of heating, cooling, and lighting structures.

Capturing the sun's heat for reducing energy bills seems a simple and inexpensive opportunity—deceptively so. Thousands of people have tried, mostly in vain, to make that opportunity available to those who could least afford their energy bills—the poor and destitute.

This is because the simplicity of solar heating principles makes it appear that there must be inexpensive techniques that would make it eminently accessible to every citizen's home regardless of financial means. If this were true, the results, it was believed, could work toward helping to achieve social and economic equity. Political pressure grew in the mid-1970s to bring ethnic minorities, women, and the disenfranchised into a tangible portion of government programs and the rapidly emerging solar industry.

These forces hoped to create solar concepts and products that were accessible to the less educated and poor.

What does all of this have to do with a book about solar architecture and planning in a compendium of government-sponsored solar research? Plenty. For it was primarily in housing—new construction as well as retrofitted—where these social issues were sorted out. Whether it was the construction of solar retrofits, solar weatherization projects of Community Action Programs, or good old-fashioned American ingenuity in the construction of new homes, experimentation was at fever pitch. A more thorough historical review would reveal a vast array of exciting techniques and products created by this (sometimes fringe) public effort. Batch and integral water heaters and movable window insulation are among the most obvious.

As energy costs and general overall inflation waned, and as solar systems proved not to be as simple and inexpensive as had been hoped, and as the country's social agenda shifted from issues of social equity to those of self-interest and from conservation to consumption, solar energy lost its appeal as a vehicle for bringing about social change.

1.8   Solar Tax Credits

Instead of growing naturally out of traditional building design and construction practice, the solar building industry evolved out of a federally sponsored R&D program and organized itself to maximize the sales of products that capitalized on solar tax credits.

The tax credit legislation provided rebates for products that did nothing for a building except to provide solar energy. It prohibited rebates for products and applications that performed functions in addition to providing solar energy. Thus, products such as collectors that were an integral part of walls or roofs, solar greenhouses that had multiple functions, and heat storage integral with a building's structure (such as concrete walls or floors) were excluded from tax credits and ignored by the industry that was organizing itself to supply solar products to the construction field.

Tax credit legislation dovetailed with federal research programs that developed few products that went much beyond doing anything for a building except to provide solar energy. Thus, typical solar collectors and their accompanying control, storage, and transport systems that could be produced in a factory and attached to relatively standard buildings emerged to dominate the solar industry.

Unfortunately, adding tax-credit-acceptable solar products to buildings was too often like adding sails to the *Queen Mary*. It could be done, but it was not always the most acceptable solution, and the industry that did it was unable to sustain itself when energy prices fell (even though they remained very high by historical standards) and when the solar tax credits expired December 31, 1985.

Nor were the products that emerged to dominate the solar industry necessarily the most effective. They did not need to be effective. The more they cost, the greater the tax credit received by the customer. And the more they cost, the higher the sales commission that could be paid to the salesperson; the higher the sales commission, the better the sales talent that could be attracted to the industry, resulting in more sales and more profits.

Had the products that emerged, instead, been ones that could have reduced other building costs, such as the example of collectors that could also perform the function of roof or wall, or if the products had made use of relatively traditional construction practice and skills, the solar building industry would likely have been more resilient and sustainable and would have been less vulnerable to the curtailment of the solar tax credits. Further, solar building design more likely would have continued to evolve steadily after the tax credits ended.

1.9 The Building Design Profession

In traditional (preoil-embargo) building design practice, architects designed buildings with little consideration for their subsequent energy bills. A mechanical engineer would be brought in late in the design process to do all of that "energy stuff" (mechanical systems engineering) without marring the essence of the architect's basic design.

The energy crisis changed the design process, and it changed the responsibilities of the various design professionals. In turn, these changes influenced emerging solar building design.

The early work in solar architecture and planning was in residential building design. This was logical because houses were easier to design and analyze than large buildings. Also, unlicensed building designers could play an influential role in residential design while the design of large buildings is much more tightly controlled by licensed design professionals and building codes. Almost anyone seriously involved in solar energy—a scientist, engineer, builder, architect, student, or homeowner—felt capable of designing a house that met building codes.

The large number of early solar houses that were designed by people inexperienced in building design contributed enormously to the renaissancelike proliferation of ideas. Often, the design neophyte was scrambling to develop professional architectural skills while earnestly advancing smart energy design. The architectural maturation of the leaders in solar building design coincided with the growing influence of energy techniques in the architectural and planning establishment.

In commercial buildings, the integration of energy techniques proved to be a highly analytical process, more complex and rigorous than the engineering work needed for most moderately sized buildings. If the solar systems being considered for a building were active ones, the mechanical engineer was the obvious designer because such systems had little impact on the energy performance of the building structure. But the large surface area of collectors and the large volume for thermal energy storage had a significant impact on the building design. This required collaboration between the architect and engineer that was closer—and earlier in the process—than most traditional architect/engineer relationships. This healthy trend sustained itself into the 1980s.

However, if the energy techniques being considered were architectural elements, such as windows, thermal mass, natural convection paths, sunspaces, or thermal walls and roofs, the architect took responsibility for the numerical analysis. Numerical analysis, however, is not the favorite pastime of most architects. And to make matters worse, seemingly simple natural energy systems often required extraordinarily complex computational analysis that used sophisticated calculators or computers. As a result, by the early 1980s, the culture of many architectural firms had assimilated the hardware, the software, the human skills, and the necessary changes in the design process to accommodate this analysis and to design sound solar and energy efficient buildings.

Subsequently, as energy concerns faded, this new, more technically sophisticated design culture embraced computer design aids more readily than the architectural profession would have in the absence of the energy crisis.

1.10 Progress in Solar Architecture

The major challenges in the integration of natural energy techniques into good building design are two.

The first is more an engineering challenge than an architectural one. The challenge is to match the energy output of natural energy systems with the energy needs of buildings. Natural energy levels fluctuate widely, sometimes from minute to minute and always from day to night and from season to season. The energy requirements of buildings also fluctuate, but are rarely "in sync" with the energy available from natural energy systems.

The second major challenge is largely an architectural one. The challenge is to integrate natural energy techniques, which are fairly substantial in size and which are usually visually obtrusive, into an overall coherent building design that already is constrained and buffeted by hundreds of other design requirements. In fact, typically the large number of these competing requirements forces the designer to try to eliminate, ignore, or otherwise subdue their influence to a manageable number so that it becomes possible to arrive at a design. The last thing an architect relishes is to have yet another major factor introduced that might impose a particular design on a building.

On the other hand, major constraints, such as a view, are often welcomed as a central design theme around which the overall design revolves. Thus, when public energy concerns reached crisis proportions, natural energy techniques often became that central organizing principle for the overall bulding design. But as soon as the crisis mentality waned, energy became a design issue that dropped in importance.

Early researchers of both active and passive systems initially agreed on a major point that later proved to be uneconomical. It was assumed that buildings required large collector surfaces, or apertures—as much as one-third to two-thirds of the floor area in size. Whether the surface was an active collector or an enormous south-facing window, the architectural challenge to integrate it well visually was formidable.

From 1972 to the early 1980s, energy efficiency design techniques proved cheaper than solar systems and slashed the average energy consumption of small buildings. First-generation solar buildings with enormous solar collectors on the roofs or large expanses of south-facing windows with few windows elsewhere gave way eventually to houses employing conservation measures that use perhaps 25% of the heating energy of their 1960s counterparts, but resemble them in appearance. With passive systems, ever larger solar apertures result in a drop in energy performance because of the resulting larger heat losses at night and the larger air conditioning loads in the summer. In hot and moderate climates and in cold climates where solar conditions are unfavorable, this point of diminishing returns can occur at rather small aperture sizes.

As these lessons became evident, some solar water heater companies expanded their business in the early 1980s by adding a couple of solar collectors to their basic system and selling it as a combined water and space heating system. On an efficient house, two or three panels would cut fuel bills another 15–25% at relatively little additional cost over and above the basic cost of the solar water heater.

A parallel lesson was learned in thermal energy storage. The amounts that were originally assumed to be optimal for active systems involved huge water tanks or rockbeds. Many tons of dense, heavy materials such as concrete, stone, or adobe were used with passive systems. This meant a return to heavy construction, which ran counter to construction industry trends toward lighter-weight construction.

Using large amounts of mass later proved to be wrong for two reasons. The first was that the volume of storage material shrank as the required size of collectors shrank with growing building energy efficiency. The other was that the amount considered economically optimal per square foot of collector—or aperture—grew smaller as the real costs for such materials were higher than anticipated. By the early 1980s, houses in most climates that were designed for the optimal cost/benefit of solar energy and energy efficiency were obtaining 15–35% of their heat from the sun, most likely through passive design. Experienced designers were choosing to add no additional thermal energy storage over and above the ordinary materials used in construction because the occasional inconvenience from overheating did not justify its additional cost or the affect on the design and construction process. This coincided with the trend toward minimizing the effect of the solar design on conventional design and construction practice.

1.10.1 Commercial Buildings

As the 1970s proceeded, energy efficiency professionals discovered that the energy consumption of a large modern glass building could be reduced to some extent by the modification of the walls and roof in response to climate. Window orientation and shading, double-glazing, insulation, natural lighting techniques, and passive and active solar techniques were experimented with.

However, in most large buildings, the interior loads from people, lighting, and machinery dominated building energy consumption—so much so that even in the coldest climates, internal loads generate so much heat in many large buildings that cooling, not heating, is needed even during the coldest weather. The exterior design, therefore, need not be as responsive to climate as that of smaller buildings.

This news produced a collective sigh of relief through the architectural community enamored of Modernism but feeling, perhaps, tinges of contrition for their reluctance to design energy conserving solar buildings. In fact, artificial lighting increasingly became the target of efficiency efforts by energy professionals, with glazing design to enhance natural lighting—a favorite technique toward that end. This dovetailed nicely with Modernism's love affair with glass and with soaring glass atria. As the energy crisis ebbed, traditional architectural design of the exteriors of large buildings continued to ignore energy and climate considerations, as it had over the entire decade of 1973–1983, although much progress was made inside with reduced installed lighting and more efficient mechanical systems.

1.10.2 Cooling Research

Without question, most of the federal research focused on heating, not cooling. Other aspects of space conditioning that were all but ignored included moisture control, air purification, and ventilation. Cooling was given some consistent attention in the active systems program, but architectural and passive approaches were paid little attention, except in the private sector, until the waning years of the decade.

In fact, volume 1 of the *Passive Solar Design Handbook* (T.E.A., 1980) contains a chapter that summarizes the state of the art and the relevant literature through the spring of 1978. Its 40 pages are less than 15% the entire book. Of the 20 references cited, only 4 or 5 are from technical literature published after 1973.

Further evidence of this early inattention to natural building cooling is demonstrated in the Proceedings of the Second National Passive Solar Conference (Prowler, 1978). Of nearly 200 papers and presentations, only 10 specifically addressed passive cooling.

All but 2 of them directly or indirectly relate to sky radiational cooling. This shortcoming contributed to the challenge facing building designers to integrate sound energy techniques satisfactorily into good building design and planning.

Volume 8 in this series gives more complete coverage of passive cooling.

1.10.3 Design Competitions

Building designers understood how important it was that the visual appearance of solar buildings was acceptable to the general public. As a result, national design competitions were organized to foster and reward outstanding design. They included the First Passive Home Awards (Franklin, 1979), the First Passive Solar Design Award Competition of 1980 (Cook, 1984a,b), and the Second Passive Solar Design Awards Competition of 1982 (Cook, 1983). These competitions reveal substantial, rapid progress in the ability of the building design community to integrate sound energy design techniques into good building design. The first competition was dominated by solar heated residence in cold climates. Just three years later, cooling, large buildings, and large housing developments were included, and the increasing design sophistication was apparent.

1.11 The Organization of This Volume

There are many ways in which "solar architecture and planning" can be dissected into subtopics for the purpose of presenting research work. The structure chosen for this volume proved workable as a means of attracting outstanding authors. It also permits investigation of almost all the intricacies of the topic with only minor redundancies with other volumes, while retaining overall emphasis on the major design challenge: architectural integration.

The chapters fall into three groupings. Chapter 2 covers site, community, and urban planning and design from the standpoint of professional planning. Typically, this discipline precedes building design itself.

The second group consists of chapters 3–5, which cover three areas of primary challenge in using natural energy systems in building design: building envelopes, thermal energy storage in building interiors, and thermal energy distribution in building interiors.

The final grouping integrates the topics of previous chapters into overall building design. Smaller, envelope-dominated buildings are covered in chapter 6, and larger, interior-load-dominated buildings are covered in chapter 7.

1.11.1 Site, Community, and Urban Planning and Design

Very little federal research support was given to the energy saving and solar energy opportunities that are available through good planning, whether by using a building site more wisely or by designing or redesigning communities, cities, and towns. This is made abundantly clear in Layne Ridley's chapter (Chapter 2). Therefore, by comparison with subsequent chapters, the limited federal efforts are described in some detail and the reference section is relatively complete.

Community planning involves a wide range of people, most notably community and political leaders who must simultaneously respond to public sentiment and lead with a view toward the future. Change comes slowly in this milieu compared with the relative spontaneity of, say, a private citizen deciding to purchase a solar water heater. As a result, sufficient public sentiment for attracting federal research support has not developed.

It is not surprising that the key federal research program did not begin until 1977 with the Site and Neighborhood Design (SAND) Program. Had the public anticipated a continuation of rising energy prices and dwindling supplies through the end of the century and beyond, energy concerns would have continued to penetrate community, city, and town planning policy. Eventually, with the passage of many decades, the physical landscape of our society would likely have been altered in an effort to use energy more efficiently and to rely less and less on exhaustible, conventional fuels. Instead, the last major federally supported initiative in this area was launched in 1980—the Solar Cities and Towns Program.

Ridley graphically describes the lost opportunity for our nation: by following the existing land use patterns dominated by suburban sprawl, the transportation energy consumed by a typical commuter far exceeds the energy savings of his or her superefficient house.

1.11.2 Building Envelopes

The three chapters on building envelopes and interiors are markedly different. The differences are in the relative balance between an architectural approach to the subject matter on the one hand and a technical and engineering one on the other and are appropriate to the subject matter of each chapter.

With respect to building envelopes, for example, the principal technical question facing a building design practitioner is the size of the solar aperture, which varies with its orientation and tilt angle; the energy demand of the building; climate; and energy system type(s). In fact, these are such fundamental questions that they were addressed early and so fully that analytical tools, rules of thumb, and actual experience were developed quickly to help building designers in their design work.

The fundamental challenges facing the designer are architectural ones. Don Prowler is a practitioner, researcher, and professor. His chapter, with Douglas Kelbaugh, on building envelopes (chapter 3) provides a good introduction to the federal programs and private efforts that influenced solar building design. With a design perspective, he traces the development of the state of the art of this principal architectural challenge in solar design—integrating a solar aperture satisfactorily into the appearance of the building.

Two major conclusions are:

1. The solar aperture needs to be neither as large nor as architecturally obvious as previously believed. Nor is a precisely southern orientation or perfect tilt angle as crucial as had been thought. These findings are in no small measure due to the realization that solar systems, whether active or passive, are more costly than originally thought and, therefore, should be small enough to minimize the amount of heat that has to be thrown away during mild weather.

2. A mix of different but complementary solar strategies usually works better than relying on just one. Direct gain almost always is one of these strategies, with sunrooms, thermal storage walls, and manufactured solar collectors being the other most common choices. Thermal storage roofs, thermosyphoning wall panels, and site-built collectors proved to be least popular. Solar control strategies, solar water heating, and daylighting strategies—including large sunspaces and atria—dominated commercial building design choices.

1.11.3 Building Interiors: Thermal Energy Storage

For most of the decade, technical questions dominated the issue of the integration of thermal energy storage into building design, despite the parallel and formidable architectural challenges. What kind? How much? How does it really work? Where should it be located and what difference does location make? Chapter 4 reflects this fact. Bion Howard, the principal author, is a research engineer, and Harrison Fraker, the chapter's coauthor, is an architect.

A major conclusion parallels that of solar apertures:

The amount of thermal mass does not need to be as great as had been originally thought. In fact, the thermal mass of common construction materials in well-insulated but typically built houses in northern climates is adequate when solar is designed to provide 25% or less of the heating needs. This is fortunate because integrating thermal mass into conventional building design proved to be far more costly and architecturally challenging than was first thought.

Other major conclusions include:

Finding a place to put the thermal storage for active systems was not a significant architectural issue, and it is largely ignored in this chapter.

The optimal amount of storage varies greatly from climate to climate for envelope-load dominated buildings. In fact, in hot, humid climates where nights remain warm, it should be minimal.

Commercial buildings (interior-load dominated buildings) benefit little from increased thermal mass unless nights cool significantly and a cost-effective night flushing system can be used.

Much remains to be learned about thermal energy storage.

1.11.4   Building Interiors: Thermal Energy Distribution

Interior thermal energy distribution is even more poorly understood than thermal energy storage. This is due in large part to the enormous mathematical complexity required to analyze it. Not only are the thermal processes physically complex (for example, involving radiation transfer among many and complex building surfaces and involving very, very high Rayleigh numbers) but no two building designs are quite the same, and even the smallest of design changes or variations in occupant use can significantly alter performance.

A simple example of this is a doorway. Most obviously, whether the door is opened or closed makes a big difference. But less obviously, the design of the doorway opening itself—for example, whether it extends all the way to the ceiling or not—influences performance since even small barriers across the ceiling retard air flow.

Thus, although it remains a technical issue, supreme architectural skills are needed to enhance energy performance through natural energy flows. Greg Franta, who is both a researcher and an architect, bridges this crucial gap in chapter 5. He accomplishes this by reviewing specific research projects as well as specific buildings, the mix depending on which aspect of energy distribution he is addressing. Active systems, for the most part, use traditional mechanical means of energy distribution and are not covered here.

The major conclusion of this chapter is that little research has been conducted in thermal energy distribution, and it is and remains poorly understood.

1.11.5   Architectural Integration

The third and final grouping of chapters in this volume is architectural integration—putting all of the many pieces together into a coherent whole, into a building that not only makes wise use of energy to provide human comfort but also satisfies the many other demands placed on the building, with wise and appropriate trade-offs having been made among hundreds of diverse and competing constraints and opportunities.

In the final analysis, solar energy and energy efficiency are not ends but rather means to accomplishing an end—in this case, furthering people's efforts to design, build, and operate buildings that serve society's needs, especially the needs of their occupants and owners. If solar energy and energy efficiency techniques and systems do not support this ultimate end, they have no purpose, regardless of the best intentions and hard work of researchers and advocates.

It is appropriate, then, that the two chapters on architectural integration (chapters 6 and 7) follow more than a hundred chapters in this documentation project that cover all aspects of solar technology.

1.11.5.1   Residential and Light Commercial Buildings   The first chapter on architectural integration (chapter 6) covers buildings that are envelope-load dominated. In general, these are residential and light commerical buildings. The second chapter (chapter 7) covers interior-load dominated buildings, which are generally large commercial buildings.

Ed Mazria, author of chapter 6, is, first and foremost, an architect. He understands that a building must serve the needs for which it is intended, and that solar energy and energy efficiency are means toward that end. This, together with the already substantial emphasis in this documentation project on residential applications, results in a chapter that is the least didactic and prescriptive. Instead, it recognizes the period since 1973 as a relative blink in time of the centuries-long evolution of architectural design, and it relies on other chapters to probe the blink in detail. The resulting brevity should be appreciated by the reader who has been immersed in earlier chapters and needs a breath of perspective.

1.11.5.2 Nonresidential Buildings By comparison with residential buildings, commercial ones require substantially more engineering to achieve overall design success. This is also true of their energy systems. Burt Hill Kosar Rittelmann Associates were among the leaders in balancing the engineering of innovative energy systems with architectural design. They also were immersed in federally sponsored solar research. It is appropriate then, that architects from their firm, Harry Gordon and his associates, should write the chapter (chapter 7) on the architectural integration of solar energy and energy efficiency techniques into commercial (interior-load dominated) buildings.

In light of the necessary emphasis on technical issues, it is probably appropriate that this chapter conclude with discussions of ongoing issues in human comfort, energy economics, control systems, and regulations and codes rather than with conclusions about the visual integration of solar elements into the building design.

1.12 New Frontiers

The fertile, creative learning period following 1973 challenged and expanded the limits of the then available building energy techniques. Within a decade, building design practitioners had ready (although certainly not perfect) access to the cost, performance, design opportunities and limitations, and product availability of many, many applications. Included, for example, were thermal storage walls such as Trombe walls, shading and other solar control options, glazing options, thermal storage techniques, active solar heating and cooling systems, natural daylighting techniques, and sunspaces and atria. The knowledge base (or state of the art) was readily available via numerous conferences and their proceedings, design manuals and handbooks, seminars, and product literature. Calculator and computer design tools; tables, charts, and graphs, rules-of-thumb; and other design aids were abundant. Designers and engineers were learning how to handle the new responsibilities related to building energy design process to accommodate the new energy design strategies.

This situation was in sharp contrast to 1973. At that time, there was but a handful of solar buildings and little knowledge about energy options and opportunities—let alone their costs or performance. Nor, for that matter, were there many data on the energy performance of buildings, whether conventional or designed for solar and energy efficiency.

Although substantial strides had been made relative to buildings such as houses, by the 1980s major challenges remained in commercial (internal-load dominated) buildings. Commercial buildings are much more complex, and their purpose, size, design, construction, and thermal performance vary greatly, making it difficult and time-consuming to develop a knowledge base or the simplified design tools that allow the building designer to adopt energy-saving techniques readily and to predict with confidence their cost and performance. Despite these shortcomings, the commerical buildings that were designed, built, and monitored in the U.S. Department of Energy's (DOE) Nonresidential Experimental Buildings Program achieved an average reduction in energy use of almost 50%.

As for urban, community, and neighborhood planning for energy efficiency and the use of solar and other renewable energies, very little progress was made during the solar decade. This will probably best be remedied in future federal research programs by designating this topic as a separate research area—led and championed by a planning professional.

If in building energy design there were no new technical and scientific research frontiers and opportunities, and if therefore the research challenge was to advance the energy performance of buildings by incrementally improving existing techniques and technologies, the resulting research program would include the following:

• simplified design tools for predicting energy performance of various building design solutions during the design of commercial buildings,

• measurement of the energy performance of buildings and of their individual pieces over the long term,

• architectural strategies for incorporating more daylighting into buildings, and incorporating it more effectively,

• advancing the product development of promising energy techniques such as water walls and water roofs, movable insulation, Trombe walls (especially those with selective surfaces), low cost solar water heaters, smart energy controls, and the integration of energy efficiency and solar energy techniques into factory manufactured building components (such as curtain wall panels),

• advancing the knowledge base of natural energy flows through buildings of various types, and

• advancing the knowledge base and developing design techniques for more energy efficient urban, community, and neighborhood planning and development.

It is well known that technological advances—indeed, scientific breakthroughs—may be possible that might enable building energy performance to take a quantum leap forward, rather than merely to make incremental improvements. Some of these advances were initiated with considerable progress prior to the 1980s. Low-iron, high-transmittance glass emerged early in the solar decade and achieved a high market penetration, especially in active solar system collectors. Low-emissivity coatings such as Heat Mirror™ reached the marketplace later with considerable promise.

Selective surfaces for maximizing solar absorption and minimizing heat loss through radiation (emissivity) also were developed early and achieved high market penetration in active system solar collectors. Selective surfaces that could be readily applied to surfaces such as concrete to improve the performance of Trombe walls were not yet fully developed but, again, showed promise.

Research and development of thermal storage utilizing phase-change materials (PCM) that could replace heavy, high volume materials such as stone, concrete, brick, and water continued throughout the decade but have not achieved commercialization.

But these achievements and promises did not satiate the visions of those who sought to press the frontiers of building energy design. On the contrary, they served to expand the visions and the frontiers even further.

1.12.1 Buildings as Energy Consumers

Historically, almost all buildings have been viewed as energy consumers, as have nearly all of their elements, with the hardy exception of south-facing glass. But even here, a single layer of glass facing south, except in the warmest of climates, would, over the course of a heating season, lose more heat than it returned to the building in solar gain.

Not until the decade following 1973 did this perception undergo radical transformation. Society came to realize that certain elements of a building, most notably south-facing multiple glazing, could actually be used to collect the energy that a building uses. Other elements are sunrooms, thermosyphoning wall panels, Trombe and water walls, solar collectors, and glazing for natural ventilation and natural lighting. Pushed to its limits, this new conceptualization of buildings sought to achieve a goal of 100% solar heating, and/or 100% natural cooling, and/or 100% natural (daytime) lighting.

This goal was elusive and almost invariably was compromised in favor of a financial and architectural balance between natural energy conversion techniques and conventional energy use that resulted in buildings that have energy bills that are 30–50% of those of a similar building built to pre-1973 standards.

In this new conceptualization, the designer sought individual building elements that delivered ("produced") more energy to the building than they cost the building in its operation. Further, a mix of elements was sought that complemented each other's contribution. For example, windows admit solar heat during the day and lose interior heat at night. Trombe walls delay heat gain until later in the day and on into the night. These two elements, then, complement each other thermally.

A major challenge in this concepturalization of buildings was and is in the trade-off between adding more glass for solar heat gain and minimizing the corresponding heat losses at night. An early lesson in solar building design was that there is an optimal point in sizing glass areas for solar heat gain beyond which the heat transmitted by each additional square foot cannot be used by the building and that at night a square foot will lose more heat than it contributes usefully to the building.

As the decade progressed, new energy techniques and technologies kept advancing this optimal point in favor of more energy savings; clearer, higher transmittance glazings; insulating glazing covers; triple and/or low-E glazings to reduce night heat loss; and, better design of thermal mass.

Another level of challenge is in the trade-offs among heating, cooling, and lighting. For example, more glazing for solar heating means more summer heat gain and therefore more air conditioning. More glazing for natural lighting increases night heating loads and summer heat gains.

Finding better resolutions to trade-offs, then, represents many of today's research challenges. Switchable glazings, for example, would be clear when the building needs light or solar heat gain but reflect light when it does not. Transparent insulation is another possibility. It admits light (for heating and/or lighting) but retards heat loss during the winter and heat gain during the summer.

Clearly, then, the way in which society—or at least building designers—conceive of buildings with respect to energy continues to evolve, and if building energy design research and innovation are to advance into the twenty-first century, then this evolution must continue.

1.12.2 A New Way of Thinking

Certainly one of the most significant results of the solar decade was that many people continued to evolve their conception of energy guidelines. For example, buildings can be designed and constructed that have heating and cooling loads that are but 10–20% of those of similar buildings using pre-1973 techniques. In such instances, the amount of renewable energy (primarily sun and wind) that impinges on the buildings is well in excess of the energy needed. Yet only a small fraction of that energy is being tapped by even the best of solar buildings. If buildings could be clad in advanced materials and systems that could more fully convert and use that natural energy than today's techniques are capable of doing, then there would be energy to spare. Buildings would no longer be energy "consumers" but might rather be considered energy "producers."

For example, walls and roofs may some day automatically convert daylight, and perhaps wind, directly into the forms of energy needed by the building at any particular moment, whether for lighting, heating, cooling, or electricity. The same walls and roofs may automatically modulate energy flow into and out of the building to maintain optimal comfort and direct available energy to points in the building where it is needed. While it can certainly be said that this is to some extent achievable today, pushing the limits of the physics, chemistry, and engineering of new, advanced materials and techniques could result in greater economy of materials, more sophisticated control strategies, greater efficiencies, lower costs, and more energy than a building needs. An example is roofing materials that look like shingles and that are applied as easily but that connect to each other electrically and convert 15–20% of the incident sunlight into electricity. This electricity is either used immediately, stored in high performance flywheels for later use, or pumped into the utility grid—for a profit. Or is used to recharge the family electric (commuter) car.

Another example is windows that have R-values of 8–10, yet are as clear as most windows today. Or windows that, with a slight electrical charge, "switch" their opacity—clear in cold weather but opaque during hot weather or when the building is so warm that it no longer needs more sunlight.

A third example is fiber-optic lighting fixtures that bring sunlight deep into buildings to reduce electric lighting levels without increasing solar heat gain.

Yes, many research challenges and opportunities remain for increasing the overall percentage of a building's energy requirements provided by various building elements and for reducing the building's [owners/occupants] purchases of energy from other sources.

But to make buildings net energy "producers," these concepts, as well as new ones, will have to be pushed to their limits. For example, advanced glazings must be not only switchable but also have R-values approaching 8–10 (i.e., transparent insulation). Natural lighting techniques should approach conventional lighting in cost and simplicity, and be well-integrated with it. Thermal mass techniques should carry buildings through multiday periods of unfavorable weather without sacrificing comfort. And energy conservation techniques shoud reduce loads yet further while improving air quality, reducing indoor pollutants and radon levels.

The following set of research challenges and opportunities is representative of these frontiers.

1.12.3 Research Challenges and Opportunities

The single greatest determinant of performance of solar systems and sub-systems, whether active or passive, is the glazing. It is well-known and understood that a single glazed window in a cold climate will lose more energy than it gains, even if it is facing south. On the other hand, a north-facing window using the most advanced glazing technologies actually admits more light (and heat) into a building than it loses—even in the coldest climates (Neeper, 1982). Yet even the best insulated wall is a net energy loser.

It is also well-known and understood that some passive systems, such as a Trombe wall, can add as much to the cooling requirements of a building during the summer as they save in heating during the winter, for example in hot, humid climates.

It is well accepted that the primary drawbacks of using natural energies is the inability of the building materials such as glazings to adapt automatically to the fluctuations in the available energy and in the building's need for it. The reason is that the thermal and optical properties of most materials are constant. The thermal and optical properties of some advanced glazing technologies are not constant but rather adapt to changing weather conditions and building energy requirements.

If these advanced glazing technologies fulfill their promise, then buildings can be made energy efficient regardless of the size or orientation of the building's glazings. This can significantly increase the likelihood that building designers will use energy-saving glazings.

Historically, new buildings have used new technology to accomplish what old buildings were unable to without that new technology. Invariably, new technologies have freed building designers from constraints imposed by nature. The introduction of low-transmittance glazings (heat absorbing and light-reflecting windows) in the 1950s is an example of this but in the area of cooling, rather than in heating, natural lighting, or electric power uses. These glazings allowed architects to design large all-glass buildings even in the hottest, sunniest climates, because the resulting air-conditioning requirements were far less than they would have been had only clear glass been available. While those buildings still used enormous amounts of electricity for air conditioning, the advanced glazing technology allowed architects to design them without regard to climate if they chose to do so. The removal of a constraint such as this adds immeasurably to the acceptance of energy efficient technologies.

The solar decade saw the influence of this factor. For example, early solar buildings had billboard-sized glazing areas to achieve a substantial fraction of energy savings. Architects rejected such an imposition on their building designs. But with the addition of more—and better—insulation, with improved techniques to reduce air infiltration, and with triple and/or low-E glazings, the same solar energy performance can be achieved with a building design that is hard to distinguish from its preoil-embargo predecessors. That is, the windows are not abnormally sized, a due-south orientation of the inconspicuously sized collector is not critical, windows appear on many orientations (sometimes generously), and the thermal mass is not noticeably large.

By the early 1980s, the energy-conscious building designer relied on new technologies to build energy-conserving buildings even while paying less attention to climate. This ability to permit a building's appearance to be constrained by nonenergy factors (such as home buying tastes or function) and yet to be energy-efficient means that energy savings need not be totally sacrificed. It makes energy saving and solar energy techniques far more acceptable than they would be had they continued to require radical changes in a building's appearance. This characteristic of the market place should be a major consideration in advanced building energy research.

1.12.3.1 Advanced Glazings The principal problem with the current generation and all previous generations of commercially available glazings for buildings is their high heat loss. This is true even of the low-emissivity glazings that reduce heat loss up to 50% compared with double glazing; they still lose 5–10 times more than the corresponding well-insulated wall.

Another major problem is that the transmittance of glass remains constant, regardless of the weather or the energy needs of the buildings. This makes buildings susceptible to overheating from the very glazing that may be saving heating energy during the winter.

Yet another problem is that glazing that is designed to provide natural light also admits considerable energy in the infrared and near-infrared range that does not contribute to natural lighting levels but adds to the cooling loads of the building.

1.12.3.1.1 Transparent Insulation   The challenge is to develop glazing systems that have high R-values, in the range of 8–10, yet still have high transmissivities, in the range of 50–70%. Such glazings could be called "transparent insulation." It should be noted that translucent insulation does exist with high R-values and low transmissivity but with significant visual distortion. In the 1970s and 1980s, Southwall Corporation of Palo Alto, CA, developed a glazing material that can be considered transparent insulation when compared with standard glazings. Subsequently, 3M Corporation developed a similar system glazing.

The Southwall system uses Heat Mirror™, which is a thin metal oxide coating that can be applied to glass. It is highly transmissive to light but reflects infrared heat back into the building, reducing heat loss. Combined with double-glazing, Heat Mirror™ provides an R-value of about 4 compared with an R-value of about 2 for double glazing.

An example of an advanced concept involves transparent, microporous materials called aerogels. Aerogels are formed when semisolid (colloidal) silicagels are dehydrated (supercritically dried). The individual particles (about 100 angstroms each) are much smaller than the wavelengths of visible light and so are transparent to it. Their porous, branched chains trap air, acting as an insulator. The material has an R-value of about 7 per inch of thickness. (Rubin, 1982). A double-glazed window with the evacuated spaced filled with aerogel could have an R-value approaching 10. Another example of a high performance window is being developed at the Solar Energy Research Institute (SERI) Materials Research Branch (SERI, 1985). Research shows that an evacuated, sealed glass with an integral, infrared reflective-coating could provide an R-value exceeding 12. When an electro-chromic coating (see section 12.3.1.3) is added, the insulating value is even greater.

1.12.3.1.2 Angle-Selective Glazings   Angle-selective glazings would have the optical property of a sharp drop in solar transmittance when the angle of incidence of sunlight is very small. Overhangs and other shading devices can keep the sun off this glass but too often are omitted from buildings for reasons of high cost, architectural incompatibility, or lack of durability, especially in the case of movable or adjustable mechanisms. Angle-selective glazings, on the other hand, would block out much of the direct sunlight without altering the building's appearance or requiring movable parts. During the winter larger angle-incident sunlight would be freely transmitted.

1.12.3.1.3 Switchable Glazings   The challenge is to be able to change the transmissivity of glazing easily and quickly. The principal use of such glazings would be for fenestration designed for daylighting in commercial buildings. They would allow apertures to be sized for cloudy conditions while reducing heat gain during sunny conditions. The switchable glazing concept make use of one of the following types of "optical switching materials":

• Photochromics: These are materials such as polymeric compounds that change transmittance in reaction to light.

• Electrochromics: Organic or inorganic materials, or transition metal oxides (such as WO_3) that change their transmittance when a voltage is applied to them.

• Thermochromics: These are materials that change transmittance when their temperature changes. Examples include inorganics in polymer systems and organometallics.

Japanese companies have been working on switchable glazings for some time (Holzman, 1982). The concept is an electrochromic window. Five layers of thin films are sandwiched between two layers of glass. Slight changes in electric current passing through it change the glazing from perfectly clear to slightly tinted, reflecting the infrared spectrum of light.

1.12.3.2 Daylighting The challenge is to find ways of bringing large quantities of natural light deep into a building. "Light tubes" and "light pipes" have been developed but are not commercially available.

For example, natural light reaches offices seven stories below ground at the University of Minnesota's Underground Space Center. A tracking collector funnels photons into a light pipe a square foot in cross section, which beams them downward (Holzman, 1984).

Fiber optics is a most promising opportunity for collecting, transporting, and distributing sunlight into building interiors. Other light transport systems are also possible. A major challenge is to develop methods, systems, and/or materials that collect the light and concentrate it into light guides (which invariably have low acceptance angles) and do so with no moving parts.

1.12.3.3. Photovoltaics The following research areas provide opportunity for achieving photovoltaic arrays that supply more electricity than a building uses:

• cheaper and more efficient cells (so that arrays can be less expensive and smaller-sized),

• low cost, reliable trackers that can be integrated easily into building design,

• cells that are integrated into other building elements, notably roofing elements (such as shingles), wall elements (such as siding), and glass (such as windows and skylights),

• cheaper and less complex equipment for interfacing with the utility grid,

• cheaper and smaller electrical storage,

• more efficient electrical appliances, office equipment, and light fixtures, and

• cheaper and more user-friendly electrical control systems that integrate with "smart house" electronic devices.

1.12.3.4 Other Research Areas

1.12.3.4.1 Superinsulating Materials   The standard approach to achieving higher total R-values in walls and roofs has been to make them thicker, adding to construction costs. Insulating materials that have much higher R-values per inch could reverse this trend, helping to lower overall building costs while increasing their thermal performance.

1.12.3.4.2 Phase Change Drywall   The trend in the construction industry is toward buildings that overall are ever lighter in weight. But in conflict with this trend, the principal means of adding thermal mass in buildings has been to add weight—usually concrete, brick, stone, or water.

The technical challenge is to develop thermal storage techniques that do not add noticeably to the weight of buildings, do not add significantly to the cost, and require little or no change in construction techniques.

In housing, drywall (wallboard) is a standard building product. The challenge is to find a phase-change material (PCM) that manufacturers would be willing to add to wallboard that meets the criteria outlined above. Another challenge is to develop PCMs that can be added to concrete and floor tiles, and even paint.

1.12.3.4.3 Cooling Research   A major opportunity exists for roof systems that reflect incoming sunlight and radiate ("radiator") or expel building heat to the sky. The "radiator" would absorb and store heat from the house or other building below. When it cools (usually at night), it would store "coolth" for subsequent cooling of the building.

An example of such a system would use a spectrally selective glazing material over a high emissivity surface. The glazing would be highly reflective (nontransmissive) of visible light but highly transmissive in the range of 8 to 13 microns (infrared). The emissive surface would also operate in this infrared regime. To be effective, the combined system would need to permit radiative heat rejection up to 100 watts per square meter during the day as well as at night.

This is similar to Harold Hay's Skytherm system, but this concept should avoid putting water on roofs and should avoid movable panels for controlling heat flow to and from the sky. Also, the concept described above emphasizes cooling while Skytherm is designed for both heating and cooling (Holzman, 1984).

1.12.3.4.4 Dehumidification One of the more difficult challenges in space conditioning in hot, humid climates is low-energy dehumidification that is economical both to install and to operate.

Low-cost desiccant materials, particularly liquids, that can be economically (i.e., having low energy requirements) regenerated are an attractive direction for cooling research.

1.12.4 A Different Way of Thinking

Most of our attention in this volume is devoted to the energy requirements of buildings, and to the process used by the architect and the builder to integrate solar and conventional energy sources and energy conservation measures into buildings. It is possible, and potentially more productive, to take a larger view of energy requirements—a community view.

Recent experience in Europe and Scandinavia has shown that, even in these cold and cloudy climates, it is possible to provide essentially all a community's needs for space and water heating from a central solar system employing long-term (seasonal) energy storage in rock caverns, aquifers, drilled soil and rock, or water pits. This approach frees the building designer from many solar system constraints and allows other architectural considerations to control the building's function and appearance. The challenge of integrating the solar energy system with the building is then transferred from the architect to the community planner.

The capacity of the seasonal storage subsystem must be large enough to absorb all or most of the solar collectors' summer excess output without overheating. Thus, the ratio of storage volume to collector area is much higher in a seasonal storage system than in a diurnal storage system. Seasonal storage units also must be large in an absolute sense to be efficient and cost effective since large systems have more favorable surface to volume ratios and because most construction projects have large fixed costs. Efforts to develop seasonal storage for single residences or small buildings in the United States and elsewhere have not been very successful.

The main technical advantage of seasonal storage for a solar heating system is that it allows the collector subsystem to operate at or near its peak efficiency throughout the year. As a result, collectors in seasonal storage systems can deliver two or even three times as much heat as those in diurnal systems. Economies of scale also apply to the solar collector array where the cost of manufacturing, marketing, distributing, and installing solar collectors decreases dramatically with the array size.

In addition to higher efficiencies and economies of scale that may result in lower delivered energy costs for central solar heating plants with seasonal storage (CSHPSS) systems, the central plant approach offers important benefits relative to fossil fuels and some other renewable energy technologies. CSHPSS systems achieve a solar fraction near unity and, therefore, offer security for the owner or consumer from short-term curtailment or long-term price escalation of fuels and freedom from adverse environmental impacts; also they do not represent a drain on local economies to purchase imported fuels. They provide a simple means of integrating and using low-cost energy that may be available from geographically and temporarily disparate sources—for example, the combination of solar heat, building heat rejection, and municipal waste conversion. Installation of CSHPSS systems allows the space in individual buildings that would ordinarily be devoted to the heating system to be eliminated or used for other purposes, and allows buildings that have restricted solar access to benefit from solar heating.

Although knowledge about CSHPSS technology has increased dramatically in the past ten years (Bankston, 1988), the approach has not been adopted in the United States. The barriers are primarily institutional, rather than technical, but an American genre of the technology will probably have to include cooling. The technology of central solar heating plants with seasonal storage is reviewed in detail in volume 6 of this series.

1.13   Conclusion

Certainly, the overwhelming conclusion that threads through this entire book is that the human race *knew little in 1973 about solar building design.* Yet within a decade our knowledge had progressed through so many phases that a substantial number of building designers were capable of producing outstanding buildings that make wise use of solar energy and energy efficiency techniques. Had the social, political, economic, and energy climate of 1970s continued into the 1980s, solar building design would have continued to mature on a very solid base of knowledge and experience.

A major indicator of the growing maturity was that leading solar designers and thinkers were replacing their preoccupation with solarizing single family, custom-designed houses with a broader and more realistic view. Other serious issues of the day began to include: transportation energy, land conservation, clean air, and clean water; revitalization of inner cities; creating vital, neighborhood-based communities; and sustainable agriculture. Solar energy, energy efficiency, and other alternative technologies were coming to be seen more clearly as simply other arrows in the quiver of design professionals trying to provide richer, more vital, and sustainable built environments.

Instead of the momentum continuing, the early 1980s saw the federal solar research budget cut, energy prices decline, the economy fall into recession, and the construction industry fall into near depression.

As the 1980s continued to unfold, as energy became less of a concern in building design, the frequency with which energy-efficiency techniques were used in buildings waned. Designers became yet more proficient in the design integration process, and energy elements melded ever more completely into the overall design. The resulting buildings were more energy-efficient than their preembargo counterparts (although it took a well-trained eye to discern them). Yet these buildings could have been designed to use considerably less energy since energy techniques were no longer being pushed to their limits.

This situation should not suggest that additional research and the continued advancement of the state of the art is unnecessary. Quite the contrary. Much work remains. The horizons are vast. The renaissancelike spirit of the "solar decade" proves that the human race is capable of responding with the very best it has to offer to the challenges and opportunities that lie before it in solar architecture and planning.

References

Anderson, Bruce (1973). *Solar Energy and Shelter Design*. Masters Thesis, Department of Architecture, MIT, Cambridge, MA.

Anderson, Bruce (1976). *The Solar Home Book*. Brick House Publishing Co., Andover, MA.

Butti, Ken, and John Perlin (1980). *A Golden Thread*. Cheshire Books, Palo Alto, CA.

Bankston, Charles (1988). "The Status and Potential of Central Solar Heating Plants with Seasonal Storage: An International Report." In K. Boer, *Advances in Solar Energy*. ASES and Plenum Press, New York.

Cook, Jeffrey (ed.) (1983). *Passive Solar Journal*. New York and Boulder. Passive Systems Division of the American Solar Energy Society, Vol. 2, No. 1, 2. 162 pp.

Cook, Jeffrey (1984a). *Award-Winning Passive Solar House Designs*. Garden Way Publishing. 173 pp.

Cook, Jeffery (1984b). *Award-Winning Passive Solar Building Designs*. McGraw-Hill, New York.

Franklin Research Center (1979). *The First Passive Home Awards*. U.S. HUD Contract H-2377. 226 pp.

Holzman, David (December 1982). "Wonders Loom for Passive Design." *Solar Age*. p. 512.

Holzman, David (February 1984). "Neglect Mars Passive Solar Progress." *Solar Age*. pp. 21, 23.

Löf, George (1961). *Proceeding of the UN Conference on New Sources of Energy*. Rapporteur paper, Vol. 5, Rome.

Neeper, Donald A., and Robert A. McFarland (August 1982). "Some Potential Benefits of Fundamental Research for the Passive Solar Heating and Cooling of Buildings." Los Alamos National Laboratory Report LA-9425-MS, Los Alamos, NM.

Prowler, Don (ed.) (1978). *Passive State of the Art*. Proceedings of the 2nd National Passive Solar Conference, March 16–18, 1978. Boulder, CO. The American Solar Energy Society. Three volumes. 950 pp.

Rubin, Michael, and Carl M. Lampert (June 1982). "Transparent Silica Aerogels for Window Insulation." Lawrence Berkeley Laboratory, Energy and Environment Division Report LBL-14462, Berkeley, CA.

Shurcliff, William A. (1978). *Solar Heated Buildings of North America: 120 Outstanding Examples*. Brick House Publishing Co., Andover, MA.

Solar Energy Research Institute (January 1985). *In Review*, pp. 1, 2, 3. Vol. VII, No. 1. Golden, CO.

T.E.A., Inc. (1980). *Passive Solar Design Concepts* (Vol. I of *Passive Solar Design Handbook*). U.S. Department of Energy. 340 pp.

2 Site, Community, and Urban Planning

Layne Ridley

The site is by definition the physical point of departure for any building project. For the most thoughtfully designed buildings and communities, it has always been the conceptual point of departure as well. The art of matching the design of buildings to the contours, the climate, the character of their natural and man-made surroundings is a very old one. With the fairly unanimous designation of energy as a "crisis" in the mid-1970s, another aspect of the site's influence on the building rose in priority. Although known for centuries—and routinely ignored for just about as long—the powerful and constant relationship between the characteristics of the site and the energy behavior of the building assumed a new significance. For solar buildings in particular, the site could determine not only how much and how efficiently energy was used, but to a large extent whether solar energy could be used at all.

In one sense, the "state of the art" of solar site planning has not changed radically since 1972, or in fact for thousands of years. In contrast to the technical advances in solar materials, systems, analysis techniques, equipment, even design methods—many of which either did not exist ten years ago, or have been remarkably changed over a decade of research and experience—the basic principles of placing a solar building for southern exposure, winter wind protection, and summer shade are little altered. The words of Socrates and pictures of cliff dwellings are likely to appear somewhere in even the most recent solar guidebooks.

But, beginning with the first oil shocks, solar energy quickly became an option not only for single, perfectly situated, custom-designed residences, but for tract housing, production housing, suburban communities, city neighborhoods, and commercial buildings of all sizes. Extending basic solar site considerations to the level of a subdivision, a city block, even an entire planned community, proved enormously complex, and called for a broad range of new techniques and strategies. The design necessities dictated by concern for energy efficiency and solar performance had to be reconciled with the same issues facing any "conventional" site development. And the bigger the project, the more formidable the nonenergy constraints become.

The real progress in solar site planning since 1972 has been on the community and urban scale, and it has by necessity combined the efforts not only of designers, builders, and developers, but of planners, lawyers, legislators, government on the local, state, and federal levels, and researchers in a wide variety of fields from botany to sociology. Over the past decade, they have devised innovative ways to place buildings to maximum advantage—on the site, and in the complex larger scheme of community needs and standards.

2.1   Energy and the Site: Basic Issues

In virtually every building, the climate is being modified in some way—in most modern buildings, by being overpowered with electricity or natural gas. The fundamental tenet of energy conscious site planning is that the climate can be modified using the natural features of the site, thus reducing or in some cases eliminating the need for artificial conditioning. The site's specific microclimate is a complex interaction of many factors: orientation, slope, elevation, surface materials, topography, the velocities and directions of prevailing winds, temperature patterns, humidity, precipitation, vegetation, the presence or absence of water, the seasonal availability of sunlight, and, especially in urban areas, the influence of other buildings. Microclimates can change markedly within a few feet, making generalized guidelines very difficult. "Instead of relying on standard orientations, a whole system of measures must be taken to produce an optimum local climate," wrote Kevin Lynch in *Site Planning* (1962/1971/1984).

Basic opportunities exist at most sites to affect temperature, humidity, and wind. For example, where the main objective is to make the microclimate warmer and less windy, the planner would consider maximizing solar exposure, using extensive paved or masonry surfaces to increase the absorption of radiation, and either using natural existing windbreaks or creating new ones with plants or structures. To make the microclimate cooler, the options would include positioning buildings for maximum ventilation by prevailing winds, using shade trees, vines, and planted ground covers, pruning lower growth for increased air circulation, and allowing for evaporative cooling from sprinklers, pools, ponds, or lakes. However, modifying the effects of one factor will have an impact on the effects of the others. For example, paving ground surfaces and increasing sunlight will also lower humidity, and the extensive use of plants, or of evaporative cooling, will work to raise it.

Where the use of solar energy is planned, a certain level of unobstructed southern exposure becomes the key objective. Thus, certain factors of the microclimate—slope, orientation, shading, solar availability—receive added weight, and in addition, the protection of solar access, not only for the present but for as long as the building stands, becomes an issue.

Reconciling the complicated elements of the microclimate into an energy-efficient compromise, within the context of other development considerations such as excavation, drainage, privacy, views, and access to roads and other services, is challenging enough for a single building. Groups of buildings present brand new groups of problems—but also significant opportunities, particularly if the development can be planned from the first stages with energy savings in mind.

For example, subdivisions have been a major means of new residential development in recent decades, and they present probably the most favorable scale on which careful site planning can affect the overall energy performance of a community. Most successful solar subdivisions are planned unit developments (PUDs), which offer a number of advantages. Probably the two most important from an energy perspective are density transfer—using units per acre for the overall development, rather than rigid lot size requirements, to control density, thus permitting flexible clustering of housing units—and district integration—combining single-family and multifamily housing with commercial and recreational uses, and allowing land uses to be more accessible to each other.

The development of new subdivisions is also a level where local governments can exercise basic controls that address the most important issues in energy-efficient site design:

Street Orientation   To the extent that streets in the subdivision can be oriented to run east-west, the lots in the subdivision will be able to use a north-south orientation to allow for solar. Housing located toward the north end of the lot gives good access, desirable south yard space, and flexibility for the owner in controlling plants or objects that might shade the collector. Reducing street widths and coordinating streets with bike or pedestrian paths can also save energy.

Slopes   Requiring maximum use of southern and eastern slopes will permit use of natural solar exposure, provide shelter from cold winds, and allow for the use of earth-sheltered designs. Such requirements, however, must be balanced with steep slope restrictions to prevent erosion and sewage disposal problems.

Vegetation   Requiring maximum retention of natural tree cover, as well as landscaping and shrubbery, can create natural shelter from winds, and provide shade in summer.

Building Energy Use   Allowing cluster housing, mixing of single- and multifamily units, and higher density can reduce the energy needed in each housing unit. Major uses on the site can be allocated in relation to favorable microclimatic "zones." For example, high-density housing can be placed on sites with the best solar access and the most favorable microclimate; sites with poor solar access can be used for circulation, parking, or open space.

Services   Proper planning of road patterns and service access to make possible less paving, shorter sewer lines, shorter power lines, and less outside lighting can result in smaller expenditures for embodied energy, as well as lower per unit infrastructure costs.

Accommodating solar energy may be "easiest" in low density, planned-from-scratch PUDs, where streets can be laid out with solar orientation in mind and solar access can be allowed for or protected. Even so, a number of conflicting issues arise.

For instance, even if *all* new housing developments were highly energy-efficient, but followed the existing patterns of being located farther and farther from city centers, their energy savings would be overwhelmed by the additional transportation energy involved. Calculations in a *Professional Builder* article in 1979 indicated that a typical, well-insulated, efficient passive solar house might reduce energy requirements by some 70%, for savings of 21 million BTU per year; but if even one person in the household lived 30 miles from his or her place of work, round-trip commuting at 15 miles per gallon would consume about 135 million BTU per year. An Urban Land Institute study (1980) concluded that "the form and density of housing, the land use patterns, and the resulting transportation systems have a much greater potential for energy saving than any solar application. If our community scale development is rational, residential solar applications need provide little more than marginal improvements."

And perhaps the most persuasive argument against limiting energy-conscious land use and site planning to low-density specialized subdivisions is that most people in the United States do not live there. Over 70% live in cities. Of the more than 75 million housing units in the United States, almost two-thirds fall under the broad classification of "urban." Of course, this encompasses neighborhoods of enormous diversity, from inner-city high-rises to close-in suburbs to rehabilitated rowhouses. The high density of some urban areas (such as Manhattan, where some neighborhoods might have a density of over 400 people per acre) is a formidable barrier to designing—or redesigning—areas for the use of solar energy. The problems are compounded by the necessity of working with existing buildings, where even basic conservation improvements are difficult and expensive; limited solar access due to unfavorable and unchangeable orientations; the likelihood that development is given priority over energy concerns; the high concentration of low-income occupants or, even in more prosperous sections, renters, and consequently building owners with little incentive to make improvements.

However, even in these areas, opportunities exist. City structures, with their common walls, have some inherent energy-efficiency, and a greater reliance on mass transportation is common. In central city areas, the planner's considerations are likely to be getting neighborhood support for common systems, such as collectors that serve entire buildings, or shared food production projects.

Even if most American housing is classified as "urban," relatively few areas face the density problems of a Manhattan. In fact, the average density of American cities of 100,000 in population or more is about 7 people per acre, and in most cities about half of the residential housing is comprised chiefly of one and two story detached buildings. About 100 million Americans—many more than those who live in central cities or rural areas—live in the part of the "city" most people would describe as "suburbs," the neighborhoods that sprang up in the rush to meet the burgeoning demand for housing after World War II. Most subdivisions were laid out in the "Jeffersonian" grid, rectangular blocks extending east-west and north-south, based on earlier, larger divisions oriented on the cardinal points. This layout presents obvious problems for solar orientation. In most parts of this country, streets that run straight east-west in built-up areas will be shaded during almost all of a winter day. Although streets that run straight north-south will be lighted and warmed somewhat in the winter, they would receive little shade at midday in summer. In many areas, this is the only kind of site available, and solar planners have to compensate with careful positioning of buildings on lots—for example, zero-lot-line schemes—and with building design and landscaping.

The range of options available to save energy in a project of almost any size is very wide. Land use arrangements to cut transportation costs; site planning and passive solar designs to make the most of the inherent character of the site; building design that emphasizes conservation; the use of other renewable resources such as active solar, wind, cogeneration, and district heating; and development techniques for the reduction of embodied energy are all possibilities—but which alternative or combination of alternatives can be applied to a specific project depends on the unique characteristics of that project.

Technically, the microclimate that is the basis of solar site planning on any level is made up of weather, landforms, and other natural conditions. But for all practical purposes, the "microclimate" of a site is made up of a great many social, institutional, and economic factors that may influence the building or the neighborhood's efficiency just as strongly as the wind or sun.

2.2   Planning for Solar: 1972–1982

Planners in 1972 had access to a well-developed body of knowledge about the relationship of climate to design. In fact, one of the most influential texts on the subject, Vincent and Aladar Olgyay's *Design with Climate*, had been in print since 1963. The calculations of thermal comfort zones, the bioclimatic charts, and the correlations of regional conditions to building form established by the Olgyays, who had been writing on climate-sensitive design since of the early 1950s, continue to be standard references for some of the most advanced recent research. Sophisticated procedures for dealing with climatic factors were available long before computers made such design tools commonplace. In a February 1955, *Progressive Architecture* magazine article, Imanuel S. Wiener described a mathematical and graphic method for modifying the solar orientation (fixed by the latitude of the locality) of buildings through the application of wind factors. Based on a 25-year (1924–1948) study of specific climatic conditions in Baltimore, the procedure was developed to "take advantage of the very desirable wind effects during the hot season," particularly for tall buildings such as "apartment houses, office buildings or hospitals," where devices such as windbreaks and plantings have no effect on the upper stories.

Even general texts such as the 1962 first edition of Kevin Lynch's widely used *Site Planning* were acute and explicit on the subject of development that responded in a fundamental way to the land and the environment.

That is not to say, of course, that this knowledge was used on anything like a routine basis. In 1973, commenting on the current state of urban planning (or lack thereof), California architect Richard Neutra asked, "Must we remain victims, strangled and suffocated by our own design which has surrounded us with man-devouring metropolises, drab small towns manifesting a lack of order devastating to the soul, blighted country-sides along railroad tracks and highways, studded with petty mere utility structures shaded by telephone poles and scented by gasoline fumes?" Faced with a legacy of almost three decades of practically unrestrained development fueled by population growth and cheap energy, urban planners in the early '70s were occupied with finding ways to revitalize inner cities, contain suburban sprawl, improve access to health and other public services, plan for new transportation and manpower trends, and reverse the deterioration of the physical environment. Although urban planners of today face many of the same problems, one major change is particularly striking: in 1972, energy conservation was, at best, a minor concern.

"Conservation" applied to air, water, and land resources. References to energy supply were for the most part limited to discussions of planning for utility hook-ups. Nuclear power was frequently cited as a promise of even cheaper, even more plentiful electricity, so energy was seen by many as becoming, if anything, *less* of a problem. Climate-sensitive design was viewed primarily as an issue related to human comfort, protecting the environment and making human habitats more responsive to the local ecology. There were, of course, already many outstanding examples of solar buildings, but only a very few isolated examples of community-level experiments such as the solar-oriented subdivision built in the Chicago suburb of Glenview by developer Howard Soan in 1941. Most planners and designers, along with the rest of the nation, were still working with pretty comfortable assumptions about energy availability. In 1972, these assumptions were on the very edge of radical and lasting change.

For many early advocates, the idea of a "solar transition" had as much to do with philosophy and values as with energy savings, and the gap between their vision and "conventional" business-as-usual development was very wide. Throughout the next decade, the gap steadily closed. By

1976, the National Association of Home Builders devoted a prominent section of its *Cost-Effective Site Planning* manual to energy-conserving techniques, saying "The higher costs of energy and the need for national independence for sources of energy have caused a greater need for proper planning from a new perspective."

Research began to expand on what was already known about the climate-building connection, and to provide better tools for analyzying and shaping the microclimate. G. Z. Brown of the University of Oregon and architect Barbara-Jo Novitski (1979) used Olgyay's definition of the thermal comfort zone as a starting point for characterizing 14 climates in relation to appropriate architectural responses. They analyzed each climate in terms of which design techniques worked best, how the techniques related to each other, how their functions were affected by the time of day and the time of year, and how different options applied to different scales—for example, if the required response is to block wind, that could be accomplished at the site scale by using trees for a windbreak; at the cluster scale, by creating wind shadows for outside areas; at the building scale with an enclosing envelope; or at the component scale with operable windows. Donald Watson and Keith Harrington, in a Yale School of Architecture program (1979), used computer simulations to rank 24 climate design elements for 20 different test cities, comparing the performance of various design strategies in improving the heating energy savings of a typical house. They studied six different types of strategies—geometric modifications, buffer zone additions, thermal mass additions, direct solar gain techniques, insulation additions, and indirect solar gain techniques—and were able to identify the best-performing strategies for four different regional climatic zones. Claude L. Robbins of Florida A&M University, recognizing that even within a single region it is possible for a variety of microclimates to occur simultaneously on a given site, developed a complete set of climate charts to provide the designer with 750 different variables for analyzing the microclimate. Vegetation choices that matched microclimatic factors were studied in detail, resulting in such techniques as the "precision landscaping" systems described by Florida International University researchers Danny S. Parker and John H. Parker (1979), and the Landscape Bioclimatic Chart, again based on the work of Olgyay and others, developed by Daniel A. Montgomery at the University of Virginia (1979).

Builders were breaking new ground as fast as researchers. The number of subdivisions and other community-level projects planned expressly for the use of solar energy grew rapidly. Some of the most famous "early" examples were in climates particularly favorable to solar, such as Village Homes in California and First Village in New Mexico, but innovative projects were soon in evidence throughout the country. In 1980, for example, an Urban Land Institute survey chose 23 model projects that satisfied two basic criteria: they were developed with energy efficiency as a primary decision factor from the early planning stages, and they used land planning techniques to achieve it. The projects varied widely, from subdivisions, apartment complexes, and luxury townhouses to commercial and institutional projects. Although most relied on fundamental principles of siting, clustering, landscaping, berming, and energy-conserving building construction, a few examples in particular demonstrate the striking diversity of strategies that had emerged in the past several years. In Fermont, Quebec, one very large building was used as a windbreak to shelter the greater part of the town. The developers of Pelican Cove in Sarasota, Florida, used flexible local zoning and permit rules to manipulate plot design, cluster buildings, and save trees; their policy of "no building taller than the trees" substantially reduced cooling costs. In San Francisco, building codes that prohibited the use of greenhouses as living space and required all habitable rooms to have windows to the exterior were at first an obstacle for the planners of Sunhouse Complex. But they subsequently proved that their designs effectively met the intent of the codes, and a unique "stairstepping" arrangement of townhouses on the downward sloping site created private south-facing rear yards that protected the buildings from the area's cool fog-laden winds and created warm spots for outdoor activities. The developers of Blue Skies Radiant Homes in Hemet, California, described by HUD as "the largest tract project in America employing the use of solar energy for space heating and domestic hot water," solved orientation problems by designing a flat area in each roof, so that no matter how the house was positioned, collectors could face southward. The flat portion was placed over the garage, and screened by a mansard, a design that proved highly marketable.

An important impetus to energy-efficient development was coming from local and state governments. In 1975, Oregon added energy considerations to its land-use legislation, and Colorado became the first state to enable privately negotiated solar easements. By 1980, a survey of local solar and conservation legislation identified 49 municipalities (states and towns) with energy-related ordinances, almost all of which were concerned with land use and zoning controls (NSHCIC, 1981).

In ten years, the "climate" for solar building had changed dramatically. Planners and designers in 1982 had access not only to an expanded body of technical knowledge, reflected in a new generation of manuals, guidebooks, and analysis techniques, but also to the experience of real-world projects in a wide variety of contexts, and to a new range of options for legal controls to encourage and protect the use of solar energy.

The following sections outline some of the most important examples of progress in each of these areas—information, experience, and policy—beginning with the federally funded programs that had a substantial impact on all three.

2.3   The Role of Federal Research

Most of the federal government's major community and urban design programs were underway by 1977 and winding down by 1981. During this time, the national commitment to energy conservation was relatively strong, making resources available for a remarkably wide variety of initiatives. In those days, federal funding for solar activities was operating at many different levels, not only through major agencies such as HUD and the Department of Energy (DOE), but through the four regional centers, SERI, and the other national laboratories, universities, associations, local and state governments, and private contractors. As an example, some of the climatological studies, the ULI survey, and the directory of solar ordinances mentioned in the previous section were supported in part by federal grants, as were a great many other projects during this period that were not strictly identified as "federal programs."

The knowledge base for solar planning benefited from this diversity, and from a number of other government programs not directly targeted to community and urban planning per se. For example, DOE assisted state and local governments and planning officials through the National Solar Heating and Cooling Information Center (NSHCIC), and the *Solar Law Reporter* published by SERI regularly furnished information about solar access regulations. The Comprehensive Community Energy Management Program (CCEMP), although not concerned primarily with solar site design issues, resulted in detailed information for planning officials about evaluating and affecting energy use in every community sector, and strategies for effective land use policies were an important component of CCEMP's overall recommendations.

But in addition to the "trickle down" effect of these and many other programs, the federal government—in particular, DOE—undertook two major activities specifically related to solar site design on the community and urban scale. The Site and Neighborhood Design (SAND) program began in 1977; the Solar Cities and Towns program, officially launched in 1980, brought together elements of earlier programs.

Before looking at these programs in more detail, it is important to note that perhaps one of the federal government's most significant contributions to the field of solar site planning was the compilation and publication of a number of comprehensive manuals. By 1979, for example, the two-volume *Comprehensive Community Energy Planning* workbook (1978), *Options for Passive Solar Conservation in Site Design* (1978), and *Making the Most of Energy in Real Estate* (1978) were available, as well as other references developed in cooperation with associations and local governments. And a series of three guidebooks produced by DOE, HUD, and the American Planning Association and authored by Martin Jaffe and Duncan Erley are still widely considered to be the most comprehensive standard reference manuals for builders, developers and officials: *Site Planning for Solar Access* (1980a), *Residential Solar Design Review* (1980b), and *Protecting Solar Access for Residential Development* (1980c).

The rapid proliferation of information about solar site planning and urban design that took place during this period had an importance beyond its obvious value to practitioners. The fact that so much information had become available in such a relatively short time proved extremely fortunate, because by 1983, one of the major sources of that information—DOE's research and development programs—was virtually out of the solar business.

2.4   The SAND Program

The Site and Neighborhood Design (SAND) program was based on a simple proposition: together, the residential, commercial, and transportation sectors of the economy use amost 60% of the energy consumed in the United States; energy-efficient land use and development techniques could have a substantial impact on all three sectors (DOE, 1980a). However, actually achieving the potential impact was far from simple, and would require changes in consumer expectations and lifestyles, public agency administration and building industry practices. In particular, three basic constraints were recognized:

• a lack of documented case studies that could serve as design and construction guidelines,

• state and local regulatory procedures that inhibit the incorporation of improved energy-efficient techniques, and

• the financial risk associated with the construction and marketing of something different from the accustomed norm.

The overall objective of the SAND program was to help overcome these constraints. In 1977, DOE issued a request for proposals to designers or developers who were in the preliminary design phases of a mid-large scale (50–500 acre), multibuilding site-development project. The next year, 5 developments were chosen from 31 applicants to participate in the SAND planning study. By mid-1979, concurrently with the preparation of the conventional development plan, each project team had prepared an energy efficiency plan for its site that became the basis for determining energy savings.

The five developments chosen for the SAND program encompassed a variety of climates, site conditions, development objectives, building costs, and state and local regulations. The SAND study area for each project was only part of the total project, and was selected for analysis because of its potential for immediate development at the end of the study period, possibly under the SAND energy plan. The developments included

Burke Centre, VA   17 miles west of Washington, D.C., in a rapidly growing suburban area. The planned population for the entire project was 15,000. The SAND study areas covered over 210 acres for mixed residential and major commercial development. The energy objective in the temperate climate was to create an energy-efficient design while responding to the changing developmental pressures of a major metropolitan area.

Greenbrier, VA   Located in the Norfolk-Virginia Beach area, in a humid-temperate climate, with a planned population of 14,000. The study area of 719 acres was primarily for single-family residences. Energy considerations included siting, infrastructure, and home heating and cooling systems, as well as groundwater heat pumps.

Radisson, NY 12 miles northwest of Syracuse, in a cool temperate climate. Radisson is a planned community with an estimated population of 18,000. The study sites, totaling over 140 acres, included a town commercial center and mixed residential developments. Primary energy consideration was the reduction of high winter energy demands through passive siting options.

Shenandoah, GA Located 25 miles southwest of Atlanta, a mixed residential-commercial development with a planned population of 45,000, in a humid subtropical climate. The 235-acre study site was to be developed as a residential neighborhood, with the major energy interest being the potential of large-scale application of site design and solar technology.

The Woodlands, TX 28 miles north of Houston, in a hot, humid climate, with a planned population of 150,000. Development plans for the 500-acre SAND site included a major regional center for mixed commercial, office, and light industrial uses. Energy concerns included long-range development needs over the 20-year buildout period.

All five case studies generally followed a two-step approach of initial energy-efficient option screening followed by a more detailed analysis of the more promising options. All of the analyses were based on a thorough survey of site conditions, and several teams used computer programs to simulate the effects of various options on overall energy consumption. The energy plan featured the most promising options based not only on energy performance but on cost, market acceptance, and institutional constraints. In some projects the energy plan appeared radically different from the conventional plan, and even the similarities were usually in appearance only: landscaping, for instance, provided in the conventional plan for aesthetic, or in some cases arbitrary, reasons, was used in the energy plan for maximum energy efficiency.

The study teams included the usual experts needed for large new community development—planners, engineers, architects, and landscape architects —as well as additional members where needed. Some teams added computer analysts, or used research facilities at nearby universities; in some cases, the local public utility provided technical input, or an advisory group of lenders, utility officials, local government officials, and residents of the existing projects reviewed the energy plans.

Table 2.1 lists all the energy techniques that were considered in the projects, as well as those that were eventually chosen for the energy plan, grouped by general type: land/site planning and architectural types generally represent passive options that require no moving mechanical parts; mechanical options require active devices such as fans or pumps; and community-level options include systems that improve energy-efficiency by economies of scale in meeting multibuilding needs from a shared system or a more efficient community arrangement.

The SAND program demonstrated that substantial energy savings can be achieved through modifications made to site design within the development process. In The Woodlands and Greenbrier, where sophisticated mechanical systems such as water-source heat pumps and community energy systems appeared practical, dramatic reductions in energy use of over 50% were indicated. In the other projects, the range was on the order of 20–35% of the project's conventional usage, but with a simultaneous reduction in general site development costs, primarily stemming from working with rather than against natural conditions on the site. Even where net initial costs were increased—usually due to sophisticated mechanical systems—the eventual savings in energy costs were calculated to pay back the capital investment within three years.

Some of the findings regarding each project's potential energy savings include

Burke Center   If the energy plan was implemented as proposed, land development costs would be reduced by as much as 18% while yielding the same densities, and total energy consumption of the buildings reduced by at least 33%, while causing no negative impact on either the price of the homes or the sales pace of the developer and homebuilders.

Greenbrier   The study team calculated that end-use energy consumption projected over a 30-year mortgage period would be six times higher than energy embodied in the materials and construction of the site infrastructure and buildings, so the research focused on options that would affect operational usage. For capital investments of $200–3,150, the team estimated a savings of about $750 per year.

Radisson   Energy plans focused on passive heating measures, such as wind protection (projected to save, in itself, 6–9% on detached units and 13% on townhouses units), and a doubling of the amount of south-facing glass (as compared to the conventional plan) for the town center. An integrated utility system for the town center, to replace the conventional system, was

Table 2.1
SAND energy-efficient techniques by project[a]

Technique	Burke Center	Greenbrier	Radisson R	Radisson TC	Shenandoah P	Shenandoah DS	Shenandoah CU	The Woodlands TC
Land/Site Planning								
Building/lot orientation (max south)	●	●	●	●	●	●	●	●
Pavement width/length reduction	●	◐	●	○	●	●	●	◐
Efficiency of lot to infrastructure	○	○			○	○	○	
Vegetation screening	●	◐	●	●	●	●	●	●
Landform screening	●		●	●	●	●	●	
Building arrangements (clustering)	●		●	●	●	●	●	
Increased building densities	●		●		●	●	●	
Central location of public uses	●				●	●	●	●
Pavement shading				●	●	●	●	○
Humidity control					●	●	●	
Shared parking	○			●	●	●	●	●
Exterior space locations					●	●	●	
Reduced parking								●
Compatability between uses								●
Separation of through and local traffic	●							●
Pathways to encourage nonmotorized travel	●	○						●
Decreased number of intersections	●			○				●
Microclimate modifications								●
Multiuse/MXD buildings	●							◐

Architectural

Internal space reconfiguration

Solar screening

Arkansas construction

Double/triple glazing/storm windows

Roof overhang

Slab vs. crawl space

Greenhouse

Air infiltration reductions

Trombe wall (thermal storage)

Reflective exterior materials and paint colors

Berming

Window-placement (N-min)

Solar window

Convective loop collector

Solar chimney

Increased insulation and use of thermally efficient building materials

Reduced exterior glass

Building form alteration

Reduced HR wall orientation to winds

Building entries protected from winds

Entry vestibules

Energy-efficient fireplaces

Roof pitch to deflect winter winds

Avoidance of excessive interior spaces

Daylighting

Natural ventilation

Table 2.1 (continued)

Technique	Burke Center	Greenbrier	Radisson R	Radisson TC	Shenandoah P	Shenandoah DS	Shenandoah CU	The Woodlands TC
Mechanical								
Heat pump-air to air	●	○	◑					◑
-water to air		●	○					
Active solar hot water		○	○		○	○	○	
Hot water heat reclaimer		●				●		◑
Active Solar heating-air			○		○	○	○	◑
-water						○		
Solar absorption cooling						○		
Solar heat engine						○		
Photovoltaics						○		
Woodburning devices								
Low wattage fluorescent lights								●
Return of air through light fixtures								●
Computer thermostat control								●
Variable-volume fans and control								●
Desiccant dehumidification								●
Gas heating								◑
Solid waste steam								◑
Water saving devices	●		○					●
Zone HVAC			○					●
Vented attic			○					●
Dryer heat recovery			◑					
Hot water tank insulation			◑					

Consumer/Community Systems and Operations

- Total solar community system
- Wind energy production
- Central thermal plant
- Waste recycling
- Energy monitoring device
- Multiuse of schools (day/night)
- Central utility
- TES
- MIUS plus variations
- TIES (6 alternative fuel sources)
- Transportation
  - park and ride facilities
  - van pool
  - bus
  - carpooling
  - rail commuter service
- Embodied energy reduced
- Heat recovery systems
- Agressive employment program
- Expanded central function of town center
- Increased efficiency of solid waste collection

a. key: o, considered; •, used; ◐, recommended but not included in energy plan savings. R = residential, TC = town center, P = passive, DS = dispersed systems, CU = central utility.

also proposed, to supply electric power and use ground water and natural gas on site.

Shenandoah   The study team developed and evaluated three alternative plans: level 1, focusing on passive site design, which would cut electricity use (compared to the conventional plan) by over 5% and natural gas by almost 30%; level 2, a dispersed systems plan adding active and passive decentralized heating and cooling, which would cut natural gas use by over 65%; and level 3, a central utility plan, using chilled water cooling, reducing electricity use over 33%, and completely replacing natural gas used for space and water heating.

The Woodlands   Analysis indicated that modifications to a 0.9-square-mile section of The Woodlands' Metro Center could save about 5% in embodied energy, and almost 17% in annual usage (50% in buildings). With reduced energy demands for transportation likely to result as more of the project's residents worked in The Woodlands as well as living there, and with the use of on-site power generation, the team projected a potential 30% reduction in the use of external sources of prime fuels.

Besides demonstrating that passive and energy-efficient techniques could be readily implemented in large-scale development for substantial energy savings, the SAND program also came to some conclusions about the major problems likely to be encountered:

• The effect the developer could have on energy use for transportation, even within a project the size of The Woodlands Metro Center, appeared to be negligible, and to depend mainly on overall density, modal availability, and development location.

• The annual operating energy over 3–5 years, in most cases, equaled embodied energy, so over a 30-year period, a reduction of from 6 to 10 BTU in embodied energy would be required to offset a 1-BTU reduction in annual operating energy.

• A stronger, more innovative role for the public utility in development decision making seemed to be necessary to achieve efficiencies of supply and distribution beyond the building level. The involvement of the public utility in the eventual ownership and maintenance of the energy system was seen as a key factor in overcoming questions of system reliability and salability.

• The development industry as a whole appeared not to have access to design teams with sufficient expertise for the design of total energy communities. Beyond the obvious problem of assembling such a team, the complexity of achieving consensus was also a major difficulty.

In a second phase of the program, eight communities—Schaumburg, IL; Bellevue, WA; Boston, MA; San Antonio, TX; St. Petersburg, FL; Fairfax County, VA; Sacramento, CA; and Honolulu, HI—were awarded contracts to develop regulations to foster energy efficiency through land use.

The SAND program demonstrated that improved energy productivity in communities did not have to increase costs, and could be accomplished without exotic departures from current development practices. But it also identified, in great detail, and based on actual projects with all their accompanying pressures and constraints, the changes in the development decision making process that would have to occur for those energy savings to be realized.

2.5 The Solar Cities and Towns Program

The SAND program concentrated on new suburban development. In 1980, a new initiative was launched to focus on urban areas—the inner cities and older suburbs, which provide housing or workplaces for three-fourths of the American population, and consume about 28.5% of the nation's annual energy use.

These areas are characterized by high-density, old, fuel-inefficient buildings. Rehabilitation and energy retrofit not only present difficult technical problems, but changes of any kind in cities are made very slowly. Many decision makers are involved, and an eroding tax base often prevents support of community-level improvements. The Solar Cities and Towns program was an ambitious effort to meet these problems by combining a number of elements: existing federal programs such as EMPA and HUD's UDAG; smaller limited-resource local programs; grants awarded by the National Endowment for the Arts to introduce large-scale active and passive solar and energy conservation projects in U.S. cities; and direct DOE contracts. The program funded feasibility studies, demonstration projects, and local planning and development projects for a wide variety of building types, including multifamily homes and commercial complexes. In some cases, Solar Cities and Towns funding supported technical assistance to building developers. In others, NEA grants or DOE contracts were backed by additional private, state, or local funds.

The Solar Cities and Towns program emphasized three basic objectives:

• establishment of a technical base for multi-building applications,

• identification of public agency and local institutional constraints and opportunities that form the context within which urban construction occurs, and

• provision of the above information to urban developers, along with direct financial assistance to stimulate solar applications in the urban setting.

Even a partial list of the projects undertaken illustrates the scope of the Solar Cities and Towns initiative (DeSerio, 1980; DOE, 1980d, 1981):

• *Philadelphia Broad Street Study*   The Philadelphia Art Alliance sponsored an urban design study assessing the solar and energy conservation potential of Broad Street, a nine-mile mass transit corridor that forms the major north-south axis of the city. The study examined such issues as how to use subway tunnels and other heat corridors to transfer heat to buildings, and how to match thermal demands with the passive design potential in an urban area.

• *Marin Solar Village*   DOE contracts partially funded the preliminary design and planning of this new town planned for about one-third of the 1,271-acre Hamilton Air Force Base, an abandoned federal property north of San Francisco. The design demonstrated the concept of community self-sufficiency based on ecological balance and efficient use of energy, in housing, food production, and waste recovery, and included a transit center, corporate center, and solar technology center to be occupied by institutions engaged in solar and renewable energy.

• *Daylight Zoning in Urban Design*   Specific research on concepts of solar access and daylight for urban design conducted under this project contributed to the 1980 proposed zoning regulations for New York City, developed to increase access to natural light, thus saving energy through daylit buildings and improving the quality of pedestrian street life. The zoning revisions were based on a performance approach, considering daylight, building reflectivity, and an innovative Daylight Evaluation Chart to measure the amount of natural light that reaches the street.

• *Manchester Demonstration*   In the Manchester neighborhood of Pittsburgh, the nonprofit Manchester Citizens Corporation undertook the renovation of over 1,100 historic structures and the construction of several hundred new multifamily housing units in a 50-block area. The Sheffield Street block was the first to be rebuilt with solar applications. With research funding from the Solar Cities and Towns Program, Carnegie-Mellon University established a set of national urban energy guidelines specifically tailored for Northeastern neighborhoods.

• *Massachusetts Local Energy Action Program*   Designed to assist Massachusetts communities in developing and implementing comprehensive local energy action programs, the project included publication and distribution of over 800 planning manuals, workshops for local energy coordinators, and the formation of the Association of Massachusetts Local Energy Officers.

• *Roxbury Energy Project*   A comprehensive energy strategy was devised for this low-income, densely populated urban neighborhood, including a 6-month solar building topographies study, several demonstration projects, workshops, and a community information campaign.

• *Dayton Climate Project*   The first plan in the United States to alter the environment of an entire downtown area through the strategic planting of vegetation.

• *Fort Sanders Neighborhood Design Plan*   An urban design panel of residents, designers, and developers devised a plan to preserve and renovate this historic, but rapidly deteriorating, residential neighborhood in Knoxville, TN. The plan called for building new homes in vacant lots and alleys, retrofitting existing homes, landscaping to protect solar access, and evaluating a district heating program.

• *Massachusetts Multifamily Passive Solar Program*   The project introduced passive solar heating in 17 state-financed housing projects for the elderly, including both new projects and retrofits, in building types ranging from mid-rise, high-density urban structures to two-story suburban townhouses. An additional significant by-product was the publication of a comprehensive guide to passive solar in multifamily construction.

In addition to these and many other projects ranging from competitions and redevelopment programs to climatological and computer studies, the Solar Cities and Towns program was invoved in three major projects with particularly far-reaching influence.

The Philadelphia Solar Planning Project (1980–1981; see also Burnette and Legerton, 1981) represented the first comprehensive, citywide effort to assess the potential for solar and energy conservation applications throughout a major city, and to implement them through policy changes within city departments. The project comprised 13 separate studies, involving collaboration among universities, city and regional government agencies, private consultants, neighborhood groups, and local designers and researchers.

As might be expected from a project that undertook an objective as broad as the transformation of the fourth-largest metropolis in the United States, the Philadelphia Project generated a wealth of information.

To define the market, the City Planning Commission counted all the housing types in the city's tax file. The survey indicated that 80% of Philadelphia's homes are two-story brick rowhouses, and that 90% of those homes have flat roofs, ideal for solar retrofits. In the five demonstration projects completed under the program, a number of techniques were used, including two particularly innovative solar applications appropriate for urban housing: a roof aperture (skylight) system, which saves an estimated 26% of annual heating costs for a typical building, provides daylighting, and can be locally manufactured; and a sunspace enclosure linking two adjoining rowhouses and designed to prevent heat loss during the winter (Burnette and Legerton, 1981).

The program also produced a *Buyers Guide to Saving Energy in the Home*, widely distributed throughout the city; conducted a commercial audit of 23 small businesses to determine conservation potential and to provide energy management assistance; developed a cooperative venture with the municipal utility to conduct energy conservation audits by mail, test demonstration projects, and select appropriate solar systems to be marketed as a backup to citywide water heating; completed a detailed study of the local fossil fuel industry; developed a climate data digest for designers; and provided the basis for modeling program impacts on energy use, employment, and economic conditions (Philadelphia Solar Planning Project, 1980–1981).

The 15 major reports issuing from the Philadelphia Project, combined with a series of working papers on subjects from markets and financing to codes and zoning, are specific to Philadelphia, but they provide what is probably the most comprehensive practical information available on how to redesign a city for solar.

The objective of the Passive Solar Potential in Urban Environments Project, conducted primarily by the National Bureau of Standards, was to develop a substantive procedure for assessing possible passive solar applications in urban commercial environments. The project mapped solar availability against varied building energy and uses for seven different urban environments (for example, central business districts, and suburban office parks), using five possible solar configurations. But the approach took into considerations a number of factors in addition to thermal performance. In support of the development and testing of analytical models, NBS also evaluated issues of construction, site planning, materials durability, pedestrian behavior, and other human factors, and economic variables such as the impact on real estate investment.

Three new evaluation tools were developed in the course of the project: a complete computer model to quantify solar availability in cities and towns as a function of urban geometry; a field survey method to quantify the impact that shadowing from a solar application might have upon pedestrian movement patterns; and a model to anticipate the economic impact of passive solar designs in commercial environments (Lovett, 1980; Powell, 1980; Ruberg, 1980a, 1982).

Even the most technically advanced solar application could quickly be rendered useless if it lost its access to the sun. The federal government supported a number of studies to determine the most feasible, effective, and enforceable way to establish public rights to sunlight. One of the most significant areas of inquiry was the development of the solar envelope approach to design and zoning. The Solar Access and Urban Form Project continued exploration of this important concept, first developed by Ralph Knowles at the University of Southern California in 1969.

The solar envelope is a volumetric set of limits in which development can occur without shadowing the natural or built surround at specified times of day and season. Thus, it is a conceptual synthesis of time (data about the sun's movement) and space (data about the fixed geometry of the site). The east and west boundaries of the envelope are determined by the daily movement of the sun, the north and south boundaries by the seasonal movements of the sun. The envelope can be described simply, for zoning and regulatory purposes, or it may be explored at greater levels of refinement as an aspect of building design seeking formal integration with the movements of the sun. There are a number of methods for generating solar envelopes, including visual methods with a heliodon, plane geometry, and computer methods. The limits of the solar envelope are an issue of public policy and individual design decisions about what will be allowed to be shaded by new development (all or portions of adjacent buildings, streets, properties) and when (times of day and season).

Solar envelope research, under the Solar Cities and Towns programs and others, developed concepts of generating and using envelopes, and their design, policy, and development implications. A number of publications resulted, including *Solar Envelope Concepts: Moderate Density Building Applications* (Knowles and Berry 1980) and *Solar Envelope Zoning: Application to the City Planning Process, Los Angeles Case Study* (Los Angeles, 1982), both published by SERI, and research supported by the Solar Cities and Towns Project contributed to Dr. Knowles' authoritative book *Sun Rhythm Form* (1981).

2.6   Private Sector Developments

Beginning in the mid-1970s, a great deal of research on solar applications for cities, towns, and suburbs was going on—but many builders throughout the country were not waiting around for the results. At the same time that the "state of the art" of solar site planning was being advanced in the laboratories, computers, studios, and literature, it could be found already at work in dozens of imaginatively designed neighborhoods, from sunny subdivisions in California to concrete canyons in the Bronx.

In Kingsport, TN, builder Robert W. Miller Jr. preserved the scenic terrain that was a major attraction for his company's Willowbrook development, while keeping the price for the fast-selling passive solar townhouses below $80,000. In Valparaiso, IN, on a mostly flat site in a climate that could hardly be characterized as sunny, the 42 passive solar units in Jefferson Park North worked so well that many homeowners went through entire harsh Indiana winters without turning on their furnaces. Green Meadows in Johnston, IA, used the agricultural setting of the multiuse project as a starting point for a detailed master plan that emphasized energy-efficient use of the site in every particular, providing cul-de-sacs for passive homes, and placing two-story houses at the north end of the site to provide wind shelter and earth-sheltered houses at the far southeast corner so no obstructions blocked their solar access. Richmond, VA, developer Patrick Bowe built large passive solar developments on sites where streets were already laid out, and not necessarily favorably for solar access, by treating each lot as if it were a large parcel, and more or less disregarding the street. By canting each house within its "building envelope" to the south, sufficient solar access was obtained on streets of varying orientation.

Since few sites are "textbook solar" sites, and in most cases the precise choice of site either is not up to the builder or is based on a host of economic priorities that rank before energy, most mass-market passive solar developments depend as much on flexible building design as on careful analysis and use of the site. Two speculative passive solar condominium projects near Portland, OR, are good examples of adapting building design to the site (Shea, 1981). The 58 townhouse units of Casa del Sol are on a site sloping to the south at a 24% grade, covered with a dense stand of Douglas firs. The site plan was a response to solar energy use, views, unit density and area coverage, traffic access on steep slopes, minimizing developed road area, balancing cut and fill, maintaining natural undergrowth, and minimizing tree cutting. A double-loaded street system was used that required two different unit types. The uphill unit has living areas stacked above the garage on the south side and the downhill unit places the garage atop the living areas on the north side. At the 35-unit Crystal Park, the site slopes to the south at a 16% grade, and a single loaded street plan was used, allowing each unit to have a backyard on the south side, with garages, main entries, and buffer spaces to the north. The sequence of movement runs from public, darker spaces at the north/main entrance side to sunlit, private spaces at the south. Cul-de-sacs helped reduce the traffic noise, which can be extreme in a solar dwelling that is extensively glazed on the south side. The backyards also work as buffers between traffic and the glazed south living areas of the units.

One of the most influential solar developments in the country is Village Homes, developed by Michael and Judy Corbett's Village Home Development Corporation, in Davis, CA. In 1978, the *Wall Street Journal* said that "Davis has done more for energy conservation than any other city in the nation," and indeed, the energy conservation building ordinances established by the City of Davis (see the following section on solar access regulations) are an important factor in the success of Village Homes. But Village Homes is also a prime example of a development with a comprehensive approach to energy use, including much more than the building of energy-efficient buildings. In a paper presented by the Corbetts at the 1979 3rd Passive Conference, the development guidelines for accommodating passive solar houses were fairly straightforward—north-south orientation for lots, appropriate setback requirements, narrow, shaded streets, lots on the north side that accommodated side or rear entrances, careful choice of tree plantings, and attention to protection of solar rights. But other, less easily summarized elements of effective community design were emphasized just as strongly.

For example, the amount of energy required to construct the subdivision was reduced by paving less land, using fewer and more durable materials, locally produced where possible, and hiring local residents; and the residents were given opportunities to live a less energy-consuming "lifestyle," by the provision of neighborhood areas for food production, recreation, and work opportunities. The design of Village Homes also offers an illustration of subtler factors that work toward more energy-efficient communities by developing a stronger sense of cohesiveness: appropriate scale and definable boundaries to encourage a sense of community, common ownership of a substantial amount of acreage, and common ownership of income property, including apartment houses and the commercial center, to provide money for the economic and social welfare of the community.

Innovative developments have not been limited to residential suburban neighborhoods. When the southwestern Wisconsin village of Soldiers Grove received federal funding after a disastrous flood to relocate its central business district, the village officials decided to emphasize the use of renewable energy. A master plan was eventually passed that provided for the construction of solar municipal buildings, governed the placement and landscaping of town center buildings to assure solar access, set strict thermal efficiency standards for all new commercial buildings, and required that each of the new buildings receive at least half its heating energy from the sun. Soldiers Grove was probably the first solar-heated business district in the country, and included the usual mix of buildings—among the first solar buildings completed were a clinic, a bank, an office building, a glassware shop, and a 7,000-square-foot supermarket that used no fossil fuels for heating during its first winter because of high thermal efficiency and passive solar techniques combined with heat from refrigeration compressors. Architect Rodney Wright, president of the Hawkweed Group, a design firm instrumental in Soldiers Groves' master plan and in the construction of several of the new buildings, was quoted as saying "If you want to make the solar change, it can be done on a community level. Soldiers grove explodes the myth that solar is very costly" (Becker, 1981; DePrato, 1978).

The tenant owners of a dilapidated 1870s tenement building in New York City demonstrated what neighborhood cooperation and innovative system design could accomplish in perhaps the most difficult environment for solar—the inner city. The five-story, 15-unit co-op at 519 East 11th Street in Manhattan was renovated by its "unskilled" tenants, using improved insulation, solar water heating, and an electric wind generator. The first year's heating bills were cut by 70%. A design for the entire block featured roof-top greenhouses for shared food and energy production, and photovoltaic cells for electricity. The "519" example has been duplicated in a number of projects in New York City, including a building in the South Bronx that uses solar collectors and roof-top gardening, and has served as a model for plans in Boston, Philadelphia, Baltimore, and Washington, D.C. (Price, 1980; U.S. Congress, 1979).

2.7 Solar Access and Land Use Regulation

Legislation, on both the local and the state levels, concerned with encouraging the use of solar energy was adopted at an unprecedented rate between 1977 and 1982. The measures varied widely. Incentives were written into property, income, and sales tax codes, modifications were made in building codes and utility rate structures, and programs were established for loans, grants, demonstration projects, and training. But perhaps the most widely used controls were legal changes to land use policy, including solar access protection. These were efforts to build energy-consciousness into standard development practice at the most fundamental level.

As with other incentive programs, the approaches varied considerably (tables 2.2 and 2.3 show examples of the kinds of measures used by communities and states as of 1980). And as with other aspects of energy-efficient development, every approach involved considerable trade-offs, particularly in the area of guaranteeing continued solar access over the life of a building without compromising the sometimes conflicting interests of neighbors, future developers, or the community as a whole.

In most states, there is no legal "right" to sunshine, unless it falls perpendicularly on your property (and since nobody's property in the United States is on the equator, that will not help your solar access rights very much). Two possible exceptions are New Mexico, where the statute declares that the right to use the natural resource of solar energy is a property right, and Wisconsin, where, in the *Prah* v. *Maretti* case, a court

Table 2.2
Communities with energy-efficient development regulations[a]

Category and county	Type of Regulation	Date accepted	Provision
Reducing Heating and Cooling Needs			
1. Port Arthur, TX	Subdivision requirements for passive solar orientation	Sept. 1979	Mandatory
2. Sacramento County, CA	Resolutions and administrative procedure for passive solar orientation	1977	Voluntary
3. Dade County, FL	Site plan view criteria for energy-efficient site design	1975	Voluntary
4. Boulder, CO	Incentives for energy-efficient site design	Aug. 1977	Incentive
5. Douglas County, KS	Zoning amendment to permit underground housing	March, 1979	Removes regulatory barrier
6. King County, WA	Regulations to permit and encourage townhouse development	Dec. 1979	Removes regulatory barrier/encourages
7. Davis, CA	Zoning amendment to permit flexible siting of fences and hedges for solar heating	1979	Removes regulatory barrier
8. Davis, CA	Zoning amendment to permit greater use of shade control devices	1979	Removes regulatory barrier
9. Davis, CA	Landscaping requirements for energy conservation	1979	Mandatory
Reducing Transportation Needs			
10. Boulder, CO	Incentives for energy-efficient location of development	Aug. 1977	Incentive
11. Windsor, CT	Incentives and requirements for energy-efficient location of development	1976	Incentive/mandatory
12. Davis, CA	Zoning amendment to expand use of home occupations	Apr. 1979	Removes regulatory barrier
Reducing Embodied Energy			
13. Windsor, CT	Reduced subdivision standards for street widths	1974	Removes regulatory barrier
14. King County, WA	Reduced subdivision standards for street widths	Proposed	Removes regulatory barrier
15. Davis, CA	Reduced subdivision standards for street widths	Proposed	Removes regulatory barrier

Using Alternative Energy Sources and Systems

16. San Diego County, CA	Mandatory use of solar water heaters in new development	1979	Mandatory
17. San Diego County, CA	Protection of solar access in new development	1979	Mandatory
18. Albuquerque, NM	Zoning provisions to protect solar access	1976	Mandatory
19. Los Alamos, NM	Zoning provisions to protect solar access	1977	Mandatory
20. Lincoln, NB	Incentives for protecting solar access	Oct. 1979	Incentive
21. Imperial County, CA	Overlay zoning provisions to manage geothermal energy development	1972	Manages and facilitates
22. Davis, CA	Deregulation of clotheslines "solar dryers"	1977	Removes regulatory barriers

[a] Within each category the examples are not listed in any particular order, except that similar techniques are grouped together. Source: American Planning Association, "Energy-Conserving Development Regulations: CURRENT PRACTICE" (ANL/CNSV-TM-38) U.S. Department of Energy and Argonne National Laboratory, Chicago, IL, May, 1980, p. 14.

Table 2.3
State initiatives to ensure solar access[a]

Colorado	1975	CH 326	Creates solar easements
California	1978	CH 1154	Creates solar easements Removes restrictive covenants Mandates passive design in subdivisions
		CH 1366	Creates solar shading/nuisance provisions
Connecticut	1978	PA 314	Enables solar access in planning/zoning
Florida	1978	CH 309	Creates solar easements
Georgia	1978	A 1446	Creates solar easements
Idaho	1978	CH 294	Creates solar easements
Kansas	1977	CH 227	Creates solar easements
Maryland	1977	CH 934	Creates solar easements Enables solar access restrictions
Minnesota	1978	CH 786	Creates solar easements Enables solar access considerations in planning/zoning
New Jersey	1978	A 561	Creates solar easements
New Mexico	1977	CH 169	Creates "sun rights" provisions
North Dakota	1977	CH 425	Creates solar easements
Oregon	1973	ORS 197	Mandates local comprehensive land use planning (which includes consideration of renewable energy sources).
Virginia	1978	CH 323	Creates solar easements

[a] Key: solar access, access to incident sunlight necessary for solar utilization; solar easement, any easement defining solar skyspace for the purpose of ensuring adequate exposure for a solar energy system.

held that an action for private nuisance may be maintained against an adjacent property owner in right-to-sunlight cases. A private nuisance was defined as "a nontrespassory invasion of another's interest in the private use of land," so the case can be interpreted as recognizing a prescriptive right to sunlight.

New Mexico's approach is based on the "prior appropriation" doctrine traditionally used in many western states to allocate water resources. It basically means "first in time is first in right." There are some inherent problems with such a precept. For example, it could limit the options for solar in already developed areas, and set up situations where a property owner could not be certain of his or her solar access rights if a neighboring property owner was able to complete a project first.

The "public nuisance" approach is not without difficulties either. The potential for frivolous lawsuits is a formidable one. Also, there would be no security for collector owners until after they install the collector and win the nuisance suit. And since a public nuisance is a crime, the state, rather than the aggrieved property owner, typically would be the plaintiff. So a homeowner might have to wait for the state to sue. The provision for compensation to owners of restricted property is also a gray area. In some cases their loss might be as great or greater than the gain achieved by owners of protected solar collectors.

Although clearly there are some problems with *every* approach, fortunately a side range of controls are possible, including

1. Modifying traditional zoning tools—for example, to provide for low density zoning, new height and grade rules, down zoning and overlays, and to remove possible barriers to solar access such as large required front yard setbacks and "gridiron" platting techniques.

2. Mandating local planning boards to include an energy conservation element in their master plans—the very adoption of such an element can often lead to greater public awareness about solar energy, and to increased support for legal alternatives ensuring solar access. Master plans are also an ideal point to provide for "internal," or on-site, protection of solar access, through good design.

3. Subdivision and site plan review ordinances—even the simplest subdivision regulations will influence the location, length, and orientation of a subdivision's streets, which in turn affects the orientation, shape, and size of platted lots, and the placement and orientation of buildings on those lots.

4. Solar envelopes and bulk plane zoning—while traditional zoning regulations define a simple "rectangular box envelope" inside which development is permitted, solar envelopes or bulk plane zoning consist of one or more planes at the top of the "box," which slope at different angles. Two western cities in particular, Alburquerque and Los Angeles, provide prototypes for this type of zoning.

5. Zoning incentives—such as the 20% density bonus offered by Lincoln, NE, for PUDs laid out for solar access, or the Boulder, CO, system, which grants extra points for solar development in the bidding for a limited number of building permits under its growth control program.

6. Mandated local energy impact statements—ordinances that require an analysis of the impact of a proposed project on local and regional energy sources, and on the human and natural environment.

7. Vesting of solar collector rights by local recording—the Environmental Law Institute recommended model legislation that would allow people to apply for permits for their solar collectors; if the permits were granted, the law would protect their solar access in a number of ways. For example, the city or town could not issue other permits for development that would result in the shading of the protected collector, and neighbors would have to keep vegetation from obscuring it. The town could repurchase the rights granted by solar collector recordation if the town decided to allow development that would interfere with solar access. The approach, however, has two shortcomings from the point of view of local governments: the "first-come-first-served" approach is difficult to integrate with comprehensive planning, since the first person to establish a solar right limits the development potential of surrounding property; and the approach places a heavy burden on local government, which must establish a system for keeping track of solar rights and must review every permit in terms of its potential to infringe on solar rights already granted.

8. Restrictive covenants and easements—a restrictive covenant is a "mutual promise" made between the members of a neighborhood, and since these promises attach to and run with the land, subsequent purchasers are also bound. Some covenants, such as height restrictions, appearance codes, or setback requirements, actually prevent the use of solar systems, and courts have traditionally been extremely reluctant to overrule neighborhood covenants (the racially discriminatory covenants broken up in the '60s are almost the only major example), but several states have passed legislation that specifically prohibits covenants that restrict solar energy use. Solar easements that can be included in the deeds for each lot are a popular method of solar access protection, even though the sale or lease of "airspace" is a confusing concept for many property owners. The best solar easements include a specific description of the area to be assessed, to clear up the concerns associated with the transfer of such nontraditional property rights.

The state of Wisconsin took a comprehensive statutory approach by developing a system that allowed local municipalities to grant solar access permits for solar home construction. The statute also grants the municipality the authority to minimize the effect of the burdens on adjacent properties and to provide for compensation. A companion statute vested the solar property owner with the right "not to be interfered with" to a greater degree than permissible under existing zoning regulation.

Statutes in Illinois, Indiana, and Utah authorize or permit local communities to regulate solar access. In Iowa, a statute requires zoning ordinances to be drafted in accordance with a comprehensive land use plan, and the plan must consider and promote conservation of energy resources and reasonable access to solar energy. The Oregon statute not only permits but actively encourages solar energy, requiring cities and counties to enact ordinances to protect solar access. These requirements complement the state's detailed mandatory comprehensive planning requirements.

Local governments have responded to unique local conditions. For example, in the hot, humid climate of Port Arthur, TX, reducing air conditioning needs was the biggest energy concern. Working with the local utility, the developer of Park Central New Town oriented two apartment projects to avoid east-west solar gain and thus achieve and estimated 10–17% energy savings. After reviewing the apartment site plans, the City Planning and Zoning Commission began recommending a density bonus for solar oriented buildings in residential PUDs. Since recorded subdivision plats often permanently determine the passive solar energy potential of a housing development, city planners were attempting to determine the optimal orientation for housing in the Port Arthur climate and encourage developers to design their subdivision plats accordingly. The Planning Commission's modifications were proposed to the city's Subdivision Code, and in 1979 the Port Arthur City Council adopted ordinances that required the following: lots and building setbacks must be designed so that at least 80% of the buildings in the subdivision could be oriented with their long axes parallel to 9° south of west with a possible variation to 6° north of west or to 25° south of west (Rapp, 1980). A previous requirement that all lots must have side lot lines radial to the abutting streets was eliminated to facilitate solar orientation. The righ-of-way width of streets was reduced from 60 to 50 feet, and when a subdivision abuts an area developed with or specified for high or mid-rise buildings, the location of open space must be such that it will protect shorter structures from shadows cast by taller buildings.

When the City of Eugene, OR, adopted amendments to the development code that required solar access to the south wall of structures in new subdivisions and PUD's, the city developed a Solar Access Checklist to assist developers in meeting the new requirements. The checklist provided detailed outlines for preparing diagrammatic, preliminary, and final plans for two separate design processes—PUDs, where the height, bulk, and location of buildings was known, and subdivisions, where buildings of as yet unspecified type and design had to be provided for.

Perhaps the definitive example of community land use policy is also one of the earliest—that of Davis, CA. The Davis "strategy" is reflected in ordinances promoting energy conservation in almost every aspect of the community, from building performance standards to the reduction of energy used for transportation. As a result, Davis has been instrumental in demonstrating where all the opportunities are for saving energy through thoughtful planning, and in identifying the most workable and innovative techniques—for lot orientation and size, building setback margins, fence setbacks, street width, landscaping, shading of parking lots, use of alternative parking lot materials, the construction and operation of swimming pools, the encouragement of home occupations, even the use of clotheslines (Vine, 1981).

In the area of solar rights, an ordinance was developed and proposed that would require every developer to include a deed restriction describing the allowable height and shade of an "envelope zone" for structure and evergreen vegetation. The envelope was designed to minimize the shading of adjacent properties, and the shading patterns cast by the envelope on December 21 from 10 AM to 2 PM were to be written in an easement or covenant to be included in property deeds. The City of Davis, however, did not adopt this policy, hoping to use less complicated and controversial methods to protect solar access—for example, using a Housing and Resale Inspection Ordinance (which prohibited unauthorized construction and was enforced by presale inspections) to prevent solar obstructions on existing homes. But subsequent California state legislation went further. Among its provisions was the prohibition, after January 1, 1979, of any tree or shrub being placed or grown after the installation of a solar collector on another's property, if the vegetation would cast a shadow over 10% of the collector between 10 AM and 2 PM any day during the year.

Clearly, a wide range of useful tools for promoting and protecting solar access were in use by 1982, even though no "perfect" method had been—or is likely to be—found. Solar access as a policy tends to be compatible with most other development objectives, but even at the level of the PUD, where the number of possible options is the highest, conflicts have to be resolved

between protecting solar access and meeting other important development goals, such as hillside and topography protection, tree preservation,
existing or planned high-density land use with high or mid-rise buildings,
architectural controls, and the temptation for some communities to use
solar access as a justification for exclusionary zoning practices, since large
lots give owners greater control over their solar collectors.

However, by 1982 designers, developers, builders, and planning officials
could approach a specific situation with a growing number of models for
reconciling these issues.

Some of the compromises worked better than others. This is true, of
course, not only for solar access regulations and land use controls but for
every other aspect of solar site, community, and urban design. And in the
years after 1982, the "climate" for solar once again began to change. Many
of the most remarkable advances in planning for solar—technical research,
large-scale demonstration projects, aggressive federal initiatives, far-rang-
ing legislative changes—took place in an atmosphere of urgency about
energy issues. A common assumption was that, as the price and availability
of nonrenewable energy sources continued to be a national problem,
momentun would gather for a broadly based "solar transition." Instead, a
period of general complacency about energy, in some senses comparable to
the pre-1972 attitudes, followed what had been a growth decade for solar
building. Many of the problems connected with community-level solar
use—for example, solar access in the cities, better and cheaper retrofit
methods, the technology for neighborhood-scale solar collectors, and
wider efforts to educate and inform developers and builders—still await
solution.

But despite the apparent diminished motivation for finding those solutions—during a period of "reprieve" from energy concerns that many
observers consider temporary at best—in a very real sense much of the
progress since 1972 is irreversible. New techniques for saving energy through
intelligent site design have been developed and proved, and old ones refined
for new situations. They have been built into neighborhoods across the
country, and written into the community standards of states and towns, to
affect the shape and character of developments far into the futrue, regardless of changes in oil prices or presidents. The people who design and build
and live in communities may decide they do not want to plan for solar, but
they will not be able to say they do not know how.

References

The author wishes to thank for their special assistance the staffs of the Urban Land Institute Library and of the American Planning Association, particularly Ms. Rachel German of the Planning Advisory Service—and gratefully to note that without the unique resources of the Passive Solar Industries Council library and staff, this chapter would not have been possible, since most other sources of information about federal solar programs have been dispersed.

Anderson, Bruce. "Solar Energy and Shelter Design." Master's thesis, Department of Architecture, M.I.T., Cambridge, Massachusetts, 1973.

Armen, Gary. "Solar Access for Built-Up Areas." *Plan Canada*, June, 1985, pp. 61–68.

Ashland, Oregon (City of): Zoning Ordinances, 1982. Selected solar access ordinances, Chapter 18.70.

Banas, Michael. "Alternative Methods for Protecting Solar Access." *Planning and Zoning News*, September 1984, p. 20.

Becker, William S. *The Making of a Solar Village: Case Study of a Solar Downtwon Development Project at Soldiers Grove, Wisconsin*. Madison, Wisconsin: Wisconsin Energy Extension Service, 1981.

Becker, William S., and Hirsch, Thomas. "Making of a Solar Village." Proceedings of the 6th National Passive Solar Conference, September 8–12, 1981, Portland, Oregon. Published by the American Section of the International Solar Energy Society. Vol. 6, pp. 467–470.

Blomquist, Robert F. "The Case for Local Solar Land Use Ordinances," *New Jersey Municipalities*, November, 1982, pp. 8, 11.

Brewer, Deborah Jackson. "Solar Access Laws Can Benefit Developers." Proceedings of the 6th National Passive Solar Conference, September 8–12, 1981, Portland, Oregon. Published by the American Section of the International Solar Energy Society. Vol. 6, pp. 557–561.

Brown, G. Z., and Novitski, Barbara-Jo. "Architectural Response to Climatic Patterns." Proceedings of the 3rd National Passive Solar Conference, January 1–3, 1979, San Jose, California. Published by the American Section of the International Solar Energy Society. Vol. 3, pp. 259–262.

Bryan, Harvey. "Utilitization of Daylighting as an Urban Design Strategy." Proceedings of the 5th National Passive Solar Conference, October 19–26, 1980, Amherst, Massachusetts. Published by the American Section of the International Solar Energy Society. Vol. 5, pp. 897–898.

Burbey, Raymond, et al. "Sunshine Laws: Legal Rights to Solar Access." *Carolina Planning*, Vol. 10, No. 2, Fall 1984, pp. 10–14.

Burnette, Charles, and Legerton, John. "Solar in the City." *Solar Age*, Vol. 6, No. 5, May 1981, pp. 38–42.

Center for Landscape Architecture Education and Research. *Options for Passive Energy Conservation in Site Design*. Washington, D.C.: Department of Energy, 1978.

Center for Renewable Resources. *Putting Renewable Energy to Work In Cities*. Washington, D.C.: Department of Energy, 1982.

Cheuvront, Pam. "Small Town Shares Its Vision with a Solar Architect." *Solar Age*, Vol. 7, No. 2, February 1982, pp. 46–49.

Chicago, Illinois. Zoning Ordinances, 1983. Selected provisions.

Corbett, Michael, and Corbett, Judy. "Village Homes: A Neighborhood Designed with Energy Conservation in Mind." Proceedings of the 3rd National Passive Solar Conference,

January 1–3, 1979, San Jose, California. Published by the American Section of the International Solar Energy Society. Vol. 3, pp. 15–18.

De Chiara, Joseph, and Koppelman, Lee. *Urban Planning and Design Criteria.* New York: Van Nostrand Reinhold, 1975, 2nd edition.

DePrato, Robert. "A Subdivision in the Sun." *Solar Age,* Vol. 3, No. 5, May 1978, pp. 24–29.

DeSerio, Frank. "Overview of Solar Cities and Towns Program." Proceedings of the 5th National Passive Solar Conference, October 19–26, 1980, Amherst, Massachusetts. Published by the American Section of the International Solar Energy Society. Vol. 5, pp. 832–835.

Eber, Ernest (editor). *Urban Planning in Transition.* New York: Grossman, 1970.

Fregonese, John A. "Ashland, Oregon's Solar Strategy." Proceedings of the 6th National Passive Solar Conference, September 8–12, 1981, Portland, Oregon. Published by the American Section of the International Solar Energy Society. Vol. 6, pp. 476–480.

Gallion, Arthur B. *The Urban Pattern.* Princeton: Van Nostrand, 1963, 2nd edition.

Hastings, S. Robert. "Passive Solar Design for Urban Commercial Environments." Proceedings of the 4th National Passive Solar Conference, October 3–5, 1979, Kansas City, Missouri. Published by the American Section of the International Solar Energy Society. Vol. 4, pp. 300–303.

Hayes, Gail Boyer. *Solar Access Law.* Cambridge, Massachusetts: Ballinger, 1979.

Hittman Associates. *Comprehensive Community Energy Planning* (Volumes 1 and 2). Washington, D.C.: Department of Energy, 1978.

Isakson, H. R. *Making the Most of Energy in Real Estate.* Washington, D.C.: U.S. Department of Energy, 1978.

Jaffe, Martin, and Erley, Duncan. *Site Planning for Solar Access.* For the U.S. Department of Housing and Urban Development. Chicago: American Planning Association, 1980a.

Jaffe, Martin, and Erley, Duncan. *Residential Solar Design Review.* For the U.S. Department of Housing and Urban Development. Chicago: American Planning Association, 1980b.

Jaffe, Martin, and Erley, Duncan. *Protecting Solar Access for Residential Developments.* For the U.S. Department of Housing and Urban Development. Chicago: America Planning Association, 1980c.

Jones, Ann (principle author and project planner). *Community Energy Planning: The Basic Elements.* Boulder: University of Colorado Press, 1980 (1st edition), 1981 (2nd edition), and 1982 (3rd edition).

Kaplan, Marshall. *Urban Planning in the 1960's: A Design for Irrelevancy.* New York: Praeger, 1973.

Katz, Robert D. *Design of the Housing Site, a Critique of American Practice.* Urbana: University of Illinois, 1966.

King, Sally. "Solar Siting and Access Protection in New Development." Proceedings of the 6th National Passive Solar Conference, September 8–12, 1981, Portland, Oregon. Published by the American Section of the International Solar Energy Society. Vol. 6, pp. 481–483.

Knowles, Ralph. *Sun Rhythm Form.* Cambridge, Massachusetts: M.I.T. Press, 1981.

Knowles, Ralph and Berry, Richard D. *Solar Envelope Concepts.* Golden, Colorado: Solar Energy Research Institute, 1980.

Los Angeles, California (City of). *Solar Envelope Zoning: Application to the City Planning Process. Los Angeles Case Study.* Golden, Colorado: Solar Energy Research Institute, 1982.

Lovett, Denver. "Sensitivity of the Appreciation of Passive Solar Construction to Selected Economic Parameters." Report for National Bureau of Standards, 1980.

Lynch, Kevin. *Site Planning*. Cambridge, Massachusetts: M.I.T. Press, 1962 (1st edition), 1971 (2nd edition), 1984 (3rd edition).

Martin, Steve, Noll, Scott, and Roach, Fred. "Economic Implications of Passive Retrofit Program in Albuquerque." Proceedings of the 5th National Passive Solar Conference, October 19–26, 1980, Amherst, Massachusetts. Published by the American Section of the International Solar Energy Society. Vol. 5, pp. 841–845.

McAvin, Margaret. *Site Planning for Energy Conservation*. Monticello, Illinois: Vance Bibliographies, 1981.

McHarg, Ian L. *Design with Nature*. New York: Doubleday, 1971.

Minnesota Energy Agency. "Energy Performance Zoning." *Energy Planning Guide for Minnesota Communities*, chapter 1.5: Land Use. No date.

Montgomery, Daniel A. "Climate Responsive Landscaping." Proceedings of the 4th National Passive Solar Conference, October 3–5, 1979, Kansas City, Missouri. Published by the American Section of the International Solar Energy Society. Vol. 4, pp. 57–59.

Moore, James A. "Daylight in Manhattan." *Solar Age*, Vol. 6, No. 12, December 1981, pp. 32–36.

National Association of Home Builders. *Cost Effective Site Planning: Single Family Development*. Washington, D.C., 1976.

National Solar Heating and Cooling Information Center (NSHCIC). *Directory of Local Solar and Conservation Legislation*. 1981.

Neutra, Richard. *Building with Nature*. New York: Universe Books, 1971.

New York State Legislative Commission on Energy Systems. Proceedings of A Forum on Solar Access, July 28, 1977. Reprinted by National Solar Heating and Cooling Information Center, no date.

Olgyay, Vincent, and Olgyay, Aladar. *Design With Climate*. Princeton: Princeton University Press, 1963.

Parker, Danny S., and Parker, John H. "Energy Conservation Landscaping as a Passive Solar System." Proceedings of the 3rd National Passive Solar Conference, January 1–3, 1979, San Jose, California. Published by the American Section of the International Solar Energy Society. Vol. 3, pp. 471–474.

Philadelphia Solar Planning Project. Philadelphia Project Working Papers, including Solar Access Protection, Climate Data Digest, Markets, Financing, Applications, Costs, Programs, Electric Utilities, Programs, Procurement, Audits, Fossil Fuels, Economic Impacts, Neighborhoods. Unpublished; prepared for Department of Energy, 1980–1981.

Phillips, Patrick. "Sidewalk Solar Access: Downtown Zoning for Sun and Light." *Urban Land*, February 1985, pp. 36–37.

Pollock, Peter. *The Implementation of State Solar Incentives: Land-Use Planning to Ensure Solar Access*. Golden, Colorado: Solar Energy Research Institute, 1979.

Powell, Jeanne W. "Economic Evaluation of Passive Design for Urban Environments." Proceedings of the 4th National Passive Solar Conference, October 3–5, 1979, Kansas City, Missouri. Published by the American Section of the International Solar Energy Society. Vol. 4, pp. 581–585.

Powell, Jeanne W. "An Economic Model for Passive Solar Designs in Commercial Environments." Report for National Bureau of Standards, 1980.

Price, Travis. "Energy Gudelines for an Inner City Neighborhood." Proceedings of the 5th National Passive Solar Conference, October 19–26, 1980, Amherst, Massachusetts. Published by the American Section of the International Solar Energy Society. Vol. 5, pp. 846–849.

Rapp, Gerald R. "Subdivision Requirements for Passive Solar Orientation in Pt. Arthur, Texas." Proceedings of the 5th National Passive Solar Conference, October 19–26, 1980, Amherst, Massachusetts. Published by the American Section of the International Solar Energy Society. Vol. 5, pp. 633–634.

Ridley, Layne. "Passive As Part of the Package." *Passive Solar News*. September/October 1982a, pp. 1–2.

Ridley, Layne. "Solar Developments: Success in Boulder." *Passive Solar News*, January 1982b, pp. 1, 8.

Ridley, Layne. "Selling Passive in the Heartland." *Passive Solar News*, May/June 1983, pp. 1–3.

Robbins, Claude L. "Architectural Climatology Charting: Characterizing the Microclimate." Proceedings of the 4th National Passive Solar Conference, October 3–5, 1979, Kansas City, Missouri. Published by the American Section of the International Solar Energy Society. Vol. 4, pp. 255–258.

Robinette, Gary O. (editor). *Landscape Planning for Energy Conservation*. Reston, Virginia: Environmental Design Press, 1977.

Robinette, Gary O. (editor). *Energy Efficient Site Design*. New York: Van Nostrand Reinhold, 1983.

Ruberg, Kalev. "Design and Analysis of Passive Solar Heating Applications for Prototypical Commercial Settings." Proceedings of the 4th National Passive Solar Conference, October 3–5, 1979, Kansas City, Missouri. Published by the American Section of the International Solar Energy Society. Vol. 4, pp. 576–580.

Ruberg, Kalev. "A Computer Model for Quantifying Solar Gain Through Various Types of Glazings in Any Given Urban Geometry and Climate." Report for National Bureau of Standards, 1980a.

Ruberg, Kalev. "Passive Solar Potential for Urban Environments." Proceedings of the 5th National Passive Solar Conference, October 19–26, 1980b, Amherst, Massachusetts. Published by the American Section of the International Solar Energy Society. Vol. 5, pp. 836–840.

Ruberg, Kalev. "Solar Availability in Cities and Towns: A Computer Model." Report for National Bureau of Standards, 1982.

San Diego, California (City of): Zoning Ordinances, 1983. Selected provisions.

Schwolsky, Rick. "Micro-Siting The Building" *Solar Age*, Vol. 5, No. 6, June 1980, p. 56.

Shea, Michael. "Passive Solar in the City: 93 Portland Townhomes." Proceedings of the 6th National Passive Solar Conference, September 8–12, 1981, Portland, Oregon. Published by the American Section of the International Solar Energy Society. Vol. 6, pp. 467–470.

Soldiers Grove, Wisconsin (City of): Zoning Ordinances, 1983. Selected provisions.

Stahl, Fred. "A Pilot Study to Predict the Effects of Passive Solar Configurations Shading Pedestrians." Report for National Bureau of Standards, 1980.

Stahl, Fred, Conway, Don, and Goglia, Margaret. "Human Behavioral Considerations in Planning and Design of Passive Solar for Commercial Settings." Proceedings of the 4th National Passive Solar Conference, October 3–5, 1979, Kansas City, Missouri. Published by the American Section of the International Solar Energy Society. Vol. 4, pp. 26–29.

Tabb, Phillip. *Solar Energy Planning*. New York: McGraw-Hill, 1984.

United States Congress. "Renewable Energy and The City." Testimony form the Joint Hearings before the Subcommittee on the City, of the Committee on Banking, Finance and Urban Affairs; and the Subcommittee on Oversight and Investigations of the Committee on Foreign Commerce; U.S. House of Representatives, October 16–17, 1979.

United States Department of Energy (DOE). Interim Report: National Program Plan for Passive and Hybrid, 1979.

United States Department of Energy (DOE). "Energy-Efficient Community Development Techniques: Five Large-Scale Case Studies." Reports published by Argonne National Laboratory on the Site and Neighborhood Design Program, 1980a.

United States Department of Energy (DOE). Proceedings of the Passive and Hybrid Solar Energy Program Update Meeting, September 21–24, 1980b, Washington, D.C.

United State Department of Energy (DOE). Progress Report on the Passive and Hybrid Solar Energy Program, November 1980c.

United States Department of Energy (DOE) Solar Cities and Towns Multi-Year Plan, 1980d.

United States Department of Energy (DOE) Solar Cities and Towns Program Information Kit, 1981.

Urban Land Institute. *Focus On Energy Conservation: A Second Project List*. Washington, D.C., 1980.

Vine, Edward L. *Solarizing America: The Davis Experience*. Washington, D.C.: Conference on Alternative State and Local Policies, 1981.

Washington, Jenkins. "A Materials Performance Data Base for Modeling the Thermal and Economic Performance of Passive Solar Configurations in Urban Commercial Environments." Report for National Bureau of Standards, 1980.

Watson, Donald, and Harrington, Keith. "Research on Climate Design for Home Builders." Proceedings of the 4th National Passive Solar Conference, October 3–5, 1979, Kansas City, Missouri. Published by the American Section of the International Solar Energy Society. Vol. 4, pp. 636–639.

Weiss, Stuart. *Survey of State Legislative Programs That Include Passive Solar Energy*. Washington, D.C.: Department of Energy, 1979.

Wiener, Imanuel S. "Solar Orientation: Application of Local Wind Factors." *Progressive Architecture*, Vol. 36, No. 2, February 1955, pp. 112–118.

Wisconsin Statutes, 1981. Selected sections, Chapter 354, Solar access protection.

Zanetto, James. "Planning Solar Neighborhoods." Proceedings of the 3rd National Passive Solar Conference, January 1–3, 1979, San Jose, California. Published by the American Section of the International Solar Energy Society. Vol. 3, pp. 88–92.

3 Building Envelopes

Donald Prowler and Douglas Kelbaugh

3.1. Introduction

In this chapter, a "building envelope" is taken to be any surface that separates the thermally conditioned interior of a building from its environment. The building envelope includes roofs, exterior walls, floors, slabs on grade, and foundation walls. Although we will focus on envelope design, it is impossible to separate this issue from whole building design; indeed, one of the accepted measures of good architecture is unity and integration, in which parts are related to the whole and the whole, in turn, to its parts.

3.2 Building Envelope Functions

The envelope of a building, like the skin on our bodies, is called upon to perform a multitude of simultaneous functions in a relatively thin dimension. These functions can be energy related (e.g., to control heat loss from the interior of the building) or nonenergy related (e.g., to present an aesthetic position).

3.2.1 Nonenergy-Related Functions

Many nonenergy-related requirements are also indirectly related to issues of thermal performance. For example

1. *Aesthetic Concerns* In its role as building facade, the building envelope often communicates important cultural and social information such as a sense of grandeur or permanence. Consequently, architects tend to differentiate between the visually exposed and the visually hidden elements of a building envelope. The majority of architects are willing to allow the design of hidden elements to be dictated by functional constraints such as thermal performance, cost, and durability. However, when energy requirements conflict with architectural expression, for many architects decisions become more difficult.

2. *Structural Concerns* Throughout most of the history of Western architecture, the exterior wall has been the predominant load-bearing element. Thus, the envelope of a building was also its structure. In residential architecture this is still largely true; wood frame walls acts as structural membranes. In nonresidential designs after the mid-1800s steel and concrete frames gradually replaced the exterior bearing wall as structural

supports. The skin became a "curtain wall"—a largely autonomous sub-system with surface continuity in an overall building assembly. As it was no longer necessary to accommodate a restrictive set of structural requirements, the design of a building's facade could respond readily to changes in style and technology.

At the same time, the rationalization of mechanical systems made interior planning more regimented and systematic. Increasingly, the distinctions between types of commercial buildings could be read only in the aesthetic interpretation of the building envelope and not in the articulation of its plan and section.

3. *Environmental Concerns*   Building envelopes shelter inhabitants from the exterior environment. They are expected to be waterproof and water-vapor resistant, to provide thermal comfort and good interior air quality, and to control the transmission of ambient noise and light. As the principal defense between the climate outside and the fragile human "comfort zone" inside, building envelopes function as environmental filters (see figure 3.1).

This filtering role sometimes places mutually exclusive design demands on the building envelope. For example, windows can be designed to be inoperable to provide acoustical privacy in noisy locations or operable to provide ventilation, but often cannot be designed to meet both demands.

4. *Construction Concerns*   The building envelope must shelter not only the building's inhabitants but also the building itself from destructive environmental forces. Whereas many buildings are expediently conceived and built to accommodate the demands of an expanding and changing society, others are regarded as long-term investments requiring special respect and care. In the latter, the design of the building envelope often has the greatest impact on longevity and durability.

3.2.2   Energy-Related Requirements

Many designers characterize buildings as either "skin-load-dominated" or "internally load-dominated." In a skin-load-dominated structure, energy consumption is primarily determined by exterior climate conditions and the thermal loads imposed on the building through its envelope. In an internally load-dominated structure, energy consumption is primarily determined by the internal sources of energy flows within the building itself such as the energy used for electrical lighting or the energy used to cool spaces heated by people, lights, and equipment.

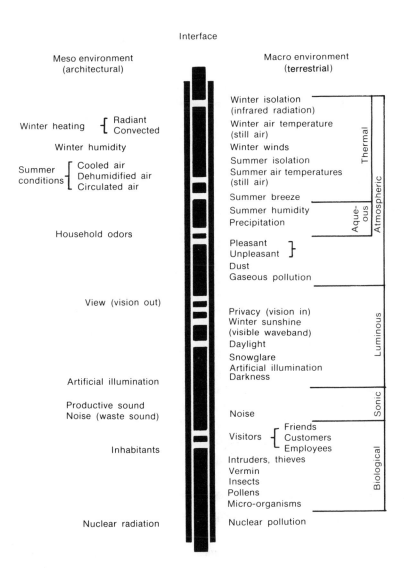

Figure 3.1
"Only with modern science and technology did it become possible to separate the load-bearing task of architectural structure from the environmental-control function of enclosing membrane. Only then could the wall be conceptualized as a selective filter...."
Source: Fitch (1972).

Generally, small buildings with load-bearing envelopes tend to be skin-load-dominated, while larger buildings with structural frames and non-structural "curtain" walls tend to be internally load-dominated. There are many exceptions to this rule, such as large warehouses that might be skin-load-dominated or small computer centers that might be internally load-dominated as well as small buildings that may have curtain walls and large buildings with load-bearing walls. However, it is convenient to use the term residential as a shorthand for skin-loaded-dominated (and, for the most part, bearing wall) structures and the term commercial as a shorthand for internally loaded (and, for the most part, curtain wall) structures as we discuss the various issues involved in envelope performance and design. In this context, "commercial" buildings should also be understood to encompass all nonresidential structures including institutional, factory, and other large buildings.

To understand the full complexity of the influence of the envelope on building energy performance, it is helpful to isolate its many energy-related functions. In a simplified model, the envelope functions as a thermal valve; a radiant filter; an air infiltration barrier; a moisture membrane; an energy collection or distribution device; a thermal, electrical, or chemical store; and a dynamic filter.

In its function as a thermal valve the building envelope, through its thermal resistance (R value), regulates the flow of thermal energy from the interior to the exterior environment (or visa versa). The classic, steady-state heat loss equation $\Delta Q = U \times A \times d\mathrm{T}$ characterizes this flow.

In its function as a radiant filter the envelope transmits, absorbs, or reflects radiant energy. This is true for any of the various wavelength radiations that it encounters: ultraviolet, the visible spectrum, infrared, or terrestrial.

In its function as an air infiltration barrier the envelope breathes by allowing exterior air to seep through cracks and openings or by intentionally introducing air through vents and fans. As unconditioned ambient air enters buildings, energy must be expended either to heat or cool the air to a desired temperature and humidify or to dehumidify it to a desired level. The design of the envelope is one of the principal factors that determine the level of air infiltration into a building. The envelope also acts as a barrier to airborne substances, such as pollutants and odors.

In its function as a moisture membrane the envelope controls moisture content within the building. All buildings contain water vapor that typically seeks to migrate outside where vapor pressure is lower. This vapor can be extremely deleterious to the integrity and performance of the building envelope if the moisture is allowed to condense within the envelope cavity. It is thus essential that building envelopes provide adequate vapor barriers to retard the flow of water vapor from the inside out (in hot, humid climates with air-conditioned interiors, a barrier that works in the opposite direction is often required). Moisture can be a source of serious maintenance problems and unnecessary heat loss.

In its function as an energy collection or distribution device the envelope regulates energy flows to the building interior. Many solar thermal systems collect radiant energy at the building envelope to enhance the building's thermal performance. Designers have also begun to regard building envelopes as plenums or chases that distribute essential building services. For example, in some commercial buildings the exterior walls house ductwork, "light shelves" that distribute natural light (see figure 3.2), or plenums that collect and distribute thermal heat (see figure 3.3).

Figure 3.2
Light shelves, such as this one on the exterior of an office building in Sacramento, CA, bounce daylight deeper into working spaces (design by MBT Associates with Sam Davis; photograph by D. Prowler).

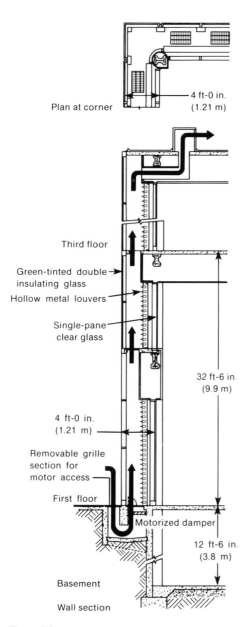

Plan at corner

4 ft-0 in.
(1.21 m)

Third floor

Green-tinted double
insulating glass

Hollow metal louvers

Single-pane
clear glass

32 ft-6 in.
(9.9 m)

4 ft-0 in.
(1.21 m)

Removable grille
section for
motor access

First floor

Motorized damper

12 ft-6 in.
(3.8 m)

Basement

Wall section

Figure 3.3
The Hooker Chemical Building incorporates aluminum louvers within a double envelope
of glass. Source: Dixon (1983).

Figure 3.4
This early experimental solar house located in Newark, DE, incorporates active solar air collectors, photovoltaics, and direct-gain south-facing windows with eutectic storage all within the building envelope (photograph by D. Prowler).

By adding photovoltaic devices, electrical energy can also be collected by the envelope (see figure 3.4).

In its function as a thermal, electrical, or chemical store the building envelope can store energy. Some passive solar applications (such as mass walls) use the skin of the building to provide thermal capacity in which heat can be stored for later use. Generally, this capacity is provided by massive materials such as concrete block or brick, but water or eutectic chemical phase-change thermal storage materials have also been used in numerous demonstration projects (see figure 3.4).

Finally, in its function as a dynamic filter the building envelope can moderate climatic extremes. Buildings have been able to change their faces in the past, with shutters, awnings, and other movable devices. But envelopes may soon become even more intelligent dynamic filters by using computer-controlled devices for selective shading (see figure 3.5) or movable insulating systems (see figure 3.6), or by using building materials whose properties change in response to changes in the environment. For

Figure 3.5
Bright-colored, exterior awnings are automatically controlled on this east facade of the
Gregory Bateson State Office Building in Sacramento, CA (design by the Office of the
State Architect, California; photograph by D. Prowler).

example, work is under way at the Solar Energy Research Institute and
elsewhere to develop glazings whose transmissivity can be changed by
applying variable electrical currents.

The interaction of all these energy-related functions results in a thermal
load on the building that must be factored into the overall building load
that can then be translated into a building energy consumption rate, once
building system efficiencies are known. Thus, the diverse aesthetic and
functional requirements we place on a building's envelope make a simple
deterministic resolution of its form impossible.

3.3   The State of the Art of Envelope Design in 1972

3.3.1   Nonenergy-Related Design Issues

When the first "energy crisis" occurred in the early 1970s, the prevailing
architectural style could be called late International Style Functionalism.
Modernism, the theoretical basis for this style, generally held that "less is

Figure 3.6
This off-the-shelf, movable insulating shade can roll up out of the way in the daytime
(photograph by D. Prowler).

Figure 3.7
Late Modernism tended to foster a uniformity of design and a lack of orientation differentiation (photograph by D. Prowler).

more," that beauty emanates from the expression of an assembly's physical structure. The commercial buildings of the era were generally designed as abstract, nonfigurative compositions lacking orientational differentiation, with repetitive bays stripped of ornamentation, and often lacking hierarchical ordering and human scale in the poorer examples (see figure 3.7). More and more of a building's facade was becoming anonymous glass or glass-spandrel panels.

In contrast to the excesses of later Modernism, the Post-Modernism of the 1980s was rooted in a belief that historical references, figuration, and typology should be the theoretical basis for architectural design. Today, there is considerable agreement about the need for energy efficiency in buildings, but the notion that this need—a functional requirement—should play a fundamental role in building appearance is opposed to most contemporary theory and practice.

3.3.2   Energy-Related Design Issues

In 1972, the envelope's influence on building energy consumption was not a major issue in architectural design. From a performance perspective, the primary question was less energy consumption than peak-load calculation for sizing mechanical equipment. As much as possible, annual energy consumption was estimated from installed system capacity. By 1972, detailed loads and systems calculation computer programs such as Trace and E-cube were being used. However, they were primarily used by mechanical engineers for postdesign analysis. Architects rarely used these calculations or considered alternatives early enough in the design process to influence basic design decisions.

In this context, envelope performance was measured in terms of instantaneous heat gain or heat loss. The common practice was to select a worst-case peak hour for calculating building loads. Typically, a late-summer afternoon would be used to determine peak cooling loads and a midwinter night to determine peak heating loads (ASHRAE, 1972). It was necessary to know the U value of the envelope and the extent and transmissivity of the glazing in the building to complete the necessary equations. To determine cooling loads, a modest amount of additional information about envelope color (light or dark) and mass (high or low) was required in the recommended ASHRAE procedures. Although the cooling calculations were less precise than the heating calculations, in most instances they were adequate for equipment sizing at a time when saving energy was not a major concern.

Then, designers did not use the terms internally load-dominated and skin-load-dominated, nor was there an organized, comprehensive data base of the energy consumption patterns of existing buildings to turn to for design information. Little data existed that distinguished energy consumption by categories (such as the percentage of building energy consumed for lighting as opposed to heating, cooling, or ventilation, etc.), nor was there any significant understanding of the influence of the building envelope on each of the categories. There was even less understanding of the impact of the envelope on the energy performance of whole buildings.

The best-known and most accessible literature directed toward architects on building design and energy consumption, including such books as those by Olgyay (1963), Fitch (1972), Givoni (1969), Aronin (1953), and Fry and Drew (1964), tended to stress "climate-responsive design" and not specifically "energy-efficient" design. The perspective of most of these authors was to optimize building envelope design before mechanical systems intervened. They skirted the complex question of whether an optimal design that assumed natural conditioning was still the most energy-efficient design when such systems were employed. For example, an office with natural ventilation would opt for the maximum operable sash, while a totally air-conditioned office might benefit from not having operable windows to decrease air infiltration. The primary envelope strategy discussed was solar control, typically by shading, in warm climates. Mathematical modeling in this literature was rudimentary, and severely hampered by tedious hand calculation procedures.

Architectural theory began to develop the notion that the International Style had encouraged too much uniformity in building facades, which resulted in climate-insensitive designs. For some, the main concern was less for excess energy consumption than for the lack of architectural "honesty." Others argued that buildings should respond to their context and that an important part of this context was the climate. In light of the monotony of skyscrapers of the 1960s (on the Avenue of the Americas in New York City, for example), the message that orientation should affect fenestration—that northern elevations should be different than southern, western, or eastern elevations—was a welcome idea in many quarters. Nevertheless, architectural expression was more the goal than energy efficiency.

In 1972, then, the average design practitioner probably perceived two strategies for effecting the "climate responsiveness" of a facade: altering the U value and controlling solar radiation (sun control). Altering the U value generally translated into increasing the insulation levels in the building's envelope. Sun control implied solutions ranging from reflective glass to reduce shading coefficients to the use of explicit exterior shading devices like overhangs, louvers, or fins (see Olgyay and Olgyay, 1976, and figure 3.8). Any analysis performed during the design process tended to be a component analysis as opposed to a whole-building analysis in which sets of parameters were allowed to vary.

With respect to solar design, the basic design philosophy was defensive. Usually, the goal was to protect the building envelope from climatic extremes rather than to employ solar radiation for heating or lighting. In fact, the term solar meant little to the design practitioner in 1972. Even architects familiar with the term would probably have grouped several distinct technologies (active solar, passive solar, daylighting, and photovoltaics) under the same "solar" heading. The various demands that these technologies place on a building's envelope design were, at best, blurred.

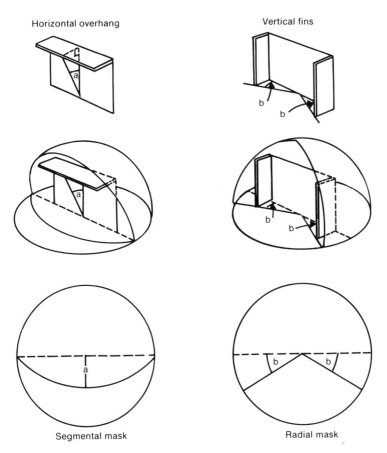

Horizontal overhang

Vertical fins

Segmental mask

Radial mask

Figure 3.8
Sun control achieved through exterior shading. Any exterior shading device has a
characteristic shading mask that can be overlaid on sun path diagrams to determine the
portions of the year during which an aperture will be shaded. Source: Anderson (1976)
after Olgyay and Olgyay (1976).

3.4   Research, Development, and Demonstration from 1972 to 1982 on Building Envelopes

From 1972 to 1982, considerable resources were expended to understand better the energy performance of building envelopes and the impact of solar applications on envelope design. Related work included pure research, applied research, information transfer, design competition, and demonstration project—all competing for attention and funding.

The efforts of both publicly and privately funded research, development, and demonstration (RD&D) can be grouped roughly into three phases. Phase one, from 1973 through about 1979, stressed research and development (R&D) to identify and articulate possible solar strategies and demonstrations to validate the solar designs available when the first energy crisis occurred in late 1973. In phase one, significant effort was also expended to increase the data base of actual energy consumption data for buildings. One of the most notable works in this regard was the AIA Research Corporation's (AIARC) program to collect baseline data to develop energy performance standards for new buildings (AIA, 1978). Data were also collected and compiled on passive solar buildings (for example, Stromberg and Woodall, 1977; AIARC, 1979), active systems (for example, NBS, 1974), and commercial building performance (for example, Ternoey et al., 1985; see table 3.1).

Phase two, the longest phase, began in the mid-1970s and was substantially completed by the mid-1980s. Its primary thrust was basic research to characterize building envelope design, manufacture, fabrication, assembly,

Table 3.1
An example of the interpretation of actual energy consumption data showing the percentage of energy need by cause in five different building types

Building type	Energy allotment (%)		
	Envelope	Contents	Lighting
School	15	45	40
Housing	50	30	20
Office	11	39	50
Hospital	10	40	50
Commercial	15	45	40

Source: Ternoey et al. (1985).

and performance and to determine the costs and benefits of the interventions being studied. By January 1980, with the publication of the *Passive Solar Handbook*, volumes I and II (Balcomb, 1980), on the heels of active solar textbooks by Kreider and Kreith (1975) and Beckman, Klein, and Duffy (1977), the basic physical principles involved in solar systems were available to and understood by a wide audience. Since 1980, R&D efforts have stressed basic materials research and improved envelope design to mitigate cooling loads and to provide daylighting.

In phase three, which began in approximately 1977 and ended abruptly in 1981, RD&D focused on the impacts on building envelope design and marketing of design tools, seminars, and other educational opportunities, design competitions, and local market incentives.

These three phases certainly overlap. But these dates highlight the shifting focus on various facets of building envelopes in the research community during the decade.

3.4.1   Phase One: Early R&D and Demonstrations

In 1972, a building was perceived as a kind of appliance that required energy to operate, much like a toaster or a vacuum cleaner. When the energy shortage of the 1970s became severe, an early reaction was to find new energy sources to power these conventional appliances. One solution was to use solar energy in "active" systems that could operate almost independently of the buildings they were powering. Active systems were conceived as additional hardware that would allow conventional mechanical systems to be smaller or used less frequently and thus consume less energy. Therefore, early government-funded solar demonstration programs such as the National Science Foundation's (NSF) "proof-of-concept" projects and the Department of Housing and Urban Development's (HUD) Residential Demonstration Program (HUD, 1976; see figure 3.9) focused on attaching active solar systems to traditional building envelopes. Modifications to the envelope were minimal, limited to attachment details and pipe chase design. Most of the demonstration projects had an active solar system as the principle space heating energy source and a conventional backup system. In many cases, the active solar system also provided domestic hot water.

The HUD program successfully demonstrated that active solar collectors could heat residences in most locations throughout the United States. The program also demonstrated that the initial costs of these systems were

Figure 3.9
This active solar installation on a home in New Jersey was one of those funded in the first cycle of HUD Residential Demonstration Projects. The collectors are discretely placed above the garage on the gabled roof (design and photograph by Korman Corporation).

high, in part because of the lack of mass-produced solar collectors, in part because of inadequate installation expertise, and in part because of the unavoidable capital costs associated with such hardware-intensive systems. It was not uncommon for systems to freeze in cold climates, and there were many installations with very low overall efficiencies. Even in properly functioning active solar space heating systems, payback periods (without subsidies) inevitably exceeded 10 years, often by a wide margin. However, the program did encourage the formation of many small solar collector manufacturing companies whose efforts have improved the systems' performance. Today, unlike the HUD demonstrations, most new active solar installations are designed to provide domestic hot water exclusively rather than space heating. This year-round application pays back its investment more quickly than space heating installations that can save energy only during the winter months.

The term passive solar design did not formally exist until 1974 and did not come into common use until after the First National Passive Solar Conference of 1976 in Albuquerque, NM, hosted by Los Alamos National

Laboratory (LANL). Consequently, the first HUD solar demonstration cycles stressed active solar collection; however, by 1978 passive solar designs were being highlighted in the last round of the HUD demonstrations. The same design sensibility that embraced passive solar designs also paved the way for better integration of active and passive solar systems with building envelopes.

To the average design practitioner, the greatest impact of the first government-sponsored programs was probably to distinguish clearly between conservation-envelope design strategies and solar-envelope design strategies, i.e., the idea that buildings can be energy sources as well as energy conservers. For example, one government-sponsored publication, *Solar Dwelling Design Concepts* (AIA Research Corporation, 1976), explained in simple terms how building envelopes could respond to various solar strategies (see figure 3.10). Here was a clear message to architects that solar applications could be coincident with, and have a direct impact on, the envelopes of buildings. These conceptual diagrams clearly spoke to architects in a visual language, demonstrating what a solar building could be. Soon afterward, a variety of publications (Anderson; 1976; Mazria, 1979; Balcomb, 1980; Kreider and Kreith, 1975; Beckman, Klein, and Duffie, 1977) lent technical support to these simple diagrams.

Somewhat later, the DOE Passive Solar Commercial Buildings Design Assistance and Demonstration Program, begun in 1979, played a role in commercial building design similar to that played by HUD's Residential Demonstration Program. Though the actual performance data from this commercial program (Booz Allen and Hamilton, 1983) has not been widely disseminated, the Commercial Demonstration Project has made the design community aware of the potential efficacy of such envelope design elements as light shelves and high apertures for daylighting, overhangs, automatic louvers and tinted films for shading, and plenums and stratified atriums for heating.

As the demonstration programs progressed, the economics of the various solar systems were becoming clearer. Early cost estimates by Saunders (1976), Haggard (1976), and Fraker (1976) in passive systems and Thomason (NBS, 1974) in active ones suggested that the incremental cost of solar systems would prove minimal. This encouraged hopes for the short-term diffusion of solar technologies and the immediate application of these technologies in millions of new buildings. But it was difficult to determine the incremental cost of variations in the envelope. The question was, how

94   D. Prowler and D. Kelbaugh

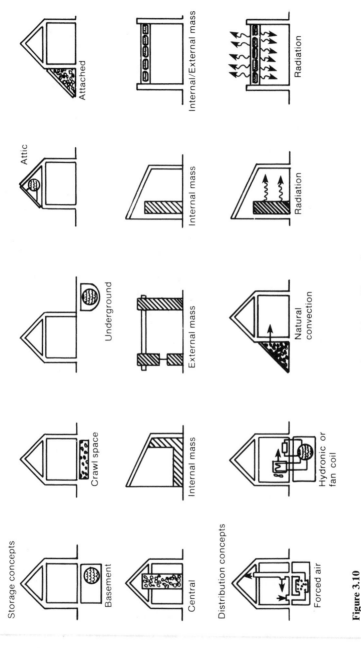

Figure 3.10
These simple diagrams were an important conceptual design tool for architects. Source: AIA Research Corp. (1976).

does one allocate incremental costs when the solar aperture is fundamental to the aesthetic expression of the building? When a solar system was simply perched on an already completed structure, as in an active solar thermal panel system, determining the cost of the system was manageable. It became far more difficult when the skin of a building was also a solar collector. We will return to the debate surrounding the cost of solar envelope interventions when we review phase two.

3.4.2 Phase Two: Research into Building Envelope Components

More precise system design and performance information was obviously needed. Research, design, and development began on a wide range of issues affecting envelope design. But what was the structure of this R&D?

Many of the researchers, who were scientists and technicians by training, organized the R&D according to thermal principles. Thus, conservation and solar energy were distinguished first, then solar thermal versus solar electric, then active solar versus passive solar, on down to direct-gain versus indirect-gain or isolated-gain systems. On the other hand, many designers and builders, more in tune with actual practice, preferred morphological, three-dimensional rather than thermodynamic concepts. They began to think in terms of roof systems, wall systems, sunspaces, atria, etc. While this approach tended to obscure some of the thermal functioning of the various systems, it did conform more closely to familiar construction and design practices in which building subassemblies, not thermal analogies, are the organizing elements.

These distinctions had consequences in term of research funding. Support tended to flow to programs of related physical and thermal characteristics rather than to those involving related end forms or end uses. Thus, at the various national laboratories containing solar groups, cooling and lighting programs were established in relative isolation and, in fact, funded from different sections within DOE—sometimes from the solar branch, sometimes from the conservation branch, and sometimes from the technology transfer branch. For example, LANL might be studying roof apertures for thermal performance in mobile homes in isolation of the daylighting potential of the same formal element, a clerestory, that was being studied at the same time at Lawrence Berkeley Laboratory—such was the diversity of funding sources and programs.

This specialization of task makes thermal research sense, but it left to the design practitioner the difficult task of recombining and synthesizing the research data into a format for envelope design. Some applied research into this design synthesis was conducted, largely in the form of design competitions, summer design institutes for architectural faculty, or curriculum development for educators (Prowler and Fraker, 1981) and practitioners (AIA, 1981).

The architectural classification system of roof, wall, and sunspace/atrium is used in the rest of this section to discuss envelope components. In each case, the extent to which R&D and demonstrations influenced the design, manufacture, fabrication, assembly, and performance of the various systems is addressed.

3.4.2.1   Roof and Roof Apertures

Roof and Roof Aperture Design   The major design issues addressed from 1973 to 1983 were the optimal orientation, tilt, size, shape, and image of solar applications on roofs.

Among the earliest questions asked was, "How should the solar aperture be oriented to collect maximum solar radiation?" In reply, "windows" of acceptable solar orientation and tilt were soon articulated. A window of 15° on either side of due south was generally accepted as the rule of thumb for acceptable collector orientation in most locations. The rule of thumb for optimal tilt (the angle between the collector and the horizontal) for active solar domestic hot water (DHW) collection was determined to be equal to the latitude angle at which the installation was located. Thus, the collector in an active DHW system for New York City, whose latitude is approximately 40° would be best tilted at 40° to the horizontal. For space heating, the optimal tilt was determined to be the latitude plus 15°. The penalty for deviations of up to 20° from these optima was found to be modest (see figure 3.11). In fact, calulations showed that vertical surfaces with additional reflections from snow or reflectors in the foreground would intercept almost as much radiation during the heating season as optimally sloped surfaces. This supported the case for the many vertical-wall passive solar homes that were constructed throughout the period.

Unfortunately, the diagrams that appeared in the solar literature to help explain the concept of optimal tilts caused a misconception about what the roofs of solar-responsive buildings should look like. These simple schematic diagrams, with their dramatically sloped roofs, often became the literal design response. One critic referred to these forms as belonging to the "flying wedge of cheese school of solar design" (see figure 3.12). The roof overwhelmed the rest of the building and sometime obscured other impor-

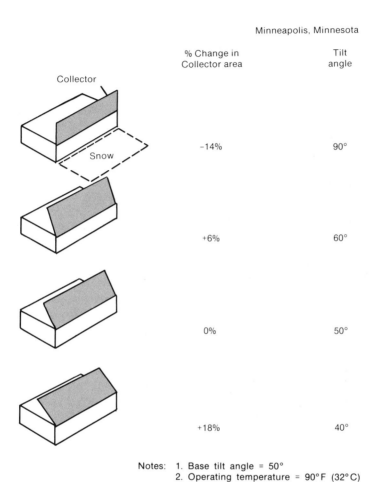

Minneapolis, Minnesota

% Change in Collector area	Tilt angle
−14%	90°
+6%	60°
0%	50°
+18%	40°

Notes: 1. Base tilt angle = 50°
2. Operating temperature = 90°F (32°C)
3. Due south orientation

Figure 3.11
Small changes in collector area are required when the tilt angle differs from the optimum.
(The figure assumes a south-facing orientation.) Source: Anderson (1976).

Figure 3.12
A "solar wedge of cheese" (photograph by D. Prowler).

Figure 3.13
Greenhouses, Trombe walls, direct-gain windows, and colorful awnings contribute to a lively composition in this housing development for the elderly in Roosevelt, NJ (design by Kelbaugh + Lee; photograph by D. Prowler).

tant visual information. As a result, solar buildings were often criticized by the design community.

The second generation of residential solar buildings employed more sophisticated roof forms and images. Aperture areas were often scaled down or integrated better into the overall building design, more often employing traditional roof forms (see figure 3.13). Similarly, in many second-generation commercial buildings, roofs were no longer the location of the principal solar intervention as daylighting or thermal collection from vertical curtain walls became the primary energy-conservation strategies.

Roof and Roof Aperture Manufacture, Fabrication, and Assembly Early Energy Research and Development Administration (ERDA), NSF, and DOE programs stressed the application of functionally separate pieces of hardware, predominantly flat-plate solar collectors designed for low- and medium-temperature working fluids. In most cases, this apparatus was placed on the roof of either a new or existing structure.

However, the high, initial cost of these systems was still a major constraint to their wide use. In new construction, the collector was sometimes integrated into the building envelope to reduce the cost of other required building subassemblies. For example, the collector might be used as the waterproof outside membrane of the roof, or the roof might be constructed as usual but configured to better accept the collectors at an optimal orientation and tilt angle to maximize solar gain (see figure 3.9).

Research and development that had at first focused on fabricating separate solar collection devices for roof applications in factories expanded to include on-site fabrication and assembly of roof aperture systems. This was true for both active and passive applications, although most of the progress occurred in passive solar applications. Some researchers developed integral roof aperture systems that had major implications for both building design and fabrication. Harold Hay's Skytherm system of heating and cooling and Norman Saunder's Solar Staircase were two of the noteworthy integrated roof aperture solar designs developed during this period.

The Skytherm system uses a flat roof to hold water-filled thermal storage bags, above which movable insulation is placed. During the daytime in the winter, the insulating panels are retracted and solar radiation is allowed to heat the water bags. At night, the insulating panels are closed and the warmed water heats the living space below by radiation from the conductive, warm ceiling (see figure 3.14). The procedure can be reversed in the summer to provide a degree of radiant cooling to the space. The Skytherm system is best suited for snowless, temperate climates where flat roofs are acceptable. Tests conducted on the original Skytherm house in Atascadero (Stromberg and Woodall, 1977) confirmed that the system was marked by excellent performance and very stable interior temperatures during much of the year. Reports differ about the incremental cost of the Skytherm system over standard flat-roof construction because the design appears in relatively few houses, but the cost certainly exceeds the $1.65/ft^2 ($17.82/m^2) (1976 dollars) originally estimated (see Haggard, 1976).

The Solar Staircase (see figure 3.15) is a roof aperture system in which alternating bands of vertical glazing and reflective, horizontal insulation create a staircaselike roof section (Solar Age, 1978). The vertical glazing ameliorates the summer overheating associated with the kind of sloped glazing found in the sloped roofs of some sunspaces. The vertical glazing also benefits from reflections from the flat, reflecting "treads." As a transparent device, the staircase has the advantage of allowing natural daylighting deep into the space, but it also requires remote thermal mass for heat storage. At present, no prefabricated staircase roof is available and the

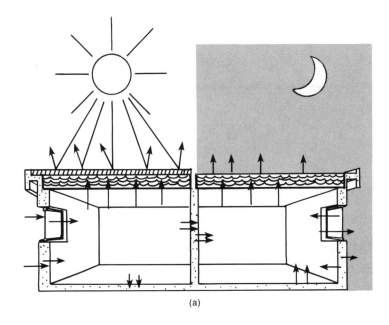

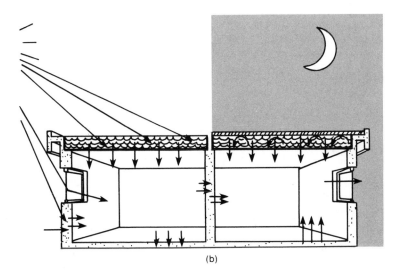

Figure 3.14
(a) Summer operation of the Skytherm system showing insulation in place over water mass during the daytime and retracted at night. (b) Winter operation of the Skytherm system showing insulation retracted during the daytime and in place at night. Source: Stromberg and Woodall (1977).

Figure 3.15
An example of a "solar staircase" roof.

labor intensity of the site-fabricated version has precluded wide application of the design.

Many designers integrated roof aperture designs into one-of-a-kind, site-specific solar buildings. For example multiple apertures were incorporated in the design of a state office building in Taos, NM (see figures 3.16 and 3.17), and one large skylight backed by movable insulating skylids capped a community center in Trenton, NJ (see figure 3.18). Daylighting and active or passive solar applications were sometimes conceived together, such as in the Princeton Professional Park complex in central New Jersey (see figures 3.19 and 3.20). In all these cases, the architectural integration of roof and floor plan suddenly became a functional necessity (Stephens, 1979; Solar Architecture, 1978; Doubilet, 1983). The roof design could no longer be divorced from the design of the whole building.

In some instances, factory-assembled active collectors also formed the waterproof membrane of the structure, so that some solar system costs could be allocated to mandated envelope costs. One well-documented

Figure 3.16
Located in Taos, NM, this low-rise office building relies on clerestories for solar collection and daylighting (design and photograph by William Mingenbach).

institutional case study of this kind is the Los Alamos Study Center (See Hedstrom and Murray, 1980). In residential construction, however, the large tolerance required in field construction makes it difficult to integrate the small tolerance, factory-assembled collectors within roofs. Thus, such systems have not been widely employed.

With a similar intention, do-it-yourselfers attempted to use the space between roof trusses or wall studs in houses to recess active solar collector panels fabricated on-site (see figure 3.21). In many cases, the collectors used air as a transfer medium with rock storage bins. Some manufacturers attempted to fabricate whole housing "systems" employing this technology. Unfortunately, low system efficiencies and high rates of energy consumption (usually by fans) plagued many of these site-built projects, often because of the inherent difficulty of site engineering and of sealing relatively complex (for residential construction) air-handling and ductwork systems. The incremental costs of such systems have varied widely, according to the literature (from $5 to $30 per square foot of glazing); the labor-intensive nature of many of these systems makes the higher estimates more likely.

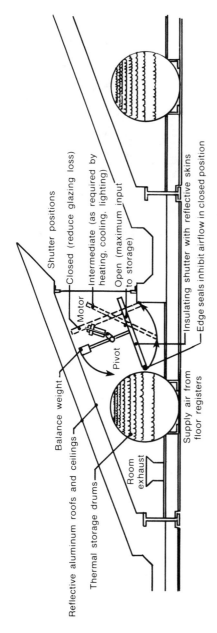

Figure 3.17
A section through the Mary Medina State Office Building in Taos, NM, showing a typical roof monitor with movable insulation and thermal storage drums. Source: Progressive Architecture (April 1979—Suzanne Stephens).

Figure 3.18
One large clerestory provides solar heating deep into a community center building in
Trenton, NJ (design by the City of Trenton, D. Kelbaugh, architect in charge;
photograph by D. Prowler).

Figure 3.19
Operable curtains can insulate and diffuse the light that enters the atrium in the single-
story Princeton Professional Park in Princeton, NJ (design by Harrison Fraker and
Associates; photograph by D. Prowler).

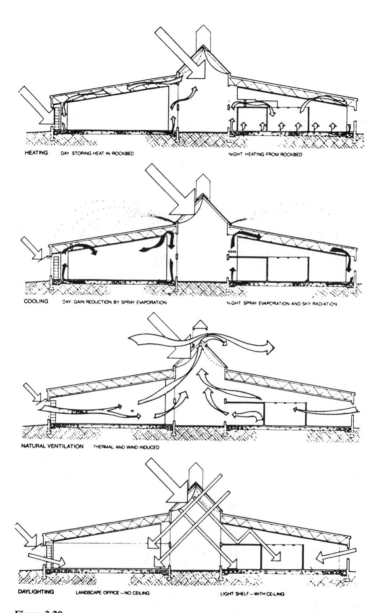

Figure 3.20
Sections through the atrium at the Princeton Professional Park showing the heating,
cooling, and ventilating modes of the building. Source: Doubilet (1983).

Figure 3.21
Site-fabricated solar air collectors are incorporated into a residential roof design (design by Malcolm Wells; photograph by D. Prowler).

In contrast to these architecturally integrated, whole-roof solutions, some manufacturers prefer the convenience and flexibility of standardized, fixturelike roof aperture devices that could be integrated into the basic roof forms. For example, Butler Manufacturing Company, a leading manufacturer of preengineered commercial and industrial buildings, undertook a research program (Butler, 1982) to incorporate preengineered roof aperture components as options on their standard building package. These apertures included integral thermal storage and movable insulation. Although full-scale prototypes were built and tested, Butler has not yet decided to make the roof aperture commercially available.

Another attempt to integrate roof aperture "fixtures" with environmental roof membranes was the LANL solar mobile home design project. In this project (see figure 3.22) a mobile home was tested that incorporated a sawtooth roof monitor with integral nighttime movable insulation. Though this design's performance met expectations (Sandia, 1979), the program has not led to any marketable products.

At present, many manufacturers offer standard residential or light commercial skylights that, they claim, can be turned into roof aperture devices with movable insulation or other control mechanisms such as reflectors and shading devices. In 1977, the Architectural Aluminum Manufacturers Association (1977) published *Voluntary Procedure for Calculating Skylight Energy Balance* to bolster the case for skylights as energy sources. To date, however, Zomeworks Corporation, in New Mexico, is one of the few manufacturers actually to offer an off-the-shelf roof aperture device that includes integral insulation and a reflector/shading device.

The integration of photovoltaic systems in roofs is still embryonic; however, it is possible to compare its progression with the design evolution of active and passive solar roof systems. For example, some designers are attempting to create solar photovoltaic shingles that can function not only as a solar electricity source but also as the waterproof membrane of the building. However, these products are still largely in the research stage.

Roof and Roof Aperture Performance   Excellent research on performance prediction and system validation was conducted throughout the period from 1973 to 1983. Completed buildings were tested in the field to measure their actual performance, and at the same time test cells were built to validate computer models. Side-by-side test facilities at Colorado State University (active systems) (see figure 3.23), LANL (passive and active heating), Lawrence Berkeley Laboratory (LBL) (daylighting), the Farallones Institute (passive heating), Trinity College (passive cooling), and

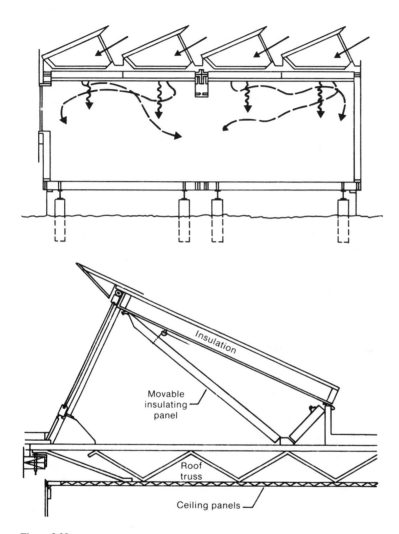

Figure 3.22
(Top) Thermal flow diagram for Mobile/Modular Home II built and tested by LASL
under funding from ERDA in 1977. (Bottom) Cross section of roof aperture construction.
Source: Sandia (1979).

Figure 3.23
These side-by-side test houses at Colorado State University provided important comparative performance information (photograph by CSU).

Arizona State University (passive heating and cooling), among others, provided useful information to compare performance of active and passive heating and cooling systems.

Performance results were not usually broken down in occupied demonstration buildings to reflect the energy flows through specific sections of an envelope. The performance of the solar envelope was usually inferred from the performance of the whole building. There are some notable exceptions to this rule, however. A detailed analysis of Unit One First Village, for example, released by LANL, quantified specific energy flows through various envelope components of the residence (Balcomb, Hedstrom, and Perry, 1981). Several Brookhaven National Lab studies also quantified actual energy flows through residential envelopes (see, for example, Hagan and Jones, 1983).

Early roof aperture sizing research was conducted primarily in the field of active solar collection using flat-plate collectors. The active load collector ratio (LCR) method developed at LANL and the F-chart calculation procedure developed at the University of Wisconsin pioneered in providing designers with reasonably accurate estimates of active solar collection area.

The load collector ratio method was a schematic design tool that required the designer to know only the general heat-loss rate of his design [expressed in Btu/ft^2 per degree day (the so-called "building load coefficient" BLC (Balcomb and Hedstrom, 1976)] and to have access to maps of the United States that contained iso-LCR lines. With these data, the designer could estimate the approximate active solar collection area required to achieve either 25%, 50%, or 75% solar heating. The designer could then determine the impact this collection area might have on a preferred building and roof design. The LCR method assumed a "standard" flat-plate collector in a "standard" system configuration for its calculations. Deviations from this standard required correcting the schematic results. This procedure was the conceptual basis for the more well-known LANL passive SLR (solar load ratio) method, which provides quick design-phase information on passive systems.

The F-chart procedure is a more detailed active solar calculation procedure that employs collector performance curves and such system performance parameters as inlet water temperatures and thermostat settings. This procedure can be more precise than the LCR method, but it requires more data and more calculations and is best performed on a computer. The F-chart procedure also allows domestic hot water to be sized, which the LCR method does not. Although it was not the case at the beginning of the decade, it is the case today that most reliable collector manufacturers provide buyers with accurate DHW sizing information. In most continental American climates, one can assume that a DHW collection area of from 80 to 100 ft^2 (7–9 m^2) will be required for a family of four to achieve a 50–60% contribution to the DHW load. Each additional family member will necessitate another 20 ft^2 (2 m^2) of collector area.

To predict the performance of residential and light commercial passive solar roofs and roof apertures, the *Passive Solar Heating Analysis* handbook (Balcomb et al., 1984) currently provides the most complete and rigorous verified procedures. This handbook grew out of extensive research conducted at LANL, also summarized in the *Passive Solar Handbook, volume III*, that included the extension of the LCR method to passive configurations. Side-by-side test cell data and computer code validation led to the correlation method on which the SLR procedure is based. The performance of most roof aperture designs without integral thermal mass can be predicted using the examples for direct gain in the handbook.

For the daylighting performance of roof apertures there is no comparative single source for design guidelines. However, early daylight calculation procedures, like the daylight factor method developed by Hopkinson and others in Great Britain in the 1950s, have been extended in recent years largely through the work of the Daylighting Group at Lawrence Berkeley Laboratory. Today, computer codes such as Superlite (LBL, 1985) allow the daylighting performance of roof apertures to be factored into whole-building analyses such as the hour-by-hour simulation programs typified by DOE-2. Most microprocessor-based daylighting programs are only beginning to incorporate roof aperture algorithms.

Although performance data on solar applications to commercial buildings are being collected, whole-building performance guidelines are still lacking, largely because of the complexity of the trade-offs involved. Consequently, no single source in the literature clarifies the simultaneous schematic design implication of changes to roof aperture area in a commercial structure for heating, cooling, peak-load demand, and daylighting performance. At present, designers who need this information must simulate the building's performance on a computer and study parametric changes to the envelope design.

In addition, basic research still remains to be done in roof cooling systems and roof aperture daylighting (the difficult task of assessing daylighting quality has hardly begun). Nevertheless, compared with the largely intuitive procedures used in 1973, quantitative performance prediction is one of the unquestionable success stories of solar research, whether it is for roof apertures, wall systems, or sunspaces (see section 3.4.2.2 for additional performance information).

3.4.2.2 Wall and Wall Apertures

Wall and Wall Aperture Design Early in the decade, data showed that in most locations in the United States, vertical south-facing walls received approximately 90% of the solar radiation during the heating season that was available to an equal area of optimally tilted surface. This led to a great deal of interest in structurally integrated wall and wall aperture solar systems, particularly passive systems.

The idea that the walls of homes could be modified to make use of solar energy was at first introduced into the building community by means of a small group of passive solar homes designed and built by private individuals—notably, the Baer residence in Albuquerque, NM, the Wright residence in Santa Fe, NM, and the Kelbaugh residence in Princeton, NJ. Each structure made significant aesthetic and technical contributions to our understanding of the role of solar walls.

The Baer residence, designed by Steve Baer, is the earliest of the three structures, actually predating the first oil crisis of 1973. By strongly differentiating the glazed southern facade from the opaque aluminum sandwich panels of his Zome structure, Baer was making an early statement about the importance of orientation in thermal performance (see figures 3.24 and 3.25). His use of movable exterior reflecting panels, which also provided movable insulation at night, foreshadowed the use of operable facade elements in the energy-efficient designs of the next decade. Also, the water-filled thermal storage containers (55-gallon drums) used in the house provided an early performance validation of passive solar mass walls. Bear showed that the envelope could be a dynamic filter with shading, insulation, and transmission functions changing in response to changing environmental stimuli.

The Wright residence, designed by David Wright, besides providing experimental validation of direct-gain passive solar heating, demonstrated that a solar envelope could still be a vernacular envelope. Whereas Baer was using a new wall construction and geometry (Zomes), Wright's non-south walls appear to be of more traditional design (see figure 3.26). In fact, the adobe-looking exterior finish on this structure is actually stucco covering insulation. The insulation is placed on the outside of the interior adobe masonry wall, which functions as thermal storage within the structure to trap the heat inside an insulated envelope. Truth in tectonic expression was not the design issue here; the issue was a desire to show that solar collection could be achieved within an existing regional style.

The Kelbaugh residence, designed by Doug Kelbaugh and built in 1974, incorporated the first Trombe wall constructed in the United States (see figures 3.27 and 3.28). It demonstrated that the Trombe wall principle first employed in the Pyrenees at the Odeillo house could work in this country. Perhaps more important, it suggested in its rigorous application of Modernist design principles that solar design could also be serious architecture; it displayed a stylistic purity that made a consciously architectural statement.

Along with these custom homes, one of the most important trends during the 1973–1983 period in solar wall design was an attempt to integrate solar design with traditional construction. Many demonstration programs—often funded by local utility companies such as Pennsylvania Power & Light (PP&L), Detroit Edison, and the Tennessee Valley Authority

Figure 3.24
South facade of the Baer House showing the water wall and movable insulation (design by
Steve Baer: photograph by D. Prowler).

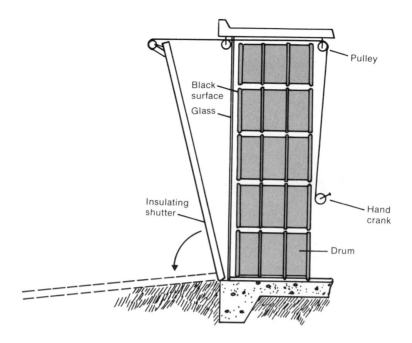

Figure 3.25
A section through the south wall of the Baer House showing the hand-operated insulating shutter and drumwall. Source: Anderson, (1976).

Figure 3.26
The Wright House appears to be constructed of solid adobe; in fact, the exterior is stucco over insulation (design by David Wright; photograph by D. Prowler).

Figure 3.27
A square glazing grid covers the south elevation of the Kelbaugh House (design by
D. Kelbaugh; photograph by D. Prowler).

(TVA)—were launched to provide prototype solar designs for the general
housing market. These programs met with varying degrees of success. The
PP&L program, for example, created six prototype passive solar residences
using wall and wall aperture systems (see figure 3.29). More than 50,000
people visited these six structures during a two-month open house. In other
areas of the country, such as New Mexico and Colorado, demonstration
projects met with equal interest and response.

Although many passive systems were integrated quickly into building
facades, active systems were not. Most active solar collectors are designed
to serve both the retrofit and the new construction markets; manufacturers
do not want sales to be limited to systems for which the building envelope
must be predesigned. Hence, active systems have not generally been integrated with wall systems to the extent that passive systems have been. Few
first-generation active solar structures made use of vertical collection surfaces; however, the PP&L research home in Allentown, PA, is a notable
exception (see figure 3.30).

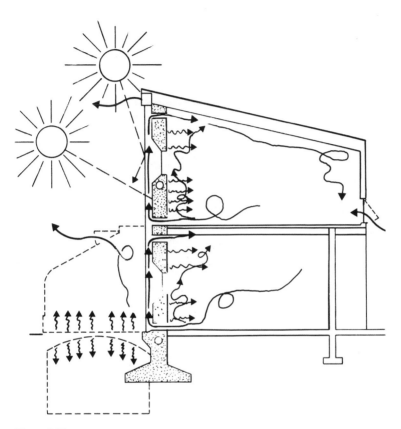

Figure 3.28
Section through the Kelbaugh House showing thermal flows caused by convection and
radiation (design by D. Kelbaugh; photograph by D. Prowler).

Figure 3.29
One of six passive solar homes included in the PP&L Passive Solar Demonstration
Program. Notice the formal relationship it shares with its next-door neighbor. (design by
South Street Design and Kelbaugh + Lee; photograph by D. Prolwer).

Among the passive system designs studied in detail were those for direct-
gain windows and mass walls (particularly Trombe wall systems). Direct-
gain systems rely on expanses of south-facing window glass to admit
sunlight to the building's interior. The sunlight changes to heat on contact
with a dark surface and, in most cases, is stored in massive, thermal storage
materials for later use. For moderately well-insulated houses [6–10 Btu/ft²
DD (0.02–0.03 KWh/m² DD)] in temperate climates, when the ratio of
south-facing glazing to house floor area does not exceed 10%, the additional
heat can be used almost immediately and no additional thermal storage is
necessary. Nevertheless, the south-facing exterior wall of even such a "sun-
tempered" house can be expected to have three to four times more glazing
than is normally found in the south facade of a tract home.

For larger expanses of glass, thermal storage must be provided within the
house. The amount of thermal storage required ranges from 60 lb of
masonry or 12 lb of water per square foot of glazing (from 293 kg of
masonry or 59 kg of water per square meter of glazing) at low solar savings
fractions (20%) to 210 lb of masonry or 42 lb of water per square foot of

Figure 3.30
The balcony railing and garden fence are actually active solar collectors in this early solar
home from 1974 located in Allentwon, PA (design by PP&L; photograph by D. Prowler).

glazing (to 1,026 kg of masonry or 59 kg of water per square meter of
glazing) at high solar savings fractions (70%). For more complete sizing
information, see the *Passive Solar Design Handbook* (Balcomb, 1980). In
general, experience has shown that direct-gain designs that hope to achieve
high solar fractions are more constrained by the difficulty of locating large
amounts of effective thermal mass within the structure than they are by the
difficulty of placing sufficient solar glazing on the building's facade.

Mass walls integrate thermal storage and solar collection within the
thickness of the wall. The thermal storage can be in the form of water or
masonry, but more typically it is masonry so that it can be self-contained
and structural. Mass walls constructed of masonry, most commonly called
Trombe walls, have been employed in several thousand houses.

Many passive solar building facades use a mix of different solar
applications—mass walls, direct gain, sunspaces—to give them design
variety, to provide different scales to the building, and to avoid a mono-
lithic appearance (see figure 3.13). From both the design and performance
perspectives, experience suggests that modestly sized wall aperture system
(i.e., those designed to provide from a quarter to a third of the heating load)

have been the most successful. The amount of thermal storage they require is not prohibitive, and they do not obscure the building's facade under a sheet of glass. Payback periods of 10–30 years for mass walls have been reported in the literature, based on a wide range of assumption about system costs and alternative fuel costs.

Whether the system is active or passive, as its size increases and the solar contribution to the heating load approaches 100%, the law of diminishing returns begins to apply. Each square foot of additional collector area contributes a smaller and smaller increment to the building's heating needs. Yet each square foot of system, with its necessary glass and mass, usually costs at least as much to build per square foot as the square foot that preceded it. Some designers argue that as 100% solar heating is approached auxiliary heating systems can be disgarded at considerable savings. This, they contend, makes attempting 100% solar heating a more viable alternative than it may first appear. Unfortunately, many lending institutions and building codes require auxiliary heaters in all homes regardless of their solar contributions.

All passive heating systems—roof, wall, or sunspace—should be constructed so they do not exacerbate summer cooling requirements. Often, this will have an impact on the function and appearance of the wall of a structure in the form of awnings, overhangs, films, or other shading devices. Optimized shading algorithms have been proposed that are sensitive to the lack of congruence between peak sun angles and peak cooling seasons (see Lau 1983, for example). Nevertheless, Olgyay and Olgyay's *Solar Control and Shading Devices* remains one of the best references for designing permanent shading devices for wall systems, while ASHRAE provides detailed information on the shading coefficients and characteristics of various louvers, blinds, and protective films.

There is little experience with incorporating solar thermal systems into commercial building facades. In fact, some conservation-based building codes restrict U-values and thus, indirectly, glass areas on commercial walls. This tends to discourage solar experimentation (see ASHRAE Standard 90A-80 for an example of a primarily prescriptive code). Nevertheless, some demonstration projects have integrated solar collectors with building curtain walls. One of the first was an experimental building at Odeillo in the Pyrenees in which a passive, thermosiphoning wall panel substituted for sprandel panels in a multiple-story office building (Anderson, 1976). In this case, the solar system provided a significant portion of the building's heating requirement.

In a similar manner more recent experimental projects have employed active double-wall collectors. For example, at the Enerplex Complex in Princeton, NJ (no author cited, 1982) (see figure 3.31), air is circulated through a glazed exterior cavity wall. As the air is pulled through the plenum it is warmed; the heat is then stored in a rock bin located under an atrium space on the south of the building. The Hooker Chemical Building in Niagara Falls, NY (Dixon, 1983) (figure 3.3), also makes use of the double skin of glass as a place to circulate a buffering blanket of solar-heated warm air. Both buildings were conceived as demonstration projects; however, the cost of the systems and the apparent long payback periods have been barriers to disseminating either approach.

In its form as daylight, solar energy is having a greater impact on designs of commercial building facades. Designs are beginning to incorporate high windows, light shelves, and other devices that bounce daylight deeper into building interiors or control glare at the building perimeter to reduce some of the energy used in artificial illumination. It is possible to reduce installed lighting levels at rooms adjoining glazed facades from 2.7 W/ft^2 to levels between 1.8 and 1.3 W/ft^2, assuming that appropriate lighting controls, task lighting, fenestration design, and other daylighting techniques are employed (see figure 3.32). However, considerable additional work needs to be done on the parametric effect of different facade designs in commercial buildings before the full energy impact of these techniques—including lighting, heating, cooling, and utility peak demands—is known.

Wall and Wall Aperture Manufacture, Fabrication, and Assembly From a manufacturing perspective, the focus of the 1973–1983 period was on developing such new materials as glazing products with improved radiation transmission and reflection properties, selective surfaces, and eutectic thermal storage materials.

Low-iron-content glass with higher solar transmissivity became more commonly available as the demand for this product grew. Considerable research was also conducted on low-emissivity glass coatings and films for windows, which significantly reduced long-wave heat radiation from windows and consequently lowered window U-values. One of the earliest products of this type brought to market was the "heat-mirror" window from the Southwall Corporation, which was developed with support from

Figure 3.31
The Enerplex Building in Princeton, NJ, uses an atrium and a double curtain wall of
glass to collect excess heat for storage in a rock bed below the atrium (design by SOM;
photograph by D. Prowler).

DOE. The heat mirror is a film consisting of a wavelength-selective coating
on a weatherable polyester substrate.

The U-value for double-glazed windows using low-emissivity coatings or
films can be expected to drop from approximately 0.55 to 0.25 (compared
with about 0.35 for triple glazing). At present, several manufacturers offer
windows with integral low-emissivity of heat-mirror-type barriers at a
premium price over double-glazed windows, and these windows are beginning to make a significant impact in the residential market.

Selective surfaces using nickel and chrome foils, which absorb shortwave
solar radiation readily but inhibit the reradiation of long-wave heat radiation, were developed during 1973–1983. These foils are being used extensively in active solar collectors and are beginning to be used in Trombe
walls as well. The application of these foils to Trombe walls is fairly labor-
intensive; coupled with the product cost, these costs have limited the
diffusion of this technology in site-fabricated systems. Nevertheless,
the increases in efficiency possible with these surfaces have been well-

Figure 3.31 (continued)

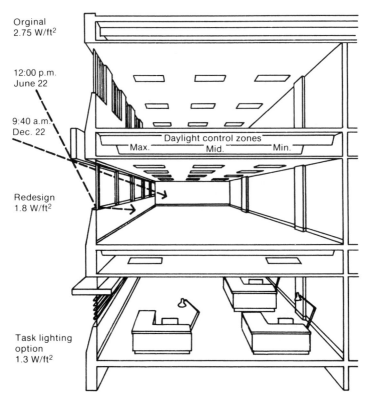

Orginal
2.75 W/ft²

12:00 p.m.
June 22

9:40 a.m.
Dec. 22

Redesign
1.8 W/ft²

Task lighting
option
1.3 W/ft²

Daylight control zones
Max.   Mid.   Min.

Figure 3.32
Three different office daylighting strategies are summarized in this section through the
perimeter office of a multistory office building. Source: *Progressive Architecture*, April
1982, p. 114.

documented. For example, the *Passive Solar Handbook* concludes that using selective surfaces on Trombe walls "is a very effective strategy and ... the performance increase may be larger than ... predicted ..." (p. 105). Tests have shown that selective surfaces in mass walls provide a performance increase roughly comparable to using an effective R-9 nighttime movable insulation system for the wall (see Balcomb, 1980).

Several companies have marketed water-storage containers for use with mass wall collecting systems. Two of the most well-known are Kalwall and One Design. Kalwall offers an FRP (fiberglass-reinforced polyester) cylinder in various diameters and heights, while One Design has stressed the stackable water "trough." Other companies have produced prefabricated mass walls using poured concrete slabs with integral water containers, but these products have yet to find a viable market. Many companies sell products in which water can be held in small amounts in containers for use with other thermal storage. In general, however, water has lagged behind masonry as the thermal storage material of choice in mass wall applications.

Considerable effort was also expended during 1973–1983 to bring an economically viable eutectic thermal storage material to the marketplace for use with wall and wall aperture systems. Such a system, which could store a large amount of heat in a relatively small volume by taking advantage of the heat required to change the state of the chemicals from a liquid to a solid, has enormous conceptual appeal because it eliminates the need for bulky and heavy water or masonry thermal storage. However, the cost of these chemicals, the problem of obtaining inexpensive containers, and the lifetimes of these chemical suspensions during numerous freezing and thawing cycles have, to date, proved to be major economic obstacles to using these systems. Nevertheless, eutectic storage containers are commercially available and are beginning to compete with alternative thermal storage strategies.

Fabrication research, under programs such as SERI's 1980 *Marketable Products for Passive Solar Applications*, stressed the development of new wall components that could be easily integrated in building envelopes and new techniques of erection that might lower the cost of solar applications. Most of these efforts—such as the "thermal diode" concept developed at MIT (Buckley, 1976) in which a factory-fabricated panel with integral water thermal storage and a one-way thermosiphoning oil valve is used as the structure, solar collector, thermal storage, and radiation distribution surface—have yet to be developed beyond the laboratory prototype stage.

Products that were developed during this decade, largely with government funding, include new selectively transmitting glass, solar integrated metal manufactured building skins, and photovoltaic arrays and selective surfaces. Equally impressive, however, is the list of wall components that were invented or developed without any government support, including movable insulating systems, such as Beadwall from Zomeworks Corporation; operable exterior reflective louvers, such as Moore Products' louvers (see figure 3.33); operable lateral arm awnings, such as those produced by Sunshade Corporation; and a wide variety of site-fabricated solar collector systems.

Manufacturing and fabricating building materials often involve capital-intensive processes and are subject to large-scale technology and economics; however, building assembly is still largely the result of craft and site labor. To a great extent, the purpose of the research and demonstration done on the fabrication of solar wall systems focused on the constraints and opportunities of traditional construction procedures and how solar systems could be implemented cost-effectively within established practice. The question was, "How can solar be implemented within today's construction industry?" rather than, "How would the construction industry have to change to make better use of solar applications?"

The LANL mobile home program and SERI's Passive and Hybrid Solar Manufactured Housing and Buildings Program addressed the first question. The SERI program introduced a number of major American prefabricated building companies, including Ryan Homes, National Homes, and Butler Manufacturing, to solar designs. Many of these companies benefited from that experience and produced solar "options" for their basic product lines. Nevertheless, in most instances the solar innovations did not influence basic corporate practice (SERI, 1984).

Wall and Wall Aperture Performance   The performance of wall systems was studied extensively during the decade. Advanced mathematical simulations of the performance of both opaque and solar wall aperture systems were validated in test facilities (see section 3.4.2.1). This information was soon translated into programs for both handheld and microcomputers (such as TEAnet and Psoup) and mainframe computer codes (such as DOE-2 and Blast). From this work, rules of thumb were formulated (Anderson, 1976; Mazria, 1979) that provided performance information to the general public.

Figure 3.33
(Top) An exterior view of an office building in Sacramento that uses exterior louvers to control interior light levels. (Bottom) A view looking out of the office with the louvers closed (design by Nacht and Lewis; photograph by D. Prowler).

The bulk of this work concerned passive solar heating wall applications. The SLR method developed under DOE funding by the Solar Group at LANL under J. D. Balcomb is the primary tool for calculating the performance of wall passive systems, as it is for roof and sunspace passive solar systems. Volume III of the *Passive Solar Design* handbook presents tables for a wide variety of direct-gain and mass wall parametric conditions, including various wall thicknesses, amounts of thermal mass, whether movable insulation or selective surfaces are used, the number of glazing layers, and the geographic location of the building. The performance information generated at LANL has been processed at different levels of complexity for different phases of the design process—schematic, design development, and construction documents. Private vendors have computerized these calculation procedures and several different versions are now available for purchase.

In mass wall construction practice, solid or filled concrete block Trombe walls 12 in. (30 cm) thick appear to be the most practical. Although somewhat thicker walls would provide better termperature flows in many locations, this increase in performance does not justify the added expense of deviating from the more commonly available 12-in. (30-cm) block width. In most climates, particularly temperate to cold climates, it is necessary to double glaze the wall surface to achieve acceptable performance. Triple glazing is advisable in very cold climates. Using movable insulation is also beneficial, although the practical problems of locating such insulation in a Trombe wall system between the glazing and the mass or outside the glazing has discouraged its use in most applications. Applying a selective surface to the mass wall has been shown to be the equivalent of adding an additional layer of glass.

While most early Trombe walls included thermocirculation vents for daytime convection of warm air from the glazed cavity in front of the wall to the living space, the most recent trend throughout the country has been toward stagnating Trombe walls without vents. Although a 5–10% overall system efficiency is sacrificed with this wall, construction is simplified, initial costs are lower, and the problems of dust on the glazing and nighttime reverse thermocirculation are reduced. Sealing off the Trombe wall to prevent overheating in summer is also simplified with this approach, although care must still be taken to vent the Trombe cavity to the outside, or to shade the glazing positively, or both.

Even though satisfactory, simplified small-computer techniques exist for modeling residential wall systems, designers must still rely on relatively sophisticated modeling techniques for large commercial building wall systems. The difficulties of factoring the dynamic performance of wall systems and determining the effect of wall systems on peak utility power demand have slowed the development of simple, intuitive commercial building design tools. Thus, as with roof and roof aperture devices, an hour-by-hour computer simulation will be needed, using programs such as DOE-2 to obtain detailed parametric design sensitivity results. Considerable applied research, such as reducing the parametric results of studies of each major building type to visual diagrams, still needs to be conducted in this field (see section 3.4.2.1).

To summarize, we can now predict the performance, expressed as a solar saving fraction (SSF), of residential direct-gain and mass walls for all U.S. climates. Using this information, rules of thumb have been developed for predicting schematic design performance. For example, we know that "a solar collection area of from 15 to 29% of the floor area can be expected to reduce the annual heating load of a well-insulated small building (i.e., a building with a heat-loss rate of not more than 6 Btu/ft^2 per degree day) located in Philadelphia, Pennsylvania, by 19–29%, or, if R-9 night insulation is used, by 38–62%" (Balcomb, 1980). More general conclusions can also be abstracted from the predicted performance data. These results show, among other things, that direct-gain systems without night insulation work less well in colder climates and that Trombe walls with selective surfaces perform well, although this has not been fully verified in the field.

3.4.2.3 Sunspaces and Atria

Sunspace and Atrium Design From a performance perspective, many design methods treat sunspaces as a form of the direct-gain passive solar wall system. However, from an architectural standpoint, sunspaces and atria affect building design in a way that distinguishes them from wall systems. Consequently, they are presented here as a different category of system.

The fact that the envelope of a building can expand to provide a functional space is one of the reasons for the popularity of sunspace, attached greenhouse, and atrium solar designs. Unlike many solar interventions, such as rooftop active collectors and Trombe wall passive systems, sunspaces and atria offer the advantage of adding to the usable space of the main structure. As the tentative economics of many solar designs became

Figure 3.34
Unit One First Village in Santa Fe, NM, uses an atrium to organize spaces; all the
rooms connect to and share in the heat generated from the sunspace (design by William
Mingenbach and Susan Nichols; photograph by D. Prowler).

clear, many designers and consumers were better able to justify solar
system costs with this extra usable space.

Sunspace designs took many forms. Formal solutions ranged from
integrally designed, site-fabricated sunspaces such as that included in Unit
One First Village, NM, designed by William Mingenbach and Susan
Nichols (see figure 3.34) to minimally connected temporary structures such
as those marketed by the Solar Room Company, composed of flexible
plastic film glazing. In some cases, the spaces were used as living space
within the home, such as dining rooms or circulation space (see figures 3.35
and 3.36); in other cases, they were rarely occupied. The designers of the
latter apparently hoped to justify the cost of the sunspace by the energy
savings alone.

In commercial buildings, atrium spaces became popular during the decade. The theory was that splitting the envelope of a conventional commercial building by inserting a naturally tempered atrium could improve
daylighting and cooling performance (see figure 3.37). This suggested that

Figure 3.35
A sunspace links the living room and dining room with the master bedroom on the first floor of this house in eastern Pennsylvania (design by South Street Design; photograph by D. Prowler).

office building design might return to the high-surface area-to-volume ratios found in such nineteenth-century, narrow-fingered office buildings as architect Louis Sullivan's U-shaped Wainwright Building in St. Louis. It was also argued that the atrium would add a social space to the building, such as that of the Gregory Bateson State Office Building in Sacramento (see figure 3.38; Murphy, 1981). It was also suggested that the stratified warm air that collected in the atrium during the day could be stored for nighttime heating. The success of many of these recent designs from either an energy or a social perspective is only beginning to emerge and has yet to be properly summarized in the literature.

Another major trend associated with sunspace design was the enthusiasm for the "double envelope" (also called "buffered-air" or "double-shell" or, simply, "envelope" designs) that culminated in three topical conferences in the northeast in 1979 and 1980 (Booth, 1980; see figure 3.39). In a double-envelope design, a south-facing sunspace forms part of an envelope that wraps around the entire structure and, in most versions, comes in contact with the ground beneath the building before connecting

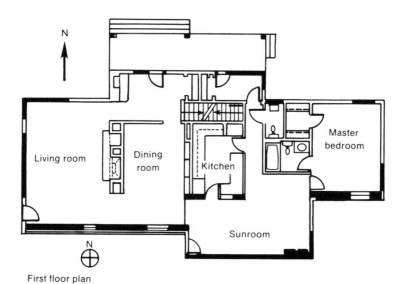

First floor plan

Figure 3.36
The first floor plan of a house in eastern Pennsylvania that utilizes a sunspace as a breakfast room and principal circulation space of the house design by South Street Design, Architects).

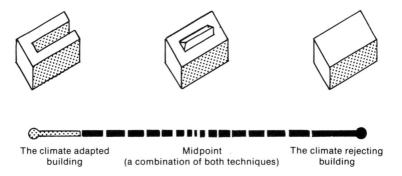

Figure 3.37
A building may be conceived with more perimeter to permit daylighting and natural convection or with a minimum surface-to-volume ratio to permit the most efficient use of mechanical systems. Source: Ternoey et al. (1985).

Figure 3.38
The atrium of the Gregory Bateson State Office Building in Sacramento, CA (design by the office of the State Architect, California; photograph by D. Prowler).

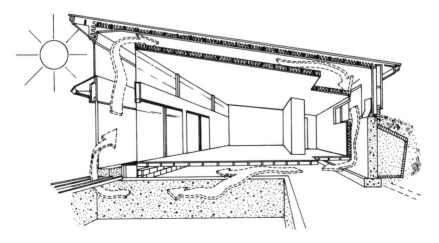

Figure 3.39
Double-envelope designs generally incorporate a south-facing sunspace to drive a thermocirculation loop that circulates completely around a building between a pair of insulated exterior walls. Source: Booth (1980).

back to the sunspace, to allow a continuous flow of air around the building. This procedure supposedly increased performance over an attached sunspace of equal size, although studies have questioned this assertion (see section 3.4.2.3).

The wide variety in sunspace and attached-greenhouse configurations caused a delay in a rigorous analysis of sizing these designs until after other passive system performance parameters had been codified. It was not until volume III of the *Passive Solar Handbook* became available in 1982 that sizing information became readily available. Questions about optimal shapes of sunspaces and greenhouses still remain, however. Although the sizing information contained in volume III provides clues to the optimal heating shapes for different climates, the negative effects of increases in cooling loads (not contained in volume III) must be factored into a complete optimizing analysis. Given the sloped glazing usually found in sunspace design and its negative effects during the cooling season, this matter merits further investigation.

Sunspace and Atrium Manufacture, Fabrication, and Assembly   Research into the manufacture, fabrication, and assembly of sunspaces and attached greenhouses generally focused on the efforts of several companies to mass produce off-the-shelf systems. Because sunspaces were perceived to represent one of the best solar retrofit markets, these companies competed to develop modular systems that could be attached to a variety of existing structures. Manufacturers experimented with issues such as curved versus straight eaves, glass versus plastic glazing materials, durable versus temporary structures, and automatic versus manual controls.

Other researchers and product manufacturers were developing components that would aid in controlling unwanted heat gain or loss from sunspaces. For example, "Big Fins," designed by Zomeworks Corporation, attempted to tap excess solar gain for passive solar hot water collection in greenhouses. Many conventional manufacturers of movable insulation for wall systems, such as Window Quilt and Solar Technology, experimented with modified versions for use on the walls and roofs of sunspaces.

Atrium designers soon saw the need for a new generation of sophisticated solar control devices. For instance, in a heavily publicized design for a TVA office building, operable, aluminized exterior louvering devices were specified. Unfortunately, the finished building included a modified louvering system. Since at present there is little standardization in components or fabrication techniques for commercial building atria, the cost of many atrium radiation control devices is high. Considerable research and demonstration in this area is still needed.

Sunspace and Atrium Performance   Volume III of the *Passive Solar Handbook* provided a basis for predicting sunspace performance; however, it did not include some important performance data. For example, it is helpful to know the effect of plant growth and water evaporation on the thermal performance of attached residential greenhouse spaces, and the degree and effectiveness of convective coupling with the parent structure offered by traditional windows and doors.

A good source for more detailed information on predicting residential sunspace performance is *The Sunspace Primer* by Jones and McFarland (1984), based on their work at LANL. For example, the authors state, "As a rule of thumb, you should assume that plants reduce the solar heating performance by the same fraction as the fraction of the sunspace floor area they occupy" as a consequence of heat loss caused by water evaporation. They also state that "common-wall openings are improtant for the transfer of heat from the sunspace to the building by the circulation of warm air. . . . For a 6'-8" door that operates as a single opening, the minimum recommended area is 8 square feet per 100 square feet of glazing area."

In general, the usable heat contributed by one square foot of "projected" glazing area in a properly designed sunspace is similar to the heat contributed by one square foot of other, comparably equipped passive solar systems (i.e., if one has movable insulation, they both do), etc. The "projected area" is defined as the projection of the sunspace glazing area onto a vertical plane that is parallel to the top (or bottom) of the main glazing. For a sunspace with vertical glazing only, the projected area is the same as the glazing area. For sunspaces with sloped glazing, the projected area is less than the glazing area. (It is the glazing area times the sine of the tilt angle relative to horizontal.) Thus, it is incorrect to assume, as some do, that increasing the floor area of a sunspace will necessarily result in more heating; rather, it is the projected area of glazing that is critical. It is also worth noting that one square foot of sunspace or atrium will invariably cost more than one square foot of a direct-gain system.

The thermal performance of double-envelope houses, in which a sunspace is usually the principal solar collecting strategy (see figure 3.39) has been debated. A noteworthy case study of a double-envelope house was conducted by Brookhaven National Laboratory of the Mastin House in 1981 (Jones et al., 1981). Brookhaven summarized in its report that the

Mastin house "ranks among the most energy-efficient building designs available today. It is concluded that that the low heating needs of the house are due primarily to the excellent insulative value of the double shell." This contradicts the claims of many proponents of the double-envelope design who propose that the performance benefits of ground thermal coupling explains the increase in the building's performance.

The performance of atria in commercial buildings can now be predicted by computer modeling (Bazjanac, 1981). However, field data on actual building performance are only beginning to validate these models. Side-by-side test modules, such as the type that launched the active and passive solar performance research, are not practical for large-scale commercial buildings.

Most of the dependable atrium performance data available at present originates with either DOE's 1979 Passive Solar Commercial Buildings Program or the series of California State office buildings designed when Sim Van der Ryn served as California State Architect (Woodbridge, 1984). As a result of these two efforts, between 20 and 30 buildings have been constructed that incorporate a variety of passive solar strategies. These range from daylighting schemes, such as buildings that use atria to provide perimeter daylighting or light shelves to bounce light deeper into office spaces and eliminate perimeter glare, to solar thermal schemes, such as buildings that use clerestories and internal thermal mass or stratified atria with rock-bed storage. Unfortunately, it is not yet possible to generalize the results of these projects to formulate national commercial envelope schematic design guidelines.

3.4.2.4 Optimization of Solar Design Strategies and Energy Conservation
In the years between 1973 and 1983 there were frequent, and sometimes bitter, debates between advocates of superinsulation of residential building envelopes and those who favored solar applications of one type or another. Obviously, the implications of these different strategies on envelope design are significant. The primarily opaque walls suggested by the superinsulation approach are in marked contrast to the glazed facades of many of the solar strategies. One of the most definitive and influential pieces of research into the role of conservation versus solar in building envelope designs was done by the LANL Solar Group and included in the ASHRAE publication *Passive Solar Heating Analysis* (Balcomb et al., 1984).

The study concluded that, for a given climate, there is an optimal mixture of energy supply by passive solar techniques and reduction of energy demand by insulation. This optimal mixture depends on the relative costs of the solar system and the insulation, but not on fuel costs. In cold, cloudy climates almost all of the energy-savings investment should be spent on insulation. The reverse is true in milder, sunny climates.

3.4.2.5 Other Envelope Performance Issues During 1973–1983, in addition to work on whole-envelope systems and on the interrelationship between the envelope and the building, research also increased our understanding of some of the basic physics of the envelope's thermal performance. Progress was made in two areas in particular: predicting heat loss from underground basements and foundations and modeling convective air flows caused by thermal gradients in houses.

The interest in underground structures in cold climates and in "cool tubes" for precooling intake air for summer ventilation in warm climates (see Labs, 1981) led to better algorithms for predicting underground temperature flows (see Kusuda et al. in ASHRAE, 1982). In regard to building envelope design, an important conclusion of this work has been the validation of the assumed efficacy and cost-effectiveness of using foundation insulation around buildings in most temperate and cold climates to retard perimeter heat losses (Govan, Greason, and McAllister, 1981).

The work on convective airflows in buildings has been useful in assessing the degree to which heat collected at the building's perimeter can be expected to flow naturally to remote spaces. A noteworthy application of these data to building envelope design has been the construction of guidelines for vent connections between sunspaces and atrium and surrounding spaces (see, for example, Balcomb and Yamaguchi, 1983).

3.4.3 Phase Three: Research to Determine Economics and Market Impact

3.4.3.1 Economics At the same time performance information was being acquired, work was under way to determine the costs of modifying envelopes for various solar strategies. Reliable information on the costs of self-contained, solar flat-plate systems was soon available through the many companies springing up to meet the perceived market demand; however, obtaining information on integrated systems proved more difficult (an integrated system is defined here as one in which one or more functions of a building's outer membrane is performed by a component of the solar system).

One important research program conducted to discover the costs versus benefits of passive solar systems was the Determination of Passive System

Costs and Cost Goals Project. This work was conducted by Total Environmental Action, Inc., for DOE's Heating and Cooling Research and Development Branch, Conservation and Solar Applications (Total Environmental Action, Inc., 1980). It provided comprehensive, specific information on passive solar heating system costs for various regions in the categories of material, labor, dollars, operation, maintenance, and life-cycle
costs. This information was not related to formal characteristics (i.e., no
value was given for the incremental costs of a roof strategy on the total cost
of the roof) but was provided in the Uniform Construction Index (UCI)
format. This procedure, widely used by architects and other building
professionals to analyze project costs, groups components into sixteen
divisions. The study defined base-case buildings, applied a range of solar
applications to each base case, and employed professional cost estimators
to determine the incremental extra costs of these solutions by UCI category
for various climatic and economic regions of the country.

Cost information for various system strategies was reported in 1978
dollars. Most of these strategies were envelope-dependent; some were
envelope-exclusive. So, for example, in the final report, mass walls are
shown to add $19.00–30.50/ft² ($205–329/m²) of collection surface, depending on the range of assumptions specified in the report (Total Environmental Action, Inc., 1980, p. 58). Cost goals were also established. According to the economic criteria set in the report, in most cases mass walls were
not found to be cost-effective at that time. Two exceptions were Denver
and Albuquerque (Total Environmental Action, Inc., 1980).

Efforts were made, frequently through local programs instituted by the
Regional Solar Energy Centers (RSECS)—which were centers established
by DOE to decentralize solar marketing and research—to obtain actual
cost information on already built solar homes. Unfortunately, inconsisten-
cies in data acquisition and methods make the results of much of this work
questionable. The data were often reduced to costs per square foot of the
entire house, which made applying this information to specific envelope
interventions difficult, if not impossible. Those who sought this information were assumed to be speculative builders and housing consumers who
were most interested in cost-per-square-foot values. This information was
much less useful to designers and cost estimators since it did not indicate
how specific changes in the envelope would effect cost.

Again, however, residential and commercial buildings must be distinguished. Some might argue that the costs of commercial building envelopes

should be easier to analyze since the cost of this kind of building's skin can be separated more easily from the rest of the structure than can the envelope in a wood frame or masonry residence. The envelope designs of commercial buildings tend to be more repetitive and can sometimes be produced in factories under quality and cost controls. Nevertheless, we have few published actual data from commercial buildings from which to draw conclusions about incremental cost. It is fair to state, however, that the driving issue in commercial, internally load-dominated structures in most climates is less heating than lighting and cooling. Consequently, traditional residential solar envelope strategies such as direct-gain windows, mass walls, and greenhouses are not likely to play a big part in the design of energy-efficient commercial structures. More important will be techniques such as daylighting, optimized shading coefficients, and new artificial lighting and load management control systems.

3.4.3.2 Market As noted, the principal program to impact the mass housing market with solar applications was the Passive and Hybrid Solar Manufactured Housing and Buildings Project. As in most market outreach programs, the focus was on whole buildings and whole-building performance. Many of the solar designs were developed to look as much like conventional housing as possible. The assumption was that consumers did not want homes with a "new" appearance, but that they could be convinced to purchase solar homes if the incremental cost was marginal *and* if the home did not readily appear to be "solar." Nevertheless, in some regional markets, sales of solar homes remained relatively strong during the housing recession of the late 1970s and early 1980s, which suggests that the energy-conscious housing consumer was really prepared to accept solar designs. A major survey of 5,000 homeowners entitled "Decisions for the 80s," published by the National Association of Homebuilders in December 1980, concluded that "the consumer is well aware of the energy situation and is very keen about an energy efficient home." This attitude seems to have extended to solar homes as well. Whether this remains the case is debatable.

Subtly, the design focus in solar envelopes had shifted from discovering a new aesthetic to fitting in as inconspicuously as possible with an old one. Nevertheless, many designers in the field believed that until solar design became an accepted if not preferred architectural style, there was little hope of a mass market penetration. Conventional economic and cost/benefit studies had confirmed what the marketplace was saying: that in many locations the economics of solar systems was not quite acceptable (even with tax credits) unless intangibles were also considered. Solar advocates countered that the true costs of conventional fuel supplies were being severely underestimated. The debate continues today, with the added public perception that we are now faced with an abundant energy supply that makes energy efficiency a less immediate problem.

3.5 The Impact of Envelope Research and Designs on Building Design

3.5.1 Impact on Building Design and the Building Design Process

Many projects and experiments conducted throughout the decade have confirmed our initial premise that we cannot separate envelope design from overall building design (see figure 3.40). We have also learned that good solar design requires that sound engineering be applied to the entire design

Figure 3.40
Thair Nature Center in eastern Pennsylvania uses a variety of roof and wall solar collection strategies within a coherent architectural vocabulary (design by Kelbaugh + Lee; photograph by D. Prowler).

process. This runs counter to current practice and may in fact intimidate some architects who fear their designs will be overwhelmed by technical requirements. The formulations of different levels of prediction tools, from easily understood rules of thumb to complex hour-by-hour simulation codes, have partially helped to alleviate this problem, but the mistrust is still strong.

Architects, however, generally appreciate that energy-sensitive envelope strategies can have a wide variety of consequences on a building's overall design. Sometimes an envelope design idea has formal implications (the shape of the building responds); sometimes only components need vary (such as a shading device on a facade); at other times a change in materials may be required with little impact on appearance (such as in the application of low-emissivity glass or films to windows); and at still other times, only a variation in building's use may be required (such as a change in occupancy schedule).

For example, a designer may be faced with the problem that an elevation has too much solar heat gain to achieve a desired energy-efficiency. Some possible responses are the following:

1. Reconfigure the building so that it receives less solar exposure (a *formal* response).

2. Change the type of glass used to one with a lower solar transmissivity (a *materials* response).

3. Shade the glass and alter the building's appearance using overhangs (a *component* response).

4. Design the mechanical systems so that the energy entering the facade can be used elsewhere in the building (both a *programmatic* and a *component* response).

5. Do not occupy the overheated portion of the building during certain parts of the day so that air conditioning can be saved (a *programmatic* response).

Any or all of these solutions (or others) might be technically possible and more than one might also be economically feasible. The approach actually selected is apt to be a function of underlying aesthetic philosophy or previous experience, as much as an objective evaluation (Pye, 1964).

Many envelope systems are not just "skin deep"; they require internal thermal storage or remote thermal storage to ensure their performance.

Nevertheless, the idea of self-contained envelope system has attracted considerable research and experiment. We are reminded, for example, of thermic diodes, Trombe walls, and roof monitors with integrated eutectic storage. The idea that interior space planning is unconstrained by the requirements of the envelope is appealing to certain designers, but it is often not possible in passive solar strategies. If photovoltaic or active solar collection systems are used with remote storage, the idea of the independent skin can be approached, but architectural separation of a passive solar envelope from the building's interior is usually neither possible nor architecturally desirable.

3.5.2 Impact on Architectural Education

Some designers argue that if solar applications are to have a significant impact on envelope designs, a major change will have to occur in architectural education to encourage the infusion of technical data earlier in the design process. This is true, they say, for both student education and the continuing education of professionals. This premise has prompted efforts to modify and to improve the education of architects and designers accordingly.

The issue of professional continuing education was addressed nationally by the American Institute of Architects (AIA) through an Energy Professional Development Program (EPDP) of educational workshops and supporting publications (AIA, 1981). This program was organized around workshops of various degress of complexity taught by members of the AIA throughout the United States.

The main programs for architectural schools were the Summer Energy Institute for architectural faculty, the Design + Energy student design competition [both coordinated by the Association of Collegiate Schools of Architecture (ACSA)], and the Teaching Passive Design in Architecture curriculum development project organized by the University of Pennsylvania (see Prowler and Fraker, 1981). All of these programs were funded by the Department of Energy.

The Summer Energy Institute provided architecture faculty with an opportunity to learn from and interact with teaching colleagues with special expertise in energy-efficient design and teaching methods. The curriculum for these institutes tended to be organized around teaching methods (such as "studio teaching" or "laboratory experiments") rather than building design principles. The Teaching Passive Design in Architecture project generated much of the early curriculum material used at the institutes. In this program, 12 schools of architecture were selected to develop curriculum packages using a variety of pedagogical models, such as design exercises, graphical analysis techniques, laboratory experiments, and computer learning programs for distribution to faculty at all the accredited schools of architecture in the United States.

All of these programs attempted to integrate solar envelope design into the overall building design process. They all had in common a search for design methods that would permit performance data to be incorporated earlier in the design process without constraining the synthetic character of architectural production.

3.6   Envelope Design Issues Meriting Further Research and Development

Further research, development, and demonstration are needed in numerous areas. Indeed, in the field of commercial building envelope design, work has barely begun on predicting building performance and exploring the aesthetic impact on envelopes. A partial list of needed R&D and demonstration would include the following:

1. studies of both the coincidences of and conflicts between solar and daylighting envelope strategies,

2. the development of additional schematic design tools for professionals to use to predict the energy performance of commercial buildings,

3. parametric studies by region of building facade interventions,

4. continued development of new envelope materials, especially glazings,

5. studies of the long-term performance of building envelope system,

6. the impact of thermal and luminous environments on human behavior and productivity,

7. studies of the role of solar envelope systems within the production of the manufactured housing industry,

8. the impact of building and envelope size, type, configuration, and orientation on commercial building performance,

9. research on the impact of new envelope technology on existing buildings,

10. research into the incorporation of innovations by the building industry and building clients, and

11. research into the prefabrication and dimensional standardization of envelope systems.

References

AIA, 1981. *Energy in Architecture*, Washington, DC: American Institute of Architects.

AIA Research Corporation, 1976. *Solar Dwelling Design Concepts*. Washington, DC: USGPO Stock No. 023-000-00334-1.

AIA Research Corporation, 1978. *Final Report: Phase One/Base Data for the Development of Energy Performance Standards for New Buildings*, Washington, DC: HUD-PDR-290-2.

AIA Research Corporation, 1979. *A Survey of Passive Solar Buildings*, Washington, DC: HUD-PDR-287(2).

Anderson, B., 1976. *The Solar Home Book*, Harrisville, NH: Cheshire Books.

Architectural Aluminum Manufacturer's Association, 1977. *Voluntary Standard Procedure for Calculating Skylight Annual Energy Balance*, Chicago: Architectural Aluminum Manufacturer's Association.

Architectural Record, May 1982. Enerplex: office complex exploring sophisticated energy solutions. New York: McGraw-Hill.

Aronin, J. E., 1953. *Climate and Architecture*. New York: Reinhold Publishing.

ASHRAE, 1972. *Handbook of Fundamentals*. New York: American Society of Heating, Refrigeration, and Air Conditioning Engineers.

ASHRAE, 1980. *Standard: Energy Conservation in New Building Design: 90A-1980*. Atlanta: ASHRAE.

ASHRAE, 1982. *Proc. ASHRAE/DOE Conference on the Thermal Performance of the Exterior Envelopes of Buildings*. Atlanta: ASHRAE.

Balcomb, J. D., 1980. *Passive Solar Design Handbook, Vols. I, II*. DOE/CS-0127/2, Springfield, VA: NTIS.

Balcomb, J. D., and J. C. Hedstrom, 1976. *Sizing Solar Collectors for Space Heating*. LA-UR-76-1334, Los Alamos, NM: Los Alamos National Laboratory.

Balcomb, J. D., and K. Yamaguchi, 1983. Heat distribution by natural convection. In *Proc. 8th National Passive Solar Conference*. Boulder: American Solar Energy Society (ASES), Inc.

Balcomb, J. D., J. C. Hedstrom, and J. E. Perry, Jr., 1981. Performance summary of the Balcomb solar house. In *Proc. 1981 ASES Conference*, Boulder: ASES, Inc.

Balcomb, J. D., R. W. Jones, R. D. McFarland, and W. Wray, 1984. *Passive Solar Heating Analysis*. Atlanta: ASHRAE.

Bazjanac, V., 1981. Energy analysis: one year later. In *Progressive Architecture*. Stamford, CT: Reinhold Publishing.

Beckman, W. A., S. A. Klein, and J. A. Duffie, 1977. *Solar Heating Design*. New York: John Wiley & Sons.

Booth, D., ed., 1980. *The Double Shell Solar House*. Canterbury, NH: Community Builders.

Booz Allen & Hamilton, 1983. *Passive Solar Commercial Building Program, Case Studies*. DOE/CE-0042, Springfield, VA: NTIS.

Buckley, B. S., 1976. *Development and Evaluation of Thermic Diode Solar Panels for Building Heating and Cooling, Phase II*. EY-76-S-02-2854, Cambridge, MA: Massachusetts Institute of

Technology, p. 40 (ERDA 76–145, *National Program Plan for Solar Heating and Cooling of Buildings Project Summaries*).

Butler Manufacturing Company, 1982. *Passive-Hybrid Heating and Daylighting Concepts for Commercial/Industrial Pre-Engineered Buildings*. PC A17/MF A01, Grandview, MO. Springfield, VA: NTIS.

Dixon, J. M., 1983. Glass under glass. In *Progressive Architecture*. Stamford, CT: Reinhold Publishing.

Doubilet, S., 1983. The decorated climate-filtering shed. In *Progressive Architecture*. Stamford, CT: Reinhold Publishing.

Fitch, J. M., 1972. *American Building, 2: The Environmental Forces That Shape It*. Second edition. Boston: Houghton Mifflin.

Fraker, H., 1976. *Proc. Passive Solar Heating and Cooling Conference and Workshop*. LA-6637-C, Springfield, VA: NTIS.

Fry, M., and J. Drew, 1964. *Tropical Architecture in the Dry and Humid Zones*. New York: Reinhold Publishing.

Givoni, B., 1969. *Man, Climate and Architecture*. First edition. London: Applied Science Publishers, Ltd.

Govan, F. A., D. M. Greason, and J. D. McAllister, eds., 1981. *Thermal Insulation, Materials and Systems for Energy Conservation in the 80's*. Philadelphia: ASTM.

Hagan, D. A., and R. F. Jones, 1983. *Case Study of the BLOVIN Superinsulated House*. BNL 51732, Springfield, VA: NTIS.

Haggard, K., 1976. *Proc. Passive Solar Heating and Cooling Conference and Workshop*. LA-6637-C, Springfield, VA: NTIS.

Hedstrom, J., and H. Murray, 1980. *Solar Heating and Cooling at the Los Alamos Study Center*. LA-8622-MS, Los Alamos, NM: Los Alamos National Laboratory.

Ike Williams Community Center, 1978. *Process Architecture: #6 Solar Architecture*. Tokyo: Bunji Murotani (American distributor: Westfield, NJ: Eastview Editions).

Jones, R. F., G. Dennehy, H. T. Ghaffari, and G. E. Munson, 1981. *Case Study of the Mastin Double-Envelope House*. BNL 51460, Springfield, VA: NTIS.

Jones, R. W., and R. D. McFarland, 1984. *The Sunspace Primer*. New York: Van Nostrand Reinhold Company.

Kreider, J. F., and F. Kreith, 1975. *Solar Heating and Cooling*. New York: McGraw-Hill.

Labs, K., 1981. *Regional Analysis of Ground and Above Ground Climate*. ORNL 40451, Oak Ridge, TN: Oak Ridge National Laboratory.

Lau, A., 1983. How to design fixed overhangs. *Solar Age*. Harrisville, NH: SolarVision.

LBL, 1985. *Evaluation Manual Superlite*. LBL Publication #19320, Berkeley; Lawrence Berkeley Laboratory.

Mazria, E., 1979. *The Passive Solar Energy Book*. Emmaus, PA: Rodale Press.

Murphy, J., 1981. State intentions. In *Progressive Architecture*. Stamford, CT: Reinhold Publishing.

NBS, 1974. In *Proc. Workshop on Solar Collectors for Heating and Cooling of Buildings*. NSF-RA-N-75-019. Gaithersburg, MD: National Bureau of Standards.

Olgyay, V., 1963. *Design with Climate*. Princeton: Princeton University Press.

Olgyay, V., and A. Olgyay, 1976. *Solar Control and Shading Devices*. Princeton: Princeton University Press.

Progressive Architecture, April 1982, p. 114.

Prowler, D., and H. Fraker, 1981. *Project Journal: Teaching Passive Design in Architecture.* Philadelphia: GSFA, University of Pennsylvania.

Pye, D., 1964. *The Nature of Design.* New York: Reinhold Publishing.

Sandia, 1979. *Passive Solar Buildings.* SAND 79–0824, Albuquerque, NM: Sandia National Laboratories.

Saunders, N., 1976. In *Proc. Passive Solar Heating and Cooling Conference and Workshop.* LA-6637-C, Springfield, VA: NTIS.

SERI, 1984. *Passive Solar Manufactured Buildings: Design, Construction, and Class B Results.* SERI/SP-271-2059, Golden, CO: Solar Energy Research Institute.

Solar Age, September 1978. In step with the sun. Harrisville, NH: *Solar Vision*, p. 16.

Stephens, S., 1979. Let the sunshine in. *Progressive Architecture.* Stamford, CT: Reinhold Publishing.

Stromberg, R. P., and S. O. Woodall, 1977. *Passive Solar Buildings: A Compilation of Data and Results.* SAND77-1204, Springfield, VA: NTIS.

Ternoey, S., L. Bickle, C. Robbins, and R. Busch, 1985. *The Design of Energy-Responsive Commercial Buildings.* New York: John Wiley & Sons.

Total Environmental Action, Inc., 1980. *Determination of Passive System Costs and Cost Goals.* Harrisville, NH: T.E.A., Inc. U.S. Department of Energy Contract No. DE-AC01-78-CS-35233.

U.S. Department of Housing and Urban Development, 1976. *Solar Heating and Cooling Demonstration Program: Cycle 1.* HUD-PDR-162, Washington, DC: U.S. HUD.

Woodbridge, S., 1984. Governing energy. *Progressive Architecture.* Stamford, CT: Reinhold Publishing.

4 Thermal Energy Storage in Building Interiors

Bion D. Howard and Harrison Fraker

4.1 Introduction

Thermal storage is an essential component in the effective use of solar energy in buildings. It acts like a reservoir that absorbs and releases intermittent sources of energy like solar radiation (or large diurnal temperature swings) to assist in providing human comfort. Although many types of solar heating systems use remote storage (such as liquid storage tank, rocks beds, air core systems or phase change materials), this chapter will address those storage techniques that are directly coupled to the interior space of buildings. These are typically surfaces of the interior building structural elements themselves. The heat capacity of interior furnishings and other contents must also be considered.

Once the solar thermal storage mechanism becomes an integral part of a building's interior, it has to satisfy many criteria other than just the efficient thermodynamic storage and distribution of energy. Thermal storage and release has to occur within an acceptable temperature range for human comfort. Thermal storage materials properly used may enhance human comfort. The thermal storage also may become part of the interior aesthetic of a building in which it is employed. Its technical function has been one of the biggest challenges to solar designers. As one developer pointed out, a major obstacle to the acceptance of passive solar design has been having floors you cannot put carpets on, walls you cannot hang things on, or having "funny" objects and materials in your living room.

In addition to the interior design considerations of the owner or operator and the amount of storage required for good performance and comfort by the climate energy source, there are other important internal sources of energy that can influence the design of any storage system. The frequency and quantity of internal heat gains supplied or generated by occupants, lights, equipment, and appliances can be as important as the amount of solar energy available. In the case of commercial buildings with rising use of personal computers, entirely new internal gains profiles are experienced, altering design considerations. The daily and weekly pattern of occupancy along with the local utility rate structure may determine for the designer whether interior thermal storage is an appropriate energy conservation strategy or not and will greatly influence design constraints. Thermal storage in commercial and industrial buildings has been shown to reduce cooling energy costs, usually when combined with ventilation.

The technical complexity of designing an effective interior thermal storage system, the importance of user interaction with the system, and its incorporation in the architecture of a building are poorly understood by most building designers and engineers. This chapter presents results from major research and development in the field over the past ten years and attempts to shed some light on these important passive building design considerations.

4.2   Background

4.2.1   Summary of Thermodynamic Mechanisms of Storage

4.2.1.1   Thermal Storage Process   The process of sensible heat thermal storage obeys the laws of thermodynamics, which state that energy flows from a warmer source to a colder (sink) object. The energy is transferred by conduction, convection, or radiation, or combinations of the three. It is useful to think of the process of thermal storage in three parts. The first part involves the collection or the absorption of energy by the storage material. In the case of solar energy (radiation) this occurs when the storage materials is directly irradiated by the sun and its surface is heated according to the amount of energy that is absorbed, reflected, reradiated, or convected. The absorption of radiant energy is a function of the absorptivity of the material's surface. Collection of energy can also occur when the air in a room is heated by convection from sunlit surfaces elsewhere, and heat is transferred to the storage material, walls, floors, or ceilings. The rate of heat transfer is controlled by the temperature difference between the air, the storage material's surface, and the film coefficients, as well as the rate of air flow. Usually the rate of transfer by natural convection is comparatively slow. It is obvious that the rate of flow and therefore the transfer coefficient can be greatly increased by creating "forced" convection, such as using fans. However, measurements do show that remarkable quantities of air do convect in passive solar buildings, from source to sink zones, without mechanical means.

The second part of the sensible heat storage process concerns the distribution of energy once it has been absorbed. It may be either convected or reradiated back to the room air and hence to the environment, or it may be conducted into the storage material. The rate of transfer into or out of storage mass is determined by the thermal diffusivity of the storage material and temperature differences. Thermal diffusivity is proportional to a material's conductance, specific heat, and its density.

These properties control the dynamic flow of energy into and out of the storage medium (i.e., the "pulse" or wave of energy) and should not be confused with the total heat capacity of the material, which is a static measure based on the material's total thickness, conductance, specific heat, and density.

The third part of the storage process involves the release of energy. Once the storage material has absorbed enough energy to be warmer than its surrounding environment, or its surrounding environment cools, it may release energy by radiation and natural convection. This process is controlled by the material's physical properties of emittance, thermal diffusivity, the temperature difference between the surface and the surrounding environment, and the convection coefficient created by the air flow over the surface (see figure 4.1 for diagram of the three parts of storage).

It should be pointed out that interior thermal storage does not increase or decrease the total energy available, nor does it change the long term heat loss/gain of the building. Thermal heat capacity in exterior envelopes, however, can reduce energy demand on space conditioning requirements under mild heating and cooling climate conditions. It changes the pattern of energy flow, i.e., the timing and amplitude of energy flow (volume). These energy balance modifications have been described as time lag (as a

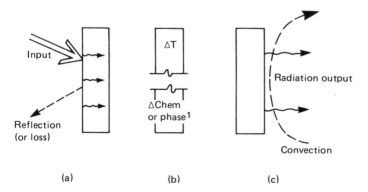

Figure 4.1
Storage functions: (a) absorption; (b) thermal diffusion; (c) release.

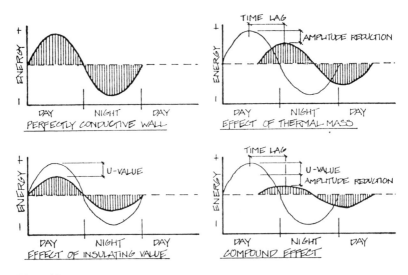

Figure 4.2
Diagramatic representation of effect of thermal mass and insulating value on the energy flow through and exterior wall. Source: T. E. A. (1978).

result of the heat capacity of the material) and amplitude reduction (primarily as a result of the conductance and diffusion of energy within the material). Time lags may be designed into buildings to displace periods of low envelope energy gain or loss into periods of elevated envelope loss or gain in which the stored energy can be used more effectively. Amplitude reduction is used to lower peak differentials (usually temperature) that the mechanical space conditioning must handle (see figure 4.2) to produce the desired level of comfort.

4.2.1.2 Chemical Storage Latent heat of fusion heat storage materials undergo reversible physical and/or chemical changes while absorbing thermal energy over narrower temperature ranges than sensible heat storage materials, such as concrete block, brick or adobe. The phase change materials (PCMs) actually do store heat through both sensible heating and latent heat of fusion processes. This is because the typical containers for solid/liquid PCMs are made of materials that do not undergo phase changes. Also, the PCMs themselves have sensible heat storage phases when not at or near their transition temperatures (melting points). Solid/solid PCMs would be essentially self-containing by definition and design, but have not yet been fully developed.

Containment of the PCMs has been one of the major challenges facing advanced PCM energy storage technology. Ideally, containers should be lightweight, compact, and leakproof when containing the often caustic salt hydrate compounds.

Typical container configurations are packets, pods, rods of various diameters and lengths, cans (usually of treated or stainless steel) and tiles with a surrounding structural material. One container design attractive to builders is a 14 × 22 in. (35.6 × 55.9 cm) panel that can fit between nominal framing dimensions common in wood frame housing. The thermal properties of the PCMs themselves have been thoroughly analyzed; however, the in-place containers monitored in real passive solar buildings have been trouble prone and have not yet reached expected levels of performance or reliability.

PCMs that have undergone the most generic research are shown in table 4.1, prepared by the NAHB-National Research Center. The values for heat content assume full "transition" or melting of the container compounds. This is a very optimistic assumption, in view of field results that have shown incongruent melting and frequent stratification within containers of PCMs.

The effective thermal capacity of PCMs is a much more important variable. Unfortunately, very little data exist on this and there are no test procedures yet standardized for its determination. Large differences between calculated and in-place heat storage capacity and duration are of great concern to builders and designers who need accurate cost to performance (benefit) information.

Another approach to PCM thermal storage enhancement is the filling of cavities frequently furnished in standard building construction. An

Table 4.1
Typical PCM salt hydrates for thermal energy storage

Compound	Transition temperature (°F)	Heat content		Range of module ($cost/MBtu)
		(Btu/#)	(Btu/ft³)	
$Na_2SO_4.10H_2O$ plus additives	89	100	9,100	11–20
$CaCl_2.6H_2O$	81	82	7,800	14–30
$Na_2SO_4.10H_2O$ plus NH_4Cl, NaCl, and additives	52–55	50	4,600	16–30
$Na_2SO_4.10H_2O$ plus NH_4Cl, KCl	45	50	4,600	16–30

example of this is the work done by Maurice Lang (1981a) at the University
of Delaware, evaluating PCM pouches placed into the cores of concrete
block. Lang's analysis showed that 100–800 Btu (102–812 kJ) can be added
to each block's heat capacity this way. Thin wall PVC (polyvinylchloride)
packages were fabricated using advanced techniques. Heat capacity, radiation and cycling tests were scheduled to be performed, but results are not
yet available.

Thermal wall panels have been designed that utilize PCM "chubs,"
which are sausagelike containers. Analysis of monitored data, by Joseph
Sliwkowski of the University of Delaware (1980), showed that 49% of
available solar radiation to a vertical triple glazing equipped with night
insulation was delivered to a heated room by a thermal wall panel system
using sodium sulphate decahydrate. The stored energy content of the panel
$(120 \text{ ft}^2/11.5 \text{ m}^2)$, by the hour of 17:00, was 17,105 Btu, or 142.5 Btu/ft^2
based on a selected day's energy balance.

Another serious problem with PCM heat storage is its high cost. F. S.
Langa (1981b) compared PCM systems cost effectiveness ($ per 1,000 Btu)
to wood, water storage, brick, concrete block, and adobe (figure 4.3). The
PCM containers alone were estimated as $9.66 per 1,000 Btu in 1981 dollars

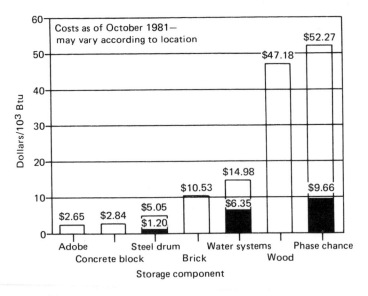

Figure 4.3
Relative heat storage cost comparison. Source: NCMA (1982).

($10.23 in 1982 dollars). By comparison, the total cost of concrete block storage per 1,000 Btu was $5.05 in 1981 dollars ($5.35 in 1982 dollars), or slightly more than half of just the PCM container cost per 1,000 Btu. Based on full rated capacity (as if the PCM always fully cycles) these costs for PCM storage would be reduced. This is an unsafe assumption since measured results show less than full transition of PCMs is quite common under operational conditions.

In a review of PCM techniques, C. J. Swet (1980) examines candidate materials. Paraffin "waxes" were mentioned as a candidate material because of high initial heats of fusion, and low vapor pressure and flash point (reasonable fire resistance). The principle disadvantages are rather high costs and difficulties of temperature matching to other solid materials that would offer structural containment of the solid-solid materials.

Swet also reported on the encasement of PCMs in building materials. He reviewed various work that tested composite wall sections, such as aluminum epoxy matrix assemblies, hollow core concrete blocks, tiles for use in ceilings, floors, and structures near windows, and Trombe walls of block masonry containing "cans" of PCMs. Findings indicated for these approaches that there were problems of heat transfer into the PCMs through the containments, and that only small initial performance improvements were obtained (Swet, 1980).

A promising encapsulation approach for concrete mixing applications is bead type PCM containers on the order of 0.5–0.66 in. (1.2–1.7 cm) in diameter. A significant constraint to placement of PCMs in concretes is "poisoning" of the mix with sulfates, reducing structural integrity. Another is the possibility of the container walls allowing a change in the water balance of the contained PCM mix, which comes under the influence of the moisture balance in the cured concrete. The concrete is likely to set up a significant water vapor pressure gradient from PCM to concrete across the container wall. Low or no permeability to liquid or vapor water is important to successful salt hydrate capsule entrainment in concrete.

Future research in PCMs is focused on "solid state" (Benson et al., 1985) materials that can permeate structural building materials, or be integrated into new building materials such as wall boards, blocks, and bricks. It is also conceivable that cast-in-place concrete may be enhanced by simple admixtures containing solid/solid PCMs. The structural mass existing in nearly every building could be much more effective in storage of thermal energy when specifically enhanced with advanced storage compounds.

4.2.1.3 Control Strategies Control of interior space comfort by architectural use of passive energy systems relies on the ability of the designer to incorporate effective thermal energy storage. The criteria for human comfort are explained in section 4.4. The successful integration of thermal protection, fenestration management, and energy storage creates successful control with minimum mechanical system intervention in the ideal passive design. If the designer is willing to incorporate hybrid elements (such as small fans or other mechanical systems), tighter control of conditioned space temperature is often facilitated. Indeed, Western society has comparatively narrow criteria for thermal comfort, expressed in acceptable ranges of indoor temperature and humidity. This is reflected in our willingness to use relatively large amounts of nonrenewable energy to obtain more tightly controlled comfort conditions than many other societies.

a. *Heat Capacity* The concept of total heat capacity of thermal storage mass is nearly useless in the context of dynamic responses to weather energy inputs and comfort demands of building occupants. The concept of effective heat capacity is helpful in understanding and designing successful thermal storage into buildings. For effective heat storage in sensible (as opposed to latent) materials, the product of the material's density and specific heat must be high per unit of thickness. Its thermal conductivity should also be high, since lower conductance tends to isolate heat from deeper in the storage during the demand side of the diurnal cycle (heating from storage).

Simple "rules-of-thumb" and builder guidelines for mass design are important, and probably will be improved and refined as more information is made available. Unfortunately, no complete guidebook on passive thermal storage systems now exists. However, much useful information is given in several important works on passive solar design.

Mazria (1979) provided classic rule-of-thumb heat storage guidelines from which numerous "first-generation" passive solar buildings were designed. A summary of these guidelines is shown in tables 4.2, 4.3, and 4.4 for several different generic passive system types. Monitored data show that homes designed with these rules perform fairly well, but that problems can occur in application of these rules to multizone or internal-loads-dominated commercial, industrial, or institutional structures.

Later work by Los Alamos National Laboratory-Solar Group (LANL), under the direction of J. Douglas Balcomb (Balcomb and Jones, 1980),

Table 4.2
Sizing solar windows for different climatic conditions[a]

Average winter outdoor temperature (°F) (degree-days/mo.)[b]	Square feet of window[c] needed for each one square foot of floor area
Cold climates	
15° (1,500)	0.27–0.42 (with night insulation over glass)
20° (1,350)	0.24–0.38 (with night insulation over glass)
25° (1,200)	0.21–0.33
30° (1,050)	0.19–0.29
Temperature climates	
35° (900)	0.16–0.25
40° (750)	0.13–0.21
45° (600)	0.11–0.17

[a] These ratios apply to a residence with a space heat loss of 8–10 $Btu/day\,ft_{fl}^2\,°F$. If space heat loss is less, lower values can be used. These ratios can also be used for other building types having similar heating requirements. Adjustments should be made for additional heat gains from lights, people, and appliances.
[b] Temperatures and degree-days are listed for December and January, usually the coldest months.
[c] Within each range, choose a ratio according to your latitude. For southern latitudes, i.e., 35°NL, use the lower window-to-floor-area ratios; for northern latitudes, i.e., 48°NL, use the higher ratios.

provided simplified passive solar analysis aides, with thermal mass assumptions built in to computer generated correlation data from which reasonable calculations of auxiliary heat requirements can be made for passive solar houses. The Los Alamos work developed a nomenclature of estimation factors based upon simulations and test cell data from generic passive systems. By using these results, LANL was able to develop some simplified guidelines for thermal mass, which have been refined in recent times into builders' guidelines and an ASHRAE *Handbook* (American Society of Heating, Refrigerating, and Air-Conditioning Engineers, 1984).

Basically, Los Alamos results show that nearly optimal mass thickness of common construction materials can be determined by analysis of the diurnal heat capacity of the materials. Figure 4.4 shows DHC responsive thicknesses of materials versus heat capacity calculated by Balcomb (1983a). A basic finding is that the density of the specific heat storage material has a major effect upon optimal thickness and effective storage capacity. An optimal storage material would have relatively high density, a specific heat above 0.25 Btu/1b °F (263.76 kJ) and reasonable, but not excessive (overly

Table 4.3
Sizing a thermal storage wall for different climatic conditions

Average winter outdoor temperature (°F) (degree-days/mo.)[a]	Square feet of wall[b] needed for each one square foot of floor area	
	Masonry wall	Water wall
Cold climates		
15° (1,500)	0.72– >1.0	0.55–1.0
20° (1,350)	0.60–1.0	0.45–0.85
25° (1,200)	0.51–0.93	0.38–0.70
30° (1,050)	0.43–0.78	0.31–0.55
Temperature climates		
35° (900)	0.35–0.60	0.25–0.43
40° (750)	0.28–0.46	0.20–0.34
45° (600)	0.22–0.35	0.16–0.25

[a] Temperatures and degree-days are listed for December and January, usually the coldest months.
[b] Within each range choose a ratio according to your latitude. For southern latitudes, i.e., 35°NL, use the lower wall-to-floor-area ratios; for northern latitudes, i.e., 48°NL, use the higher ratios. For a poorly insulated building always use a higher value. For thermal walls with a horizontal specular reflector equal to the height of the wall in length, use 67% of recommended ratios. For thermal walls with night insulation (R-8), use 85% of recommended ratios. For thermal walls with both reflectors and night insulation, use 57% of recommended ratios.

rapid) thermal diffusivity. The thermal diffusivity is expressed as the conductivity divided by density times specific heat. For common heat storing structural materials, thicknes greater than 6–8 in. (150–200 mm) has little added effect on diurnal heat storage. Lighter weight materials for heat storage are optimally thinner, and much less effective.

The Los Alamos-diurnal heat capacity (DHC) method refined by Balcomb is a very simple and useful method for analysis of storage components and of the total interior effective heat capacity of a passive design. DHC can be used to estimate the role of all the interior surfaces, whether lightweight or massive, and their properties, in temperature swings and comfort levels to tbe expected. Each type of surface is also characterized in terms of its exposure to transmitted solar radiation via the collection system to make the necessary calculations.

Figure 4.5 and tables 4.5A and 4.5B are taken from Los Alamos DHC analysis. These data show how much heat can effectively be stored in various sensible heat storing materials where the density and thickness are

Table 4.4
Sizing the attached greenhouse for different climatic conditions

Average winter outdoor temperature (°F) (degree-days/mo.)[a]	Square feet of greenhouse glass[b] needed for each one square foot of floor area	
	Masonry wall	Water wall
Cold climates		
20° (1,350)	0.9 −1.5	0.68−1.27
25° (1,200)	0.78−1.3	0.57−1.05
30° (1,050)	0.65−1.17	0.47−0.82
Temperate climates		
35° (900)	0.53−0.90	0.38−0.65
40° (750)	0.42−0.69	0.30−0.51
45° (600)	0.33−0.53	0.24−0.38

[a] Temperatures and degree-days are listed for December and January, usually the coldest months.
[b] Within each range choose a ratio according to your latitude. For southern latitudes, i.e., 35°NL, use the lower glass-to-floor-area ratios; for northern latitudes, i.e., 48°NL, use the higher ratios. For a poorly insulated greenhouse or buildings, always use slightly more glass.

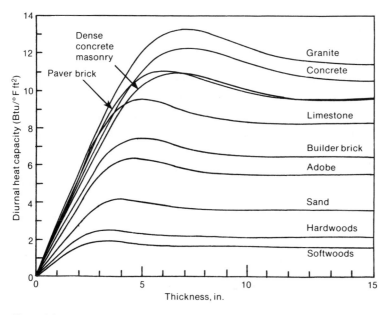

Figure 4.4
Diurnal heat capacity of various typical materials. Source: Balcomb (1983a).

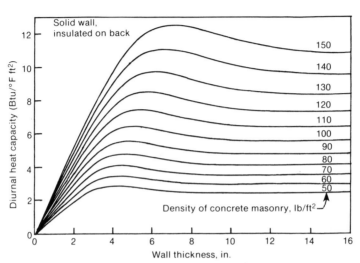

Figure 4.5
Diurnal heat capacity of "formula" materials. Source: Balcomb (1983a).

known. Observe the damping effect of increased thickness, beyond apparent optimal thicknesses for each material or "formula." For surfaces supplied diurnally with heat on both sides, effectiveness may essentially double—as in the case of a north-to-south running interior partition wall.

b. *Mass Applications* Interior mass in direct gain systems with layers greater than 6 in. of solid concrete (or equivalent material) may even be counterproductive. An exception is the case of a south-to-north running interior wall, like a partition that receives transmitted solar energy direct to both its surfaces during the daily cycle. Direct gain floor systems should receive direct sun, and be well insulated on the perimeter at least. About 4-in. thickness is correct for concrete masonry pavers, brick pavers, and cast concrete floors.

In a Trombe wall, different criteria exist to detemine optimal thickness. In Trombe wall design, it is necessary to relate the heat output desired from the wall's interior face to the wall's thickness, under typical operating conditions. Figure 4.6 shows the energy furnished by one square foot of a Trombe wall surface per hour per degree of temperature swing versus thickness. Clearly, the use of typical masonry units of 6–12 in. (depending

Table 4.5A
Diurnal heat capacity (Btu/°F ft^2) of various materials

Thickness (in.)	Granite	Concrete	Concrete masonry (140 lb.)	Paver brick	Limestone	Builder brick	Adobe	Sand	Hardwood	Softwood
Direct DHC										
1	2.78	2.50	2.44	2.70	2.80	2.20	2.00	1.50	1.12	.87
2	5.54	4.99	4.85	5.36	5.52	4.33	3.92	2.90	2.08	1.61
3	8.18	7.37	7.13	7.81	7.81	6.11	5.44	3.86	2.48	1.88
4	10.46	9.47	9.04	9.71	9.17	7.16	6.20	4.14	2.42	1.81
6	13.00	11.94	10.88	11.07	9.30	7.23	6.05	3.82	2.20	1.65
8	13.05	12.14	10.69	10.55	8.63	6.70	5.62	3.62	2.17	1.64
12	11.81	10.99	9.68	9.68	8.29	6.45	5.49	3.61	2.18	1.64
16	11.51	10.65	9.53	9.65	8.33	6.48	5.52	3.62	2.18	1.64
Indirect DHC										
1	2.48	2.28	2.23	2.42	2.48	2.03	1.86	1.43	1.08	.85
2	3.84	3.63	3.56	3.73	3.71	3.23	3.00	2.39	1.77	1.42
3	4.36	4.21	4.10	4.19	4.05	3.64	3.39	2.70	1.91	1.54
4	4.51	4.40	4.26	4.29	4.06	3.68	3.41	2.67	1.82	1.46
6	4.45	4.37	4.19	4.16	3.84	3.48	3.19	2.46	1.68	1.35
8	4.30	4.22	4.03	3.99	3.69	3.32	3.05	2.38	1.67	1.34
12	4.11	4.02	3.86	3.86	3.65	3.28	3.04	2.39	1.68	1.35
16	4.10	4.00	3.85	3.87	3.66	3.29	3.04	2.39	1.68	1.35

Table 4.5B
Diurnal heat capacity (Btu/°F ft^2) of formula materials

Thickness (in.)	Density of concrete masonry (lb/ft^3)									
	60	70	80	90	100	110	120	130	140	150
Direct DHC										
1	1.16	1.34	1.51	1.67	1.84	1.99	2.15	2.30	2.44	2.59
2	2.26	2.61	2.96	3.29	3.62	3.95	4.26	4.56	4.86	5.15
3	3.08	3.58	4.10	4.63	5.15	5.67	6.17	6.67	7.15	7.61
4	3.39	4.00	4.66	5.36	6.09	6.84	7.59	8.33	9.05	9.75
6	3.20	3.82	4.53	5.34	6.26	7.28	8.41	9.62	10.90	12.21
8	3.00	3.57	4.22	4.96	5.81	6.79	7.92	9.22	10.70	12.33
12	2.97	3.52	4.12	4.80	5.55	6.39	7.34	8.43	9.69	11.16
16	2.98	3.53	4.14	4.82	5.58	6.42	7.35	8.39	9.54	10.85
Indirect DHC										
1	1.13	1.29	1.44	1.59	1.73	1.86	1.99	2.11	2.23	2.34
2	1.98	2.23	2.46	2.68	2.88	3.07	3.25	3.41	3.56	3.70
3	2.35	2.62	2.88	3.13	3.36	3.57	3.77	3.95	4.11	4.25
4	2.38	2.66	2.93	3.19	3.44	3.68	3.89	4.09	4.27	4.43
6	2.20	2.47	2.74	3.00	3.27	3.52	3.76	3.99	4.20	4.39
8	2.10	2.36	2.61	2.86	3.10	3.35	3.58	3.81	4.03	4.23
12	2.10	2.35	2.59	2.82	3.05	3.26	3.47	3.67	3.86	4.04
16	2.10	2.35	2.60	2.83	3.06	3.28	3.48	3.67	3.85	4.02

on density) is warranted. Thicker walls than this may again be counterproductive according to the data. Certainly for a typical masonry Trombe wall, annual solar heating fractions do not increase much beyond an 8-in. (200-mm) thickness (figure 4.7). A more important concern regarding wall thickness here may be structural or seismic code requirements for life safety.

However, most Trombe walls are reinforced, and many are filled with concrete or grout to increase their heat capacity. This improves structural integrity as well.

Today's architects and designers require more information than rules of thumb to make appropriate decisions in the design phase. It is important to relate heat storage capacity of both "free" structural and surface mass and "additional" or "purchased" mass effectively in order to verify comfort and cost effectiveness. For example, if a frame house with a certain south-facing window area requires X units of thermal storage capacity to be

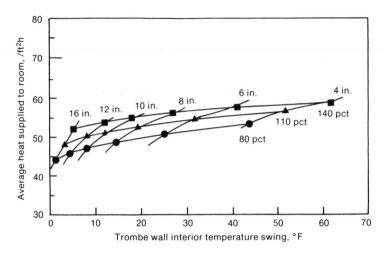

Figure 4.6
Trombe (thermal storage) wall performance versus interior air temperature swing. Source: NCMA (1982).

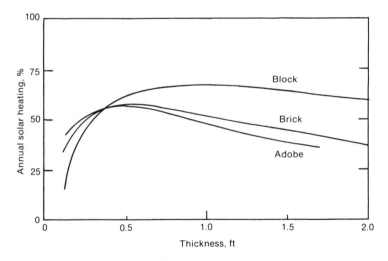

Figure 4.7
Trombe wall performance for brick, adobe and concrete block (solid): solar heating versus wall thickness. Source: Mazria (1979).

added to preserve comfort (at cost Y), how does this compare with the cost and performance of construction of the same house using heavy-mass wall materials with exterior insulation (at some added cost over frame walls) to avoid the need for "purchased" extra interior mass? Direct evaluation of temperature swings and diurnal heat capacity can help designers analyze this type of problem early on to help make appropriate decisions.

c. *Phase Change Thermal Storage*   Effects of using 5/8-in. PCM-rich wall surface area (sheetrock with PCM) while reducing the illuminated floor mass (from 4 in.) down to 5/8-in.-thick concrete (from 4 in.) was investigated (Neeper and McFarland, 1982). Floor mass has three times collector area, and the PCM walls were analyzed at 6–12 times collector area. Thirteen times wall to collector area was considered the practical limit of interior surface area for direct gain systems.

Conservative PCM properties were assumed, and absorbed radiation was divided equally between floor and walls. At 6 times glazing area, the PCM walls could provide a 50% performance increase in the direct gain system with no night insulation. At 12 times glazing area, the same system's passive heating performance nearly doubled.

The placement of glazing and its ability to directly illuminate PCMs effectively prescribes performance of typical containerized systems. The ability of the indoor-facing surfaces of the PCM module to release heat when required by the space or, conversely, to absorb heat during cooling demand is also influential. An effective absorber surface on a PCM container may be hampered by the low thermal diffusivity of typical container materials. Later, poor release of heat from the container may occur if surface emittance is low. Surface-to-air heat transfer coefficients of PCM containers must be enhanced to encourage proper release of stored energy from PCM modules.

4.2.1.4 Enhancement of Human Comfort   The parameters of human comfort have been fairly well documented by both theory and experiment. These parameters include air temperature, radiant temperatures, humidity, and air flow (ventilation). The ASHRAE *Fundamentals Handbook* (1989) contains information on the ranges of temperature and humidity conditions in which humans "feel" comfortable.

Our modern society has become accustomed to very slight thermal variations in indoor temperatures. We have learned to accept some seasonal changes like winter and summer thermostat set backs, imposed by early energy conservation efforts. Passive solar structures can be designed with acceptable (comfortable) temperature swings, and thermal mass is essential to accomplish this goal. Daily temperature swings above about 12°F (6.7°C) are considered to produce discomfort in conditioned spaces other than sunspaces and greenhouses. Sunspaces and greenhouses are expected to produce elevated temperature swings by design, unless they are to be occupied during the day; then a similar temperature swing (12°F/6.7°C) should be designed for, making them conform more closely to direct gain system criteria.

Perceptions of comfort by humans primarily depend on the interaction of the following variables describing the environment of persons in buildings:

- air and mean radiant temperature,
- nearby surface temperatures—walls, floors, ceilings,
- quantity, location, and temperature of thermal masses,
- exterior dissipator temperatures coupled to absorbers indoors,
- quantity of water vapor or "relative humidity,"
- air motion or velocity near the person,
- quantity of admitted solar radiation,
- building internal heat generation,
- level of physical activity,
- level of metabolic activity,
- amount of clothing worn, and
- physical condition and acclimitization level.

These controlling variables are of three varieties. One set is controlled by the building environment, over which we can have some influence through the design process. A second set is controlled by the physiology of occupants themselves and, to a degree, societal norms, such as dress codes or type of work done, which can determine the clothing worn. The work done and clothing worn create a complex process in which the body functions to maintain thermal equilibrium with its surroundings. The final set is beyond our control and represents the realities of the atmospheric environment (climate) in which the building exists, and our daily activites all take place.

The basic energy balance describing a human in equilibrium with the environment is

Table 4.6
Metabolic levels of various activites [kcal/h (Btu/h)]

Basal metabolism	60–70 (240–280)
Sitting at rest	90–100 (360–400)
Sedentary activity	100–120 (400–480)
Walking on a level at 4 km/h	210–270 (840–1,080)
Walking on a level at 7 km/h	300–400 (1,200–1,600)
Walking up 10% slope at 4 km/h	340–480 (1,360–1,920)
Light industrial work	150–300 (600–1,200)
Moderate industrial work	300–480 (1,200–2,400)
Heavy industrial work	450–600 (1,800–2,400)
Very heavy work	600–750 (2,400–3,000)

$$dQ = M \pm R \pm C - E,$$

where dQ is the change in energy content of the body, M is the metabolic rate, R is the long-wave radiative term, C is the convection near the body, and E is the evaporation heat loss from the body, typically as sweat or respiration. Table 4.6 contains energy output values from humans engaged in various activity levels. Active sports activities such as soccer, swimming, or motorcycle racing, are at the top ranges—similar to heavy work. When the body is clothed, the terms R, C, and E must be evaluated using empirically derived data from measurements of human responses. Much of this work is summarized by Baruch Givoni (1976).

The mean radiant temperature (MRT) is the determinant of the radiant (R) heat exchange. Givoni cites two formulas for determining MRT, one of which is more easily understood, while both are reasonable approaches:

$$\text{MRT} = Tg + 0.24 + V0.5(Tg - Ta),$$

where Tg is the black globe temperature, V is the air velocity near the subject in feet per minute, and Ta is the measured air temperature. Indoor spaces that have been designed to store heat gains effectively tend to produce somewhat elevated MRTs compared to lightweight buildings, in winter. Conversely, if the space is ventilated at night in summer, the mass may be cooler than the air temperature, lowering MRT, and can provide a cooling effect.

ASHRAE Standard 55–81 (ANSI/ASHRAE, 1981) provides a set of operative temperature and air movement requirements designed to provide reasonable comfort levels for persons doing light office work in light clothing. The operative temperature used is a weighted average of the dry bulb air temperature and the MRT. Figure 4.8 shows this in graphic form for a summer zone and an extended summer zone, if increased air movement is provided.

Other investigators believe higher air flow rates can be used without problems, according to Clark. A study from Kansas State University (Rholes et al., 1981) cited by Clark extends the summer comfort zone even further. The extended summer comfort zone could be expanded with the use of ceiling fans. ASHRAE also sets an upper dew point temperature limit at 62°F, which also may be extended to 76°F, due to relative insensitivity of humans to changes in dew point temperature. However, dew point temperatures above 62°F have been shown to promote growth of mold and mildew.

The bioclimatic chart is one way of showing some of the interrelated factors governing comfort. Developed by Victor Olgyay (1963), it shows temperature and relative humidity zones in which either comfort or discomfort will be felt by most persons. Numerous charts have been generated, reflecting the differences in aclimatization of humans in different climate zones. Figure 4.9 shows this chart for the "U.S. Moderate Zone," which is adequate for the purpose of discussion here.

Data on outdoor temperature and relative humidity can be plotted on a working copy of the chart for days, weeks, or months of the year. This will show the amounts of shade, dehumidification, and ventilation needed in a specific site. Data on temperature, relative humidity, and wind velocity is available from the U.S. National Oceanographical and Aeronautical Administration (NOAA), which maintains climatic records for over 3000 locations.

Most nations have weather bureaus that also keep similar data. It is a valuable exercise to produce a bioclimatic chart for your area, based on actual local weather data.

4.2.1.5 Cooling Thermal Mass Utilization Masonry structures have been used for many years in the subtropical areas of the United States and similar regions throughout the world. Ancient civilations realized the ability of masonry to moderate the temperature swings of summer, in buildings that took many forms. Prehistoric and more contemporary native Americans used natural overhangs of sandstone cliffs and exfoliations of

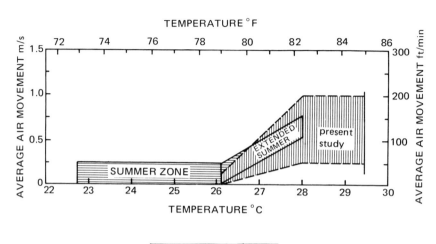

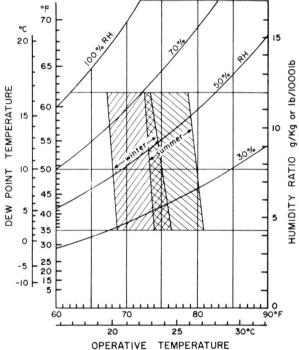

Figure 4.8
ASHRAE comfort criteria. Source: ANSI/ASHRAE (1981).

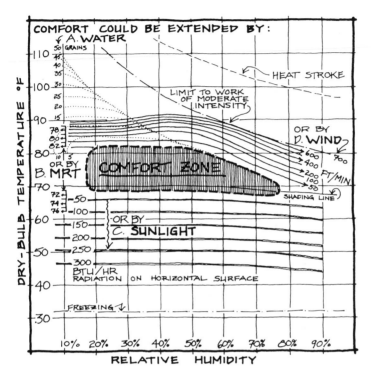

Figure 4.9
Olgyay bioclimatic chart (Moderate U.S. Zone). Source: Olgyay (1963).

rock faces for shade from the high summer sun and as collectors for low angle winter solar energy. Their massive pueblos were made of hand-formed masonry called adobe, which, while not being capable of very great heat storage, provides long delays in heat transfer through the thicknesses typically used: 18–24 in. (46–61 cm). This primitive thermal mass and insulation served these people well, buffering their living spaces year-round and reducing their need for long treks for fuel wood.

The Greeks and Romans, through their developing understanding of astronomy, physics, and mathematics, adapted thermal mass and solar techniques to heat and cool their homes, meeting places, and public baths. Numerous examples of Greco-Roman solar utilization are cited in *A Golden Thread* (Butti and Perlin, 1981). The structures were oriented to the equator so as to capture the sun's energy in winter, but exclude it by overhangs in the summer. The Romans employed windows of glass or mica that were removed in spring to promote ventilation and replaced in fall as temperatures dropped.

Masonry was used by these cultures for many reasons, energy efficiency being one. Another reason was that most wood was (or had already been) burned for cooking and heat. In fact, the destruction of the forests near Rome helped lead to its ultimate downfall.

Thermal mass in buildings reduces the temperature swings indoors and makes the mean indoor temperature less dependent upon short term variations of outdoor temperature. This fact helps massive structures stay cool in summer and warm in winter. The Thermal Mass Effect is more completely described in an overview report by Oak Ridge National Laboratories (Childs, Courville, and Bales, 1983). The effect is most pronounced in climates where outdoor temperatures swing below and above the average indoor temperature each day. If outdoor temperatures are always above the average indoor (thermostat) temperature settings, then auxiliary energy will very likely be used. Testing by the National Bureau of Standards (NBS) has shown that lightweight buildings in warm climates consume up to 37% more space cooling energy than massive buildings (Burch, Davis, and Malcomb, 1984). Further research into this effect is now underway.

What can we expect from cooling systems using thermal mass? The minimum temperature obtained depends on the total effective mass and its degree of coupling to the environmental heat sink. Of similar importance is the effectiveness of coupling the interior load to the absorber portion of the mass. Data from Givoni (1976) for houses using night flushed mass shows that the mass temerature can reach down to within $4°-6°F$ ($2°-3°C$) of the minimum night dry bulb temperature. An increase in surface area per unit load for dissipation should improve the system's ability to attain minimum temperature. This increase in surface is available in commercial buildings, which show great potential for passive and hybrid thermal mass cooling (Childs, Courville, and Bales, 1983).

4.3   Systems For Thermal Storage

The generic description of passive thermal storage components is necessary for full understanding of the wide range of typical systems and applications. The storage, or internal thermal mass, is directly linked to the comfort of the interior space, the passive collector, and the outdoors via interaction with envelope thermal integrity. The passive thermal storage components are typically part of the structure and can be less "recognizable" than the storage subsystem of the typical active system.

4.3.1 Building Based Materials, Components, and Systems

The direct, indirect, and isolated gain storage types are commonly coupled to collector apertures in varying degrees. The direct gain system's thermal storage is typically surfaces of floors, walls, or ceilings combined with the "free" mass of furniture and articles contained in the space. In contrast, a thermal storage wall system, whether brick, concrete block, concrete, water containers, or PCM, is more indirectly coupled to the space, when the glazing is considered. That is, the mass is in the path of the transmitted solar energy, rather than in the surfaces of a "cavity" absorbing direct gains.

The basic generic types of single-story passive buildings are shown in figure 4.10 illustrating typical mass placement (Franta et al., 1981). The thickness of mass layers in the drawing is not to scale. Figure 4.10 illustrates the use of direct gains, storage walls, storage roofs, sunspaces, and some combination systems in typical application.

Direct gain systems employ mass in floors and walls most commonly. Ceiling tiles of PCM have been used (Johnson, 1978) in combination with special window blinds to reflect sunlight up onto the ceiling tiles. In the heating mode, sunlight heats the mass during the day and the collected heat is released when the building load and indoor air temperature change at night. Figure 4.11 shows the direct gain system. At high solar angles in summer, much of the unwanted sun can be excluded using overhangs. Cross ventilation can reduce overheating conditions well, except in humid climates. Insufficient mass or concentration of mass into smaller surface areas has the potential to cause oveheating of the space, particularly in fall, when outdoor temperatures are mild and the sun angle is low enough to permit insolation to be transmitted into the space.

The thermal storage wall intercepts (collects and stores) transmitted solar heat from the glazing and provides this heat via the massive construction materials of the wall (or high heat capacity materials such as PCM pods or panels) to the space by thermal diffusion across the wall and hence by radiation from the inner surface and by convection of room air across the inner surface. Figure 4.12 shows a typical vented Trombe wall in a two-story building. In summer, overheating is prevented using overhangs and cross ventilation out of the cavity between the storage and glazing. Vented thermal storage walls have only slightly higher performance than unvented

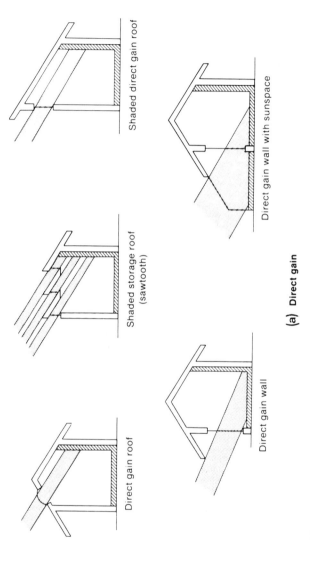

Figure 4.10
Schematics of passive heating types and mass placement within the building. Source:
Franta et al. (1981).

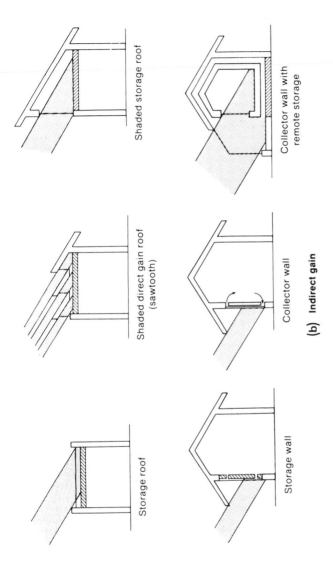

Shaded storage roof

Collector wall with remote storage

Shaded direct gain roof (sawtooth)

Collector wall

(b) Indirect gain

Storage roof

Storage wall

Figure 4.10 (continued)

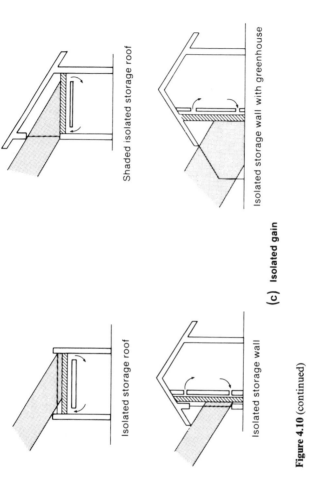

Figure 4.10 (continued)

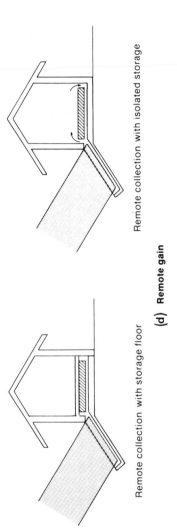

Remote collection with isolated storage

Remote collection with storage floor

(d) Remote gain

Figure 4.10 (continued)

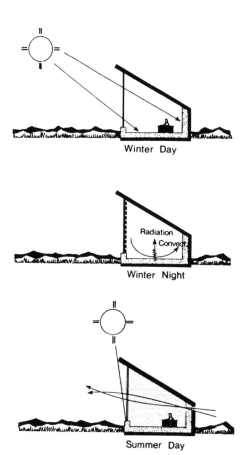

Figure 4.11
Direct gain heating—modes of operation. Source: Johnson (1978).

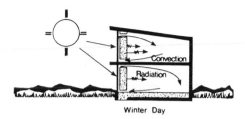

Winter Day

Storage wall in heating mode

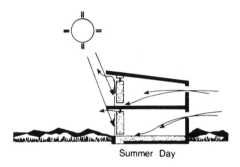

Summer Day

Storage wall in cooling mode

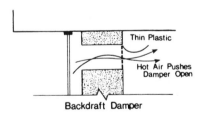

Backdraft Damper

Back draft damper for storage wall vents

Figure 4.12
Thermal storage wall—modes of operation. Source: Johnson (1978).

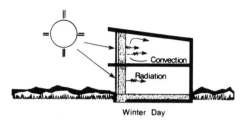

Winter Day

Storage wall in heating mode

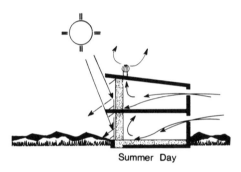

Summer Day

Storage wall in cooling mode

Figure 4.13
Unvented thermal storage wall—modes of operation. Source: Johnson (1978).

thermal storage walls, and require much more frequent cleaning. Thermo-syphon backflow is prevented using thin plastic dampers as shown. Heat is delivered during the day when outdoor temperatures are moderate. This means the vented Trombe wall may be poorly matched for low heat loss buildings (Franta et al., 1981).

The unvented Trombe wall is simpler to construct, requires less maintenance, and provides nearly equal performance to the vented types. The unvented Trombe wall, shown in figure 4.13, may also be protected by overhang shading, but both indoor venting and venting of the cavity between the glazing and the collector-storage wall are recommended in summer months.

An interesting variation on the theme of indirect gain systems is the thermal storage roof system, devised by Dr. Harold Hay in the mid-1960s. Figure 4.14 shows the modes of operation in winter and summer, and the use of controlled movable insulating decks over the storage media. Water

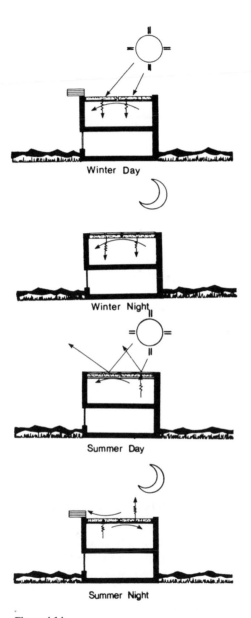

Winter Day

Winter Night

Summer Day

Summer Night

Figure 4.14
Storage roof system—modes of operation. Source: Johnson (1978).

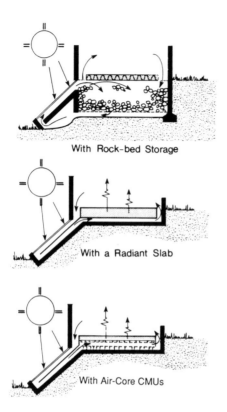

With Rock-bed Storage

With a Radiant Slab

With Air-Core CMUs

Figure 4.15
Convective loop systems, typical designs. Source: Johnson (1978).

ponds, bags, or modules are typically used for collection, storage, and summer night heat rejection. The storage heat collector/rejector medium is placed atop structural high conductance material such as steel decking topped with concrete. The control of gains and losses to and from storage media permits total passive conditioning (zero or minimal auxiliary energy use) by buildings using this system in mild climates. Variations have also been successfully demonstrated in colder climate zones such as Minnesota and New Hampshire.

The connective loop system relie on the density changes in solar heated air to drive warmer air as the heat transfer media through arrangements of rocks, concrete block or slabs typically located under floors. As shown in figure 4.15 the systems are simple, but do require collector panels mounted below floor level to enhance convective flow. There are three basic approaches: (1) A rock bed plenum, filled with fairly large diameter rocks to reduce pressure drop, is supplied by a back-pass convective loop solar air panel. Heat is radiated from the rocks to the floor topping. (2) A slab is provided with air flow paths below it using ducts, pipes, or formwork, and heat is supplied by a front pass convective loop solar air panel. (3) Concrete block is laid on its side in a stack arrangement and a slab or concrete top coat is cast over the block, with no mortar required. All these approaches should be well insulated around their perimeters for best results.

4.3.2 Mechanical Systems

The use of fans to move air through passive buildings really makes the application a "hybrid" in technical terms. Some building research shows that properly designed passive systems can very effectively distribute heat (Balcomb and Yamagichi, 1983). However, problems in design such as isolated north zones indicate that there is little or no potential for glazings to furnish direct passive gains.

Floors, ceilings, and walls can be employed for forced convective heating and/or cooling of mass using indirect radiant coupling to conditioned spaces. An example of floor and wall systems that have been constructed, operated, and monitored is the use of "free" void spaces in masonry walls or underfloor cores as in precast planks. In their simplest forms, these "air-core" systems (Howard, 1986) can be quite effective in reducing stratification in solar buildings, providing a sink for internal gains that could otherwise add to overheating and to furnish heat or cooling to isolated zones. Figures 4.16A and 4.16B show a generic block masonry system employing the air-core approach. Other high mass internal structures can also be used, such as two wythe (layer) brick partition walls, concrete cast-in-place with ducts, or pipes open at each end to conduct air flow.

The cores of concrete block provide air flow passage, and the roughness of the block surface enhances heat transfer. The system can be controlled so that the fan flushes cool night air through the mass in the summer to precool the mass. If the walls have one side exposed to ambient, it must be very well insulated, as must air-core slab floors on grade.

Plenum arrangements can be used to heat PCM tiles or pouches mounted above ceiling finish materials during the day. Passive direct gains to rooms with little internal mass, or excess gains from a sunspace, can be used to heat the PCM. Heat is provided through radiation from the ceiling. In summer, the relatively isothermal ceiling can absorb unwanted heat from the space.

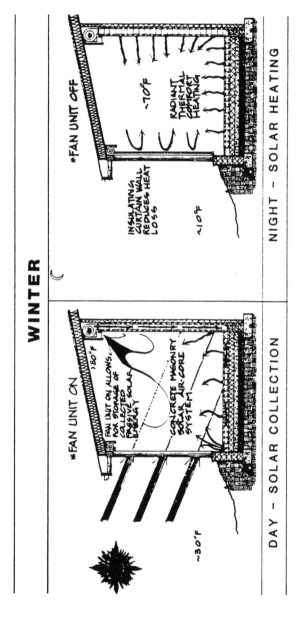

Figure 4.16A
Air-core system schematic—winter mode. Source: NCMA (1984).

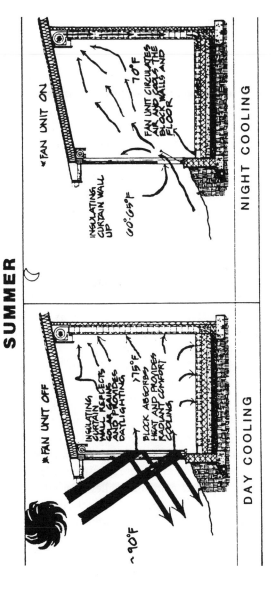

Figure 4.16B
Air-core system schematic—Summer mode. Source: NCMA (1984).

Cool night air flushed across the PCM modules can dump the heat out-doors.

4.3.3   Criteria For Successful Application

The purpose of internal thermal storage, whether provided by masonry, PCM, water, or the use of smaller windows on the south to take advantage of "free mass" without danger of overheating, is comfort and energy savings. Thermal mass use can "temper" increased solar gain. Adding thermal capacity reduces temperature swings if the mass is well distributed in the direct gain space. Centralized masses in highly solar driven spaces have not been shown to reduce temperature swings effectively. However, spreading out thinner layers of heat storage materials up to about a 12-to-1 ratio of storage layer area to glazing area provides better results. In reality, a 6-to-1 storage-to-glazing area ratio is thought to be most effective (Balcomb and Jones, 1980; Balcomb, 1983a). This ratio was increased from earlier rules of thumb, which suggested 3 to 1 was adequate. If temperature control (reducing tendency for "swings") is not adequately provided during spring and fall seasons, discomfort or cooling energy use may increase. Couple ineffective massing of direct gain space with elevated humidity levels and potential discomfort increases accordingly.

Monitored results from several DOE sponsored projects (NSDN— Howard and Pollock, 1982; SERI "Class B"—Frey, Swisher, and Holtz, 1982; LANL—Haskins and Stromberg, 1979) point to direct gains being most effective in standard construction (no added mass, insulated light frame walls) when solar glazing areas are less than 8% of interior floor area. Above this ratio, added mass is needed either in the form of heavier envelope construction or added interior thermal storage systems. Measured data point to the wisdom of using direct gains in smaller amounts, combined with indirect or isolated gains systems for heat, after the daylighting requirements are satisfied. Trombe walls, sunspaces with high-mass separation walls, or air-core type systems can satisfy this requirement.

In both NSDN and Class B monitoring projects, user participation in operation of passive control components was often a problem. Occupants are capable of offsetting much of the energy saving capability designed into solar buildings if they are not informed users. Movable insulation mis-operation is a key example.

Placement of thick carpet over heat storage floors and hanging too many plants in sunspace windows are other examples. There is a limit to the positive effect interior mass can have on comfort if it is shielded from effective solar heat absorption. Occupants of passive buildings must be well-informed of the necessity for exposure of thermal storage components to direct sunlight, or to secondary gains via reflection and convection. There have been examples of follow-on owners covering over heat storage walls with insulation and wall board to "hide" block or brick exposed on the interior, thereby eliminating its storage function. One way to prevent this kind of intervention is to provide a storage mass that is aesthetically acceptable. Also, an operator's manual for the building explaining the functions and requirements for the mass to work well can be helpful.

Construction of passive solar heat storage ranges from the very simple to the complicated. The simplest heat storage approach is to construct the building of massive structural materials insulated on the exterior to couple the mass to the indoor space. Multiple functions of the components can increase cost effectiveness. Many useful construction details are given in the *Passive Solar Construction Handbook* (1981/1984) for buildings using high-mass materials and for frame construction buildings using integrated mass materials.

A key practice is the attention to detail in construction. Careless construction can impose significant control problems in passive solar designs. For example, if glazings permit excess air leakage, effective insulation and thermal mass benefits can quickly be offset. The improper use of materials or the substitution of inferior or poorly designed components can also impose performacne and comfort penalties. In general, the simpler a passive design is, the less likely it is to encounter operational problems.

Occupants may be unable to accept the appearance of certain passive solar components. For example, PCM rods exposed in a sunspace may look "high tech," but occupants may not feel they fit with traditional furniture. Similarly, interior masonry walls are "unusual" except when associated with fireplaces. An interior designed for thermal performance and comfort may not help "sell" the building if it does not look good to the owner/buyer. Interior masonry has been successfully associated with commercial or institutional buildings, and exposed mass in this setting, as opposed to residences, may be deemed more acceptable.

A solution to improve appearance is to cover heat storage materials with noninsulating finishes such as grass cloth, plaster (parging), or wall paper. New architectural patterns for masonry surfaces provide new opportunities for exciting interior design that do not compromise the comfort and performance of the passive system. PCM materials under developement for integration into structural materials such as wall board, block, and brick hold promise for improved performance with little or no aesthetic penalties.

In past years the spatial arrangement, and even the exterior shape, of the building was thought related directly to performance. This was true in the earlier passive designs where less attention was paid to envelope thermal protection—and the emphasis was more on "glass and mass." Passive design has entered a more elegant phase since the capacity has emerged for balancing the envelope's construction with passive glass and heat storage requirements within reasonable economic constraints (Balcomb, 1980, 1983b). The new passive solar design ethic can be applied to virtually any design, and proper analysis indicates what insulation, windows, mass and arrangements of these components produces good results.

Generally, however, spaces occupied at night benefit from the use of stored solar heat in winter and night flushing of mass in summer. Spaces occupied during the day hours benefit from good natural lighting and reasonable fluctuations in temperature in both winter and summer.

4.3.4   State of the Art as of 1972

Socrates (c. 400 BC) described what has become today's "passive systems" as follows: "... in houses with a south aspect, the sun's rays penetrate into porticos in winter, but in summer the path of the sun is right over our heads and above the roof so that there is shade ... we should build the south side loftier to get the winter sun and the north side lower to keep out the cold winds" (Xenophon, *Memorabilia Socratis*).

Native Americans also knew of the use of passive solar nearly 1,000 years ago, in their arrangements of adobe buildings and the use of natural south-facing rock formations and canyons to site their villages. During the years directly before and following World War II, architects stumbled upon passive solar heating in homes again. Some gains in popularity occurred and plan books were developed, but the onset of cheaply supplied fossil fuels during the 1950s and 1960s reduced demand for such building systems.

Europeans were not so "lucky" as U.S. residents, because their post–World War II economies developed in such a way as to be dependent upon relatively expensive imported oil, coal, and natural gas resources.

The construction of the Wallasey School in 1961–1962 confirmed European commitment to improving energy efficiency. The school's design uses a huge (by today's standards) 6,210-square-foot direct gain "solar wall."

Original papers on the school's performance indicate it uses high mass construction with exterior insulation of roof and north walls (Perry, 1976). Control of comfort was achieved by choice of clothing, internal heat from lights and students, and ventilation in response to solar collection, storage, and distribution (figure 4.17). It was not until 1968 that instrumented results first became available from the school. A thermal model was established by Davies (1968), and detailed analysis of construction thermal properties ensued. At typical ventilation rates, the building's time constant was about 5–6 *days*. Davies' research monitoring showed the school was 70% solar heated with lights supplying 22% and student "body-heat" making up the other 8%.

No less revolutionary than the Wallasey School were the CNRS houses that pioneered modern use of masonry thermal storage walls. These houses, built in 1967, later known in the United States as the first Trombe wall houses, were extensively analyzed and later monitored by their designer. The Trombe wall principle is well known today, but during 1967–1974 French researchers examined many prototypes of "Trombe walls" with varying results. A key finding was that improving the insulation used on the building provided a significant boost in passive system effectiveness (Trombe et al., 1976).

Research was also performed to investigate the air flow and heat transfer characteristics of the wall systems. Radiation and convection exchange coefficients were evalutated. Studies on this type of passive system continue today, although U.S. builders have not accepted the Trombe wall very widely.

Australian researchers were also looking at passive and hybrid building design in the late 1960s and early 1970s. A direct gain building with a rock bin heat storage and an earth coupled ventilation system equipped with water sprays was described in a paper presented at 1970 ISES Conference in Melbourne (Chapman, 1970). An under-floor plenum distributed heat to and from the rock bin and simple dampers altered air flow in summer to help cool the structure. The building itself was laid from north to south in order to buffer the inner spaces from temperature swings (figure 4.18).

The solar greenhouse or "attached sunspace" was also undergoing development during the early 1970s, primarily as a food-producing tool as opposed to a method for heating buildings. Work by Bill Yanda in New Mexico proved that sunspaces were perhaps the most attractive passive systems since they do so much. They can (a) buffer wall areas normally

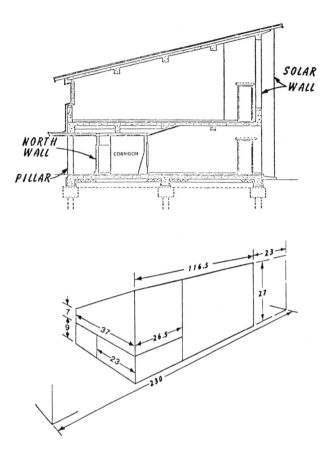

Figure 4.17
Cross section (top) and dimensions (bottom) of Wallasey School. (top) Cross section of portion of school; (bottom) approximate dimensions of the portion of the building studied (ft). Source: Perry (1976). Source: Perry (1976).

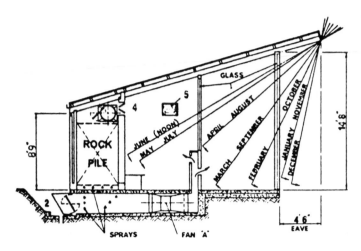

Figure 4.18
Direct gain lab facility with "rock pile." Source: Chapmain (1970).

exposed to night air in winter, (b) provide some direct heat, (c) raise humidity, and (d) provide CO_2-to-O_2 exchange via resident plants. Yanda (1976) developed some simple rules of thermal mass in solar greenhouses to keep temperatures from dropping below the threshold for plant mortality, about 35°F (1°C). Equally important is reducing summer temperatures below unpleasant levels using thermal mass.

Yanda's early greenhouses were very simple, using recycled materials, low-cost frames, and plastic films or fiberglass corregate for glazings. Concrete blocks, stone, and water drums were common heat storage materials. Using 80 pounds of concrete or 2 gallons of water storage per square foot of south-facing glazing could keep sunspace temperatures above 50°F (10°C), thereby maintaining plant health. Venting through windows to the inner space of the attached building provided indirect heating and reduced temperature swings.

We can clearly see that by 1972–1973 several independent efforts had already begun producing passive buildings and a basic understanding of their technical attributes. The forms were based somewhat on intuitive reasoning and application of existing engineering practice to new problems. This was certainly the case as passive solar form and function tied into the southwestern architecture led to rapid regional acceptance of passive solar. With mass built in, as in the traditional adobe wall, larger areas of glazing could be applied before overheating occured.

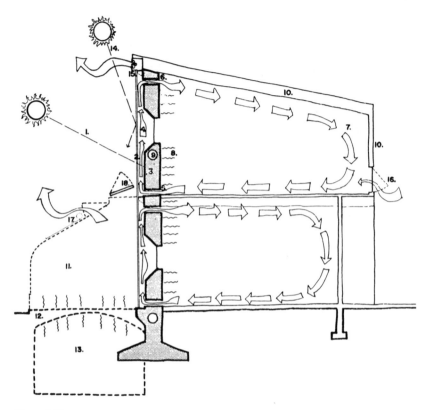

Figure 4.19
Cross section, solar heating schematic, Kelbaugh House. Source: Kelbaugh (1983).

The Trombe wall solar design was introduced in the early 1970s to the United States in Princeton, NJ (Kelbaugh, 1983). A two-story concrete cast-in-place mass wall was used in the Kelbaugh House, along with an early factory sunspace. Far from being a regional style, such as "colonial" or "ranch," this house (figure 4.19) practically shouted, "Look at me—I'm solar!"

Designers during this early period did not always understand the relationship between envelope integrity, glass, and mass. Often the form of "the passive building" took over, and function (comfort) was left to luck in some cases. Recognition of this lack of design expertise lead to pioneering research on passive systems analysis by J. Douglas Balcomb. But the period 1970–1976 was largely driven by experiment, imagination, and sometimes failure. The current state of the art, reflected in an increasing interest in passive buildings design and construction by builders, developers, architects, and the Standards organization, reflects rapid expansion of knowledge from 1976 to the present time, reflected in the next part of this chapter.

4.4   Interior Thermal Storage R&D

4.4.1   Strategies for Integrating Thermal Storage into Building Interiors

4.4.1.1   Building Strategies—Passive   This section provides information and examples of actual buildings employing passive solar interior thermal storage systems. Discussed are direct wall irradiation, wall irradiation by a clerestory or roof aperture, wall irradiation by attached sunspace, thermal storage walls, water walls, water tubes, mass "pillars," and interior walls coupled by natural convection. The relationship of the mass to its associated aperture becomes desensitized as higher levels of envelope conservation (more insulation and air tightening) are applied. Also, the results from monitored buildings suggest that substantially less mass (reduced effective heat capacity) is required. Cost to benefits may be explained by evaluating the material's in-place cost per 1,000 Btu (1,005 kJ) of heat storage capacity. This generalization is useful in comparing the various storage types. One difficult variable is proper evaluation of the role of installation costs. Obviously, a structural material that also provides necessary heat storage without imposing additional costs can be more cost effective than a non-structural material with extra container, structural upgrade, and installation costs. These added costs must be accounted for since they are a real part of what the building consumer pays for in heat storage.

We have learned that adding heavy mass to light frame structures is often problematic and costly. Within the realities of the U.S. based construction industry, in which a trend to lighter construction is occurring, later addition of masonry or water containers can cause need for reinforcement in footings or other modifications. This is one reason that for many designers the use of increased conservation to achieve net performance levels similar to those using increased passive solar often seems attractive. The real design trick is balancing conservation and passive energy flows given climate specific criteria. The use of thermal mass helps to temper interior comfort in any climate specific design, gives greater interior comfort flexibility, and is forgiving of design errors.

The following sections describe heat storage approaches used in real buildings. Where possible, measured results are reviewed from monitored buildings. Where necessary, systems that were not instrumented are included to help illustrate the generic approaches that have been utilized.

4.4.1.2 Interior Storage

a. *Direct Gain*   The use of direct transmitted solar gains is one of the more popular system types, especially among mainstream homebuilders. Mass is typically provided in walls (discussed here) or in floors or ceilings (to be discussed later). South-facing windows can provide direct gains into rooms with north-to-south oriented mass walls. Since both sides of the mass are illuminated during some of the day, the mass can be more effective. Interior partition walls that are in radiative view of objects first struck by sunlight are also effective for heat storage, but at a lower rate than directly illuminated materials. Heat storage walls can also be a part of the building envelope if well insulated on the exterior.

The NSDN (Howard and Pollock, 1982) monitored a direct gain home located near Corning, NY, that used exterior insulated structural mass walls as the primary heat storage, along with an insulated concrete floor slab (figure 4.20). The walls comprised north-south running surfaces on the east and west walls, which are 8-in.-thick solid masonry. The wall in the west bedroom heats up in the morning hours while the living room wall is heated in the mid-to-late afternoon. Additional solar gains are transmitted via clerestory apertures, which also light the space. The envelope thermal protection on this home was adequate but not superior. Storage heat loss to glazings was reduced by movable insulation (window quilts), which were not operated properly all the time. About 30% of the floor area exists in solar glazing—a very large collector area by more recent design standards. The home had 8°–10°F temperature swings, and the storage had fairly similar temperature swings. The well distributed storage stays warmer than indoor air temperatures during the night according to measurements, enhancing comfort. Figure 4.21 shows typical performance for two cold days in February 1982. Little auxiliary heat is required even after 10:00 PM. The first day was cold and had poor sun, as shown. The occupants opened the quilts too early on the second day, causing indoor air temperature to decline rapidly. Fortunately, they also turned off the auxiliary heaters at this time. Storage temperature rose from 60°F to 74°F and was higher than indoor air after 9:00 AM. The glass area lost heat rapidly, cooling indoor air despite reasonable charging of storage. Data reported by the status switches on the window quilts showed the occupants were about 70–80% "right" in setting the movable insulation. Other studies by SERI indicate that movable insulation may not be as effective as high performance glazings, or smaller glazed areas and improved envelope conservation (Frey, Swisher, and Holtz, 1982).

An early passive solar house using PCMs was designed and constructed in Dover, MA, by Dr. Maria Telkes and Eleanor Raymond in the late 1940s. The house employed a center east-west running mass wall containing eutectic salts in 5-gallon steel cans, totaling 470 cubic feet (12 m³). Natural convection was used to transfer heat through the home. It was operated in 1953, at about an 80% passive solar contribution (figure 4.22a). Data were apparently taken on temperature distributions, but the author was unable to locate them. The Peabody House was really not a direct gain case, but a cross between a sunspace, thermal storage wall, and a direct gain design.

In 1973–1974, David Wright designed and built the Sunscoop in Santa Fe, NM (figure 4.22b). Adobe walls insulated on the exterior were used along with a large expanse of south glass. The walls are 14-in.-thick (35-cm) and the floors are 24-in.-thick (61-cm) adobe. 384 square feet of south-facing double glass was used. A 4-ft single overhang helps protect the glazings. Overheating was observed, however, in spring and fall. Comfort levels in this type of design indicated the need for exterior shading over the extensive glass area, and better insulation levels.

A more typical direct gain heat storage approach than walls has been the use of insulated floor slabs directly illuminated by transmitted solar energy. Early systems like the Dasburg House in Santa Fe, designed by William Lumpkin, used brick pavers bedded on sand (4 in.—10 cm) over polyurethane insulation (figure 4.22c). His design also included movable insulating panels, which were placed over windows on the inside to reduce night time heat loss.

Despite the fact that the SERI "Class B" (Frey, Swisher, and Holtz, 1982) monitoring program did not monitor thermal storage systems, unlike the NSDN program (Howard and Pollock, 1982), some interesting thermal mass applications are shown in reviewing their case studies on Denver-Metro homes (SERI, 1984). In one direct-gain home by Tradition Homes, Inc., a full-height 8-in. (200-mm) masonry wall located in the north center of the home was used for storage mass (figure 4.23). A glass area of 167 ft² (6 m²) serves the 1,360-ft² interior. The dining room, kitchen, hallway, and

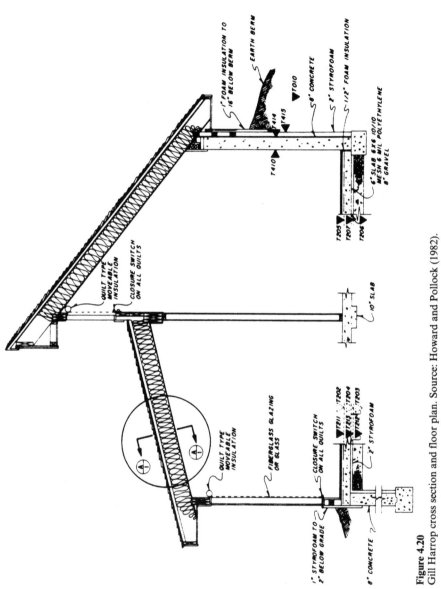

Figure 4.20
Gill Harrop cross section and floor plan. Source: Howard and Pollock (1982).

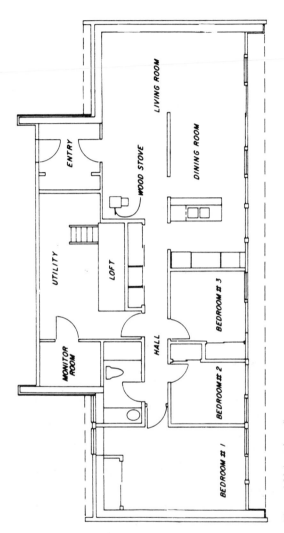

Figure 4.20 (continued)

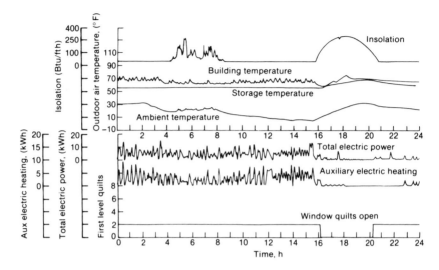

Figure 4.21
Thermal performance for two consecutive days (1982) at Gill Harrop. Source: Howard and Pollock (1982).

master bedroom areas directly face the storage wall, contained in a well insulated envelope, furnishing a 48% solar fraction. Thermal mass kept temperature swings below 10°F in the sunny Denver climate. Another home, monitored in Denver, used a brick veneer wall inside insulation on the west wall—facing the dining room. Direct gains provide direct and reflected solar energy to this mass. The below-grade level has generous south-facing glass. Heat is stored in the structural walls of the home.

b. *Clerestory Systems*   An important variant of direct gain systems is the clerestory aperture type that directs transmitted solar gains onto mass walls, water tubes, or floors. This system can also be effective for daylighting interior spaces in both residential and commercial buildings.

Fairly good measured results exist for several examples using clerestory systems. One of the first to be instrumented was the Williamson House (figure 4.24) in New Mexico. Los Alamos National Laboratory measured insolation, weather, and numerous temperatures in both the building air and mass. Both the floor and an exterior insulated mass wall were designed to store heat. Data from December and January 1978–1979 showed the house interior air had up to 25°F temperature swings, while the sunlit wall

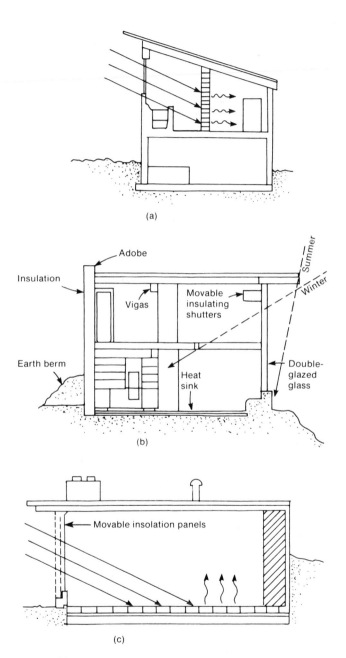

(a)

(b)

(c)

Figure 4.22
Prototype passive buildings using thermal mass: (a) Peabody House, 1949; (b) Sunscoop, 1974, (c) Dasburg House, 1974. Source: SERI (1984).

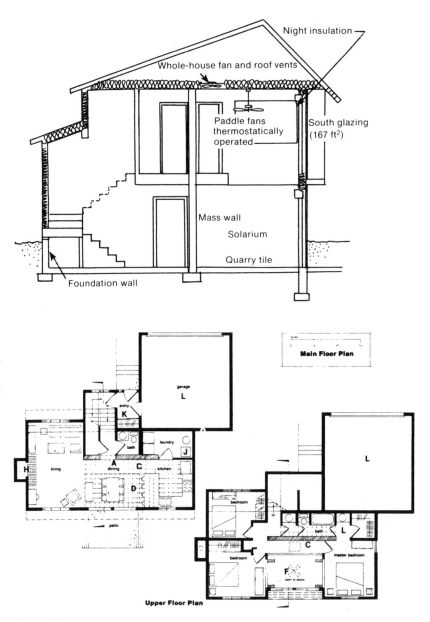

Figure 4.23
Cross section and floor plan of a direct gain home with full height interior mass wall.
Source: SERI (1984).

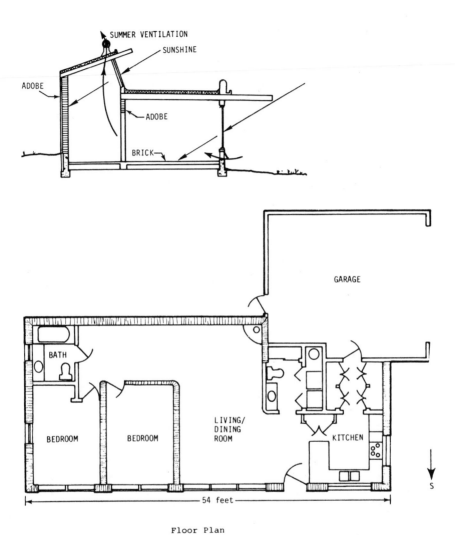

Floor Plan

Figure 4.24
Cross section and floor plan of the Williamson House.

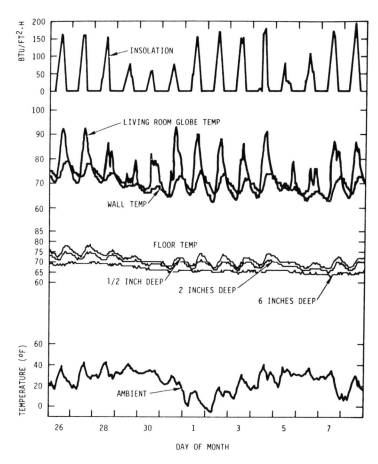

Figure 4.25
Williamson temperature profile performance data (1978–1979): (top) direct gain; (bottom) floor temperatures.

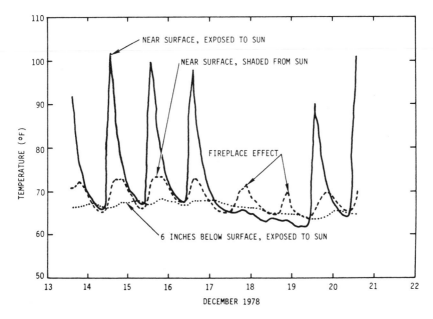

Figure 4.25 (continued)

had 10°–15°F temperature swings. The storage floor had 5°–8°F temperature swings, and was most effective for heat storage in the top 2 in. of its
material. At 6-in. depth only long-term trends in temperature (cooling)
could be detected (figure 4.25). Despite its simple layout, generous mass,
and exterior insulation, the home could be rendered uncomfortable. One
conclusion was that less glazing and somewhat better insulation levels
would be preferred in deference to high mass, which had difficulty absorbing enough of the large solar input. The heat storage floor of the Williamson House was monitored to show the difference in temperatures between
shaded and unshaded mass, near the surface. Nearly a 30°F difference in
mass temperature developed between shaded and unshaded areas (figure
4.25). This illustrates the potential effect of shading by furnishings and
carpets on heat storage floors, reducing their effectiveness.

Another interesting house monitored by LANL during this same period
is the Star-Tannery House located in Virginia. It uses both water wall and
clerestory direct gain to an exterior insulated masonry wall located to the
home's rear. The masonry veneer wall helped stabilize interior tempera-

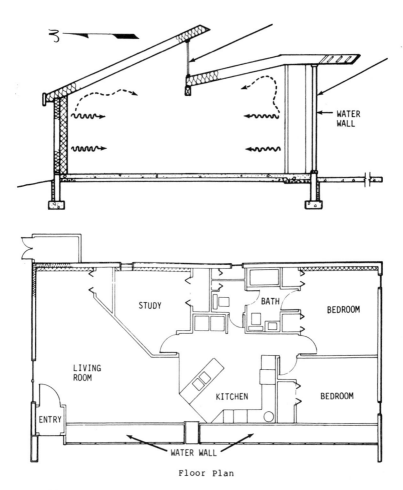

Floor Plan

Figure 4.26
Cross section, floor plan, and temperature recordings for Star-Tannergy House. Source:
LANL (1979).

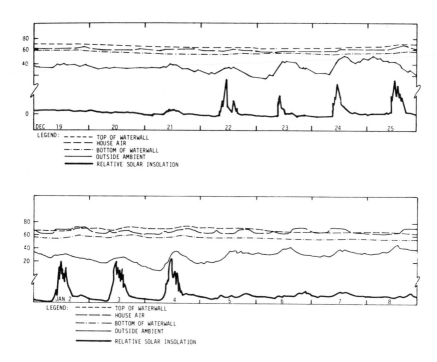

Temperature Recordings

Figure 4.26 (continued)

tures in the north zones of the small house. However, the water wall was the primary monitored thermal feature. Results showed that house air temperature swings were much lower than for some direct gain types. The clerestory shown in figure 4.26 provided light and solar heat to the back portion of the home.

The living systems Suncatcher House is a clerestory design designed to "concentrate" solar radiation slightly to a 60° tilted glazing (figure 4.27). Extensive overhang protection for summer passive cooling is provided in this design. As in other clerestory types, daylighting is enhanced. In the Suncatcher, collected solar energy is directed onto freestanding water tubes running to full ceiling height inside the envelope of the house. Insulating shutters help protect the interior from winter heat loss and summer overheating. This home also uses a direct gain south wall collector with half high water drums, protected by an insulating drape.

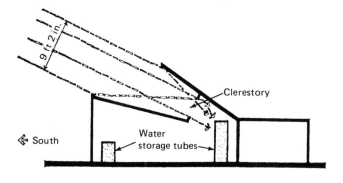

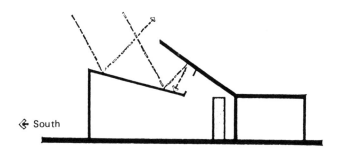

Figure 4.27
Living systems Suncatcher system: (top) December 21, noon, 26° sun angle; (bottom)
August 21, noon, 62° sun angle.

Measured data on storage temperatures show that this system is quite
sensitive to proper operation of the insulating shutter. Occupants were not
very conscientious in the shutter and drape operations, which dramatically
reduced performance. This problem of "passive house–(in)active occupants" can have an impact on even the best design intentions. Plots of
sensor data on three consecutive days in January 1981 (figure 4.28) indicate
that the water drums operated above the average temperature of the total
storage mass, and also frequently are warmer than building air. This
radiant effect adds to comfort.

The same performance data also show that the wood stove can dominate
the interior space thermally, and provided considerable heat to storage.
The quantity of mass and its location in the Suncatcher house provides
minimal 10°–12°F temperature swings on bright mild California winter
days. The home is located in Davis, CA, outside Sacramento.

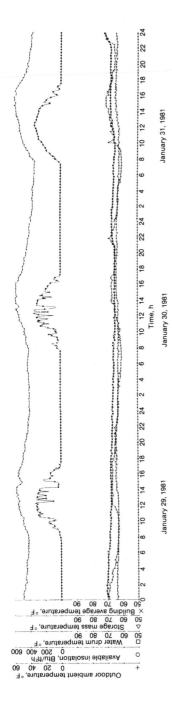

Figure 4.28
Suncatcher three-day typical performance data. Source: Howard and Pollock, 1982.

The Taos State Office Building, also monitored in the NSDN (Howard and Pollock, 1982) like Suncatcher, uses the interesting derivation of the clerestory in a water drum system. To facilitate the open floor plan needs of a medium office, the designer, William Mingenbach, placed the water storage units up in the roof superstructure near clerestory glazings. The apertures are protected by automated movable shutters that control the storage energy balance as well as the admission of daylight and direct gains thermal year-round. The heavy roof support structure is supported by insulated concrete masonry exterior walls (figure 4.29). The solar system provided over 50% of space heating requirements, and electric lighting demand was significantly reduced. By opening the thermal shutters at night in summer, day-collected unwanted indoor heat was rejected. The building was also night-flush ventilated.

Detailed data plots reveal that the storage-clerestory systems performed well, and that the automated control system operated successfully. Due to the high mass of the building, the arrival of staff in the morning occasionally called for high auxiliary use for reheat. Night setbacks were used, and weekend operation used setback all day, to 63°–65°F from the daytime 70°–72°F level. Figure 4.30 shows a workday morning following a cold night, leading into a cloudy day. The large reheat load serves to heat the air in the building, and the rate of storage temperature drop decreases after 8:00 AM. Storage temperature leveled off two days later during this cloudy period at 68°–72°F. Since the water drums are suspended in the ceiling superstructure, they reside in, and store heat from, warmer stratified air. Instead of this heat being lost directly through the roof, it is partly recycled since the overall U-value of the roof is reduced at night when the shutters close. After a good sunny day in the work week and considering night setback control, no appreciable auxiliary heat is used until very late evening/early morning (figure 4.31).

Another example of direct gain clerestory design is from the SERI Class B program (Denver-Metro) in which storage was not directly measured, but performance may be inferred from temperature swings and energy balance results. In the Arnold Home (figure 4.32) the living room and back bedroom are separated by a masonry wall. The clerestory aperture illuminates this mass on winter days. A destratification fan and duct system moves excess heat from the back of the living room to the basement. The home is modestly solar heated at about 25%. A significant time lag is provided by the mass wall to its heating of the north bedroom. The back

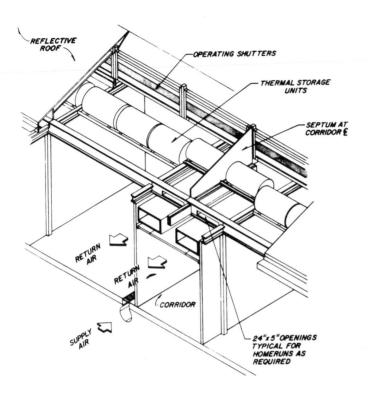

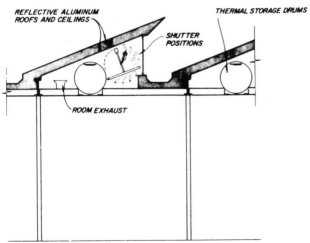

Figure 4.29
Taos State Office Building schematics: (top) office drum and sensor locations; (bottom) typical room monitor section. Source: Howard and Pollock (1982).

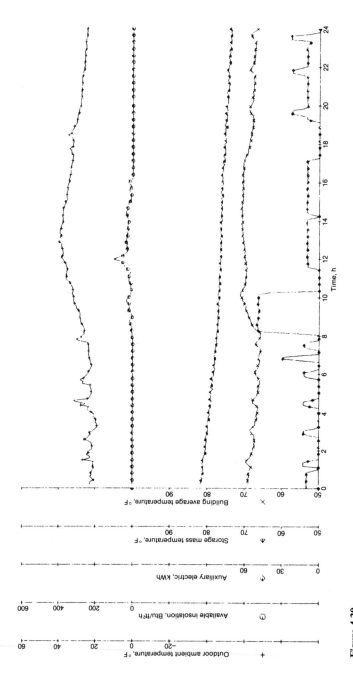

Figure 4.30
Taos performance data—cloudy day (January 1981). Source: Howard and Pollock (1982).

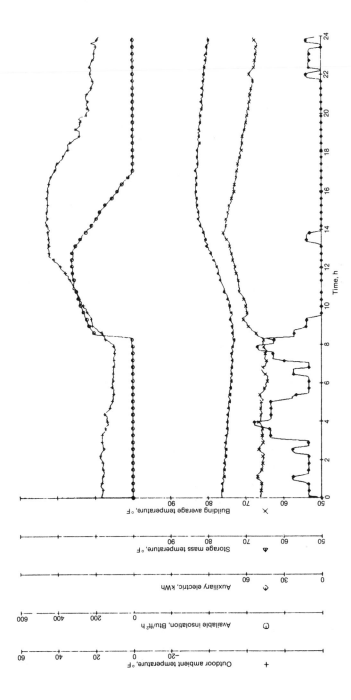

Figure 4.31
Taos performance data—sunny day (January 1981). Source: Howard and Pollock (1982).

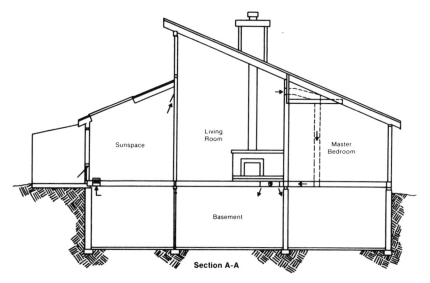

Figure 4.32
Arnold Home cross section and floor plan. Source: Frey, Swisher, and Holtz (1982).

bedroom temperature is allowed to float which increases the storage wall's effectiveness (figure 4.33). Peak auxiliary heat is used during early morning hours since a lightweight envelope encloses the home and its mass. Actually, this wall and a brick wall in a solar room on the south side are the major passive solar features.

The Pitkin County Airport Terminal in Aspen, CO, uses interior concrete block structural walls to store heat from Skylid™ protected 50° tilted clerestory roof apertures. Direct gain Beadwalls™ form the south wall of the structure storing heat in thickened, perimeter insulated floor slabs. The automatic aperture insulation systems protect the mass and the building from excess heat loss. The mass, combined with ventilation in summer, greatly reduces cooling auxiliary energy use (figure 4.34).

4.4.1.3 Thermal Storage Walls Thermal storage walls irradiated on one side, with radiative and/or convention release of heat to the other side, represent the second "classic" passive solar type.

One of the earliest attempts to prove the concept of solar collection and storage wall was by Felix Trombe in France in the middle-to-late 1960s. Trombe constructed a series of mass wall buildings for testing, including the

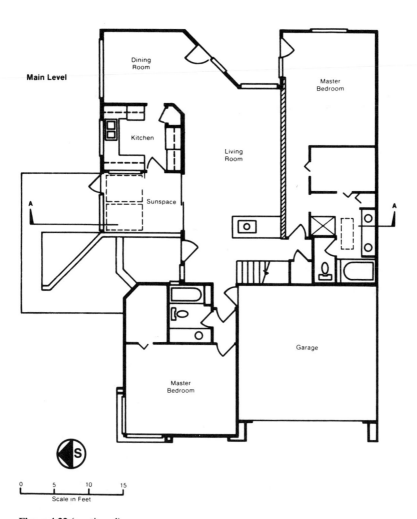

Figure 4.32 (continued)

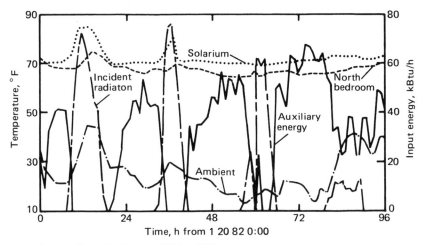

Source: Frey, Swisher, and Holtz 1982

Figure 4.33
Winter data summary—Arnold Home. Key (time, in hours, from January 19, 1982, midnight): auxiliary energy (————); incident radiation (—·—); ambient (———); north bedroom (- - -); solarium (. . .). Source: Frey, Swisher, and Holtz (1982).

famous house in Odeillo, France. He derived mathematic solutions for the thermal behavior of the system, known today as the Trombe wall. Figure 4.35 shows both the heating and ventilation cases used for simulation and measurement, reported in an early paper (Trombe et al., 1976). Several years of measured results have led to interesting guidelines for construction. Trombe was concerned with improving the net energy balance of the wall—that is reducing night losses, preventing backflow, and automatically regulating air flows. One major development over the 1967–1976 period of prototypes leading to the 1974 home was the thickness reduction from 24 in. (600 mm) to 14.5 in. (370 mm), and a corresponding reduction in the ratio of collector area to mass-volume. As the wall thickness was reduced, two times larger openings were used top and bottom, for better air flow.

The first major architectural application of the mass Trombe wall system in the United States was by Kelbaugh in 1975 (Kelbaugh, 1983). Prior to this, Steve Baer's famous Corrales, NM "Zome Home" used recycled oil drums in a water wall that employed movable insulating panels.

The Kelbaugh home (figure 4.19) has been monitored off and on for about 8 years, making it one of the better understood passive buildings.

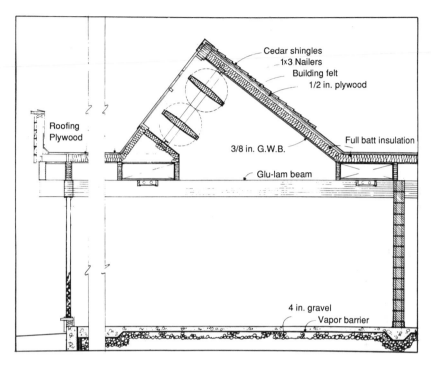

Figure 4.34
Cross section of Pitken County Airport, Aspen, CO. Source: NCMA (1977).

While many papers on thermal storage walls report on temperature profiles across the mass, Kelbaugh documented all improvements to the home and correlative energy savings. His findings, predicated on reducing heating in the Princeton, NJ climate, indicate double glazing, Trombe wall back-flow preventers (plastic film "check valves"), thermal curtains, and improvements in envelope conservation all can contribute to better performance. A series of retrofits from the winter of 1975–1976 to the winter of 1982–1983 reduced space heating consumption from over 4 Btu/ft^2/degree-day. The elimination of unwanted thermosyphoning in the Trombe wall and other minor improvements in the first winter provided the largest performance improvement.

While most of the results from Kelbaugh's monitoring were aimed at evaluating effects of design improvements on overall heating demand and comfort, the Hunn House Trombe wall (figure 4.36) was a target of

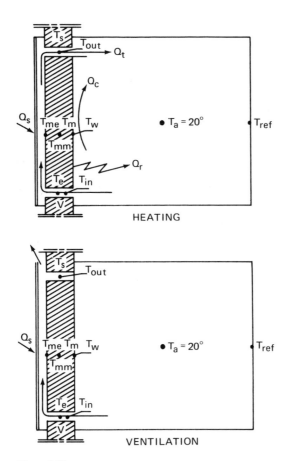

Figure 4.35
Heating and ventilating modes of Trombe wall. Source: Trombé et al. (1976).

intensive instrumented testing. A two-story mass wall of 440 ft^2 serves the major portion of a 1,955-ft^2 heated space. A 200-ft^3 rock storage bin is located under the house in an insulated crawl space. Due to the dominance of the mass wall and the rock bed's ability to reduce overheating, the indoor temperatures have an 8°–12°F daily swing which is more stable than for early direct gain types. The Trombe wall is of 12-in. (305 mm) "slump block" (a type of concrete masonry that looks like adobe). The outer wall surface typically obtained an 85°F temperature swing while the inner surface provided about 20°–25°F temperature swings for winter heating, with a 6–8 hour time lag on sunny, cold days (figure 4.37).

Observations at the home uncovered one problem with the mass walls. On the second day of poor sun in cold weather, the room air thermostat was turned up to avoid "feeling cool." This means that the discharged wall became a comfort liability under continuously cloudy, cold conditions. Movable insulation, an interior drape, or selective coating of the sunlit face to reduce its emittance could have reduced this problem. The rock bed was found to be inefficient due to excessive air leaks, high air flows, and low storage temperatures. Rock beds tend to work better if well sealed, slowly aspirated, and designed for passive heat discharge. Investigators also felt that the conservation levels, such as roof insulation, could have been improved. However, the house as designed and built provided a 57% solar fraction in a 7000 heating-degree day climate, with good solar resources.

Water has also been used successfully in collector storage walls. In the Gunderson House (Unit 4–First Village, Santa Fe), LANL monitored water wall performance in 1978–1979. The home is designed around a central patio, with two solar heated bedroom wings flanking it (figure 4.38). The water walls are equipped with movable panel-type insulation. Results showed that slightly higher indoor air temperature swings occurred, and smaller water-wall areas can produce similar passive solar benefits similar to those of masonry Trombe walls. The water temperature inside the containers exhibited a time lag of several hours and the inner surface of the containers remained cooler than the water, indicating heat flow into the room. On a sunny day in late December 1978 (figure 4.39) the inner container surface temperature was 25°–30°F warmer than room air; and 17°–20°F warmer than room air at night. Indoor temperature swings were held to 10°F due to the high overall mass of the home. Excellent passive cooling was reported by the occupants in summer. Data indicated that the overall loss coefficient for the house is rather high (11.31 Btu/ft^2/degree-

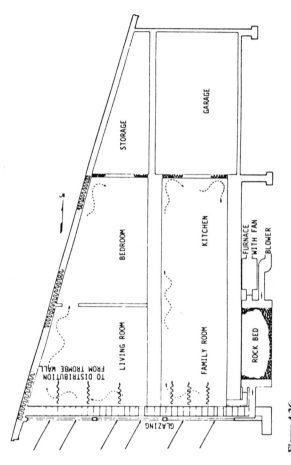

Figure 4.36
Cross section (top) and floor plan (bottom), Hunn House.

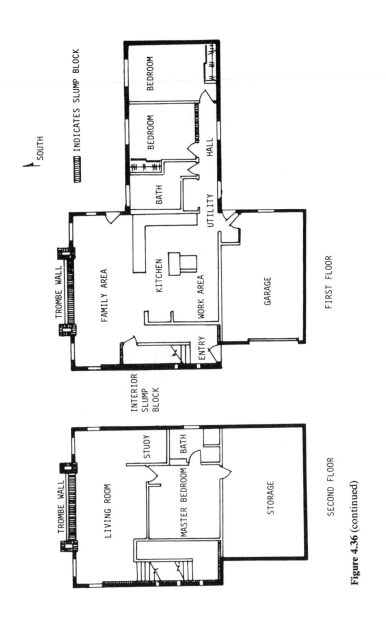

Figure 4.36 (continued)

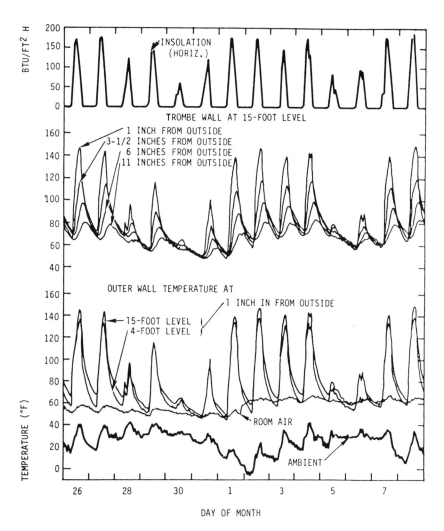

Figure 4.37
Daily temperature data in the Hunn House.

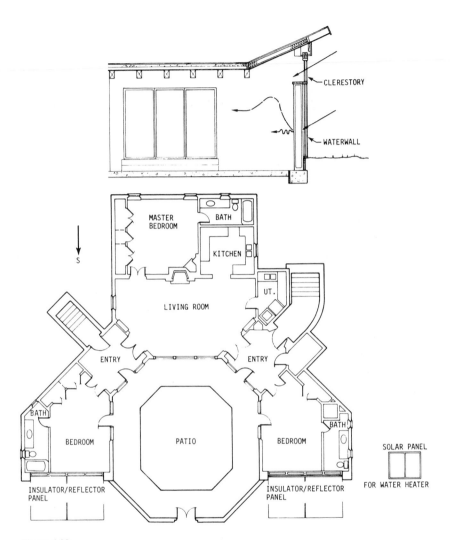

Figure 4.38
Cross section and floor plan of Unit 4–First Village.

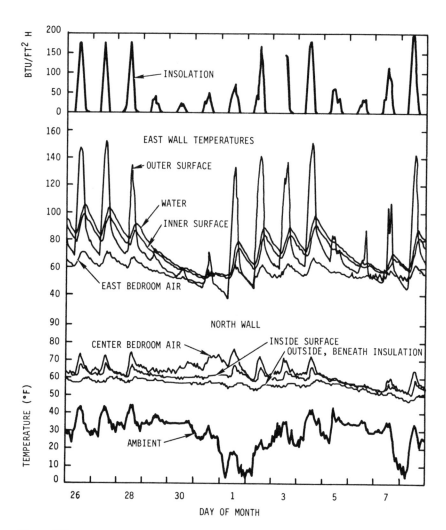

Figure 4.39
Unit 4–First Village thermal performance data.

day), indicating it might not perform well in areas less sunny and colder than the U.S. Southwest.

A successful variant on the Trombe wall design resulting from research by Jim Beir is the Vertical Solar Louver (VSL) system (Beir, 1979). VSL was the result of analysis of the disadvantages of traditional Trombe wall systems. Masonry walls can be used for heat storage and still provide daylighting and direct gains with fewer drawbacks. Less glare, fabric fading, and overheating are VSL benefits. VSLs are constructed of concrete block or brick masonry facing 45° to direct south along a SE-NW axis. This allows morning direct gains to warm the living space rapidly, provides all-day natural lighting, and intercepts maximum afternoon sun for heat storage in the mass (figure 4.40). The VSL units can be stacked for structural purposes as long as they are tied structurally at each floor level. They lend themselves either to light frame construction, where daytime overheating may be a problem, or full masonry construction, where morning heat gains from the sun must be maximized to offset mechanical reheat loads.

Franta applied this design to his own home in Colorado by providing an outer glazing, and Heat-Mirror™ between the VSLs to capture warm air in the space between VSLs and the outer glass (Franta and Hogg, 1983). Measured results from February 1983 showed that the inner wall surface remained between 88°F and 96°F on a day with 20°–30°F outdoor temperatures. Franta added glass block to the concrete masonry (slump block) walls for visual appeal and found no major construction problems that could not be overcome with proper detailing. Called a "Floating-Mass Wall," the opaque elements in such a wall appear to be floating to observers behind the wall in daytime, or outside looking in at night. Franta also believes that stained glass windows can and should be used in mass walls for aesthetic reasons.

The Trombe wall has one singular deficiency that performance data, comfort enhancements and low fuel bills cannot seem to offset. Builders in the United States today are carpentry oriented, not masonry oriented. Severe resistance to masonry and water walls has occurred (less for components type of water storage that the frame builder can integrate). But masonry construction has not been widely embraced in the United States since World War II and continues to limit the Trombe wall's wide acceptance in housing. Trombe walls have achieved moderate acceptance in commercial buildings such as churches, warehouse, and service facilities—traditionally strong users of masonry construction.

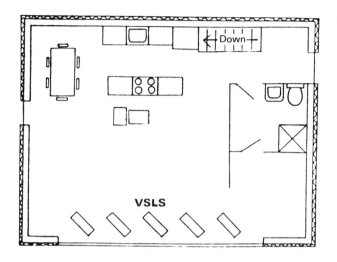

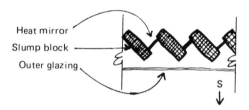

Figure 4.40
Vertical Solar Louvered mass wall systems: (top) floor plain; (bottom) detail of the
louvered mass. Source: Beir (1979).

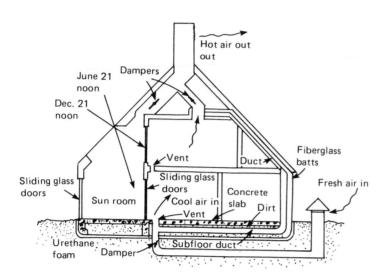

Figure 4.41A
Jackson House, Butler.

4.4.1.4 Sunspaces with Mass Walls A good deal of data has been collected at buildings using passive sunspaces with mass walls separating them from conditioned spaces. The mass wall may serve several functions according to design criteria. It can provide structural support as a building wall; it provides a buffering effect to moderate sunspace temperature swings; and it conducts heat from the sunspace (collector) to the conditioned space, thereby acting as an absorber, and to a degree provides thermal control over interior responses to solar inputs to the sunspace.

One of the first houses in the United States to use an integrated sunspace was designed by Lee Porter Butler in the early 1970s. It does not use a mass wall per se, but rather natural circulation through the house taking advantage of floor, furnishings, and finish materials mass (figure 4.41A). This design led to Butler's later "Thermal Envelope Designs."

The Hofman House, designed by Dan Skully of Total Environmental Action (T.E.A.), uses good insulation levels and a sunspace mass wall system (figure 4.41B). A concrete wall separates the fiberglass reinforced plastic glazed sunspace (greenhouse) from the lower-level conditioned space of the house. The designers indicated in reports on the house that the sunspace did produce "net gains." The home heated with three cords of wood in an average winter according to T.E.A.

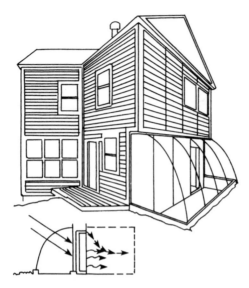

Figure 4.41B
Hofman House, By Dan Skully.

The archtypical sunspace mass wall house is Unit 1–First Village, designed by Wayne and Susan Nichols in 1974 and built under the HUD-Cycle 1 program grants in 1976 as one of the first solar homes in the program. Its owner, J. Douglas Balcomb, was responsible for its instrumentation and monitoring, and today it is one of the better understood solar buildings due to these efforts. Heat is collected in a two-story greenhouse with sloped glazing (figure 4.42). A 14-in. and a 10-in. (second-story) full height adobe walls with two "legs" running to SE and SW from a central midpoint in the home provide heat storage and separation. Two underfloor rock beds provide remote heat storage and control overheating. An overall solar heating fraction of 80–85% has been documented.

The mass wall first and second stories have been instrumented with temperature profile "rakes." Results are shown for the adobe mass performance in figure 4.43. The thinner second-story greenhouse wall reaches higher temperatures both near outside and inside surfaces compared to the more moderate temperatures of the thicker first-story adobe wall. The first-story wall has about a 5°F temperature swing near the inside surface, while the second-story wall has about a 15°F temperature swing near the inside surface, and a shorter time lag. The overall effect of the mass wall serves to dampen interior (not sunspace) air temperature swings to about 10°F. Convection through doorways and windows in the mass wall plays an important role in heat transfer to north zones. Due to the high mass of the house and its well insulated envelope, its observed peak load is about 3 kW of electric baseboard heat, compared to an expected 9.5 kW based on typical ASHRAE design calculations. Figure 4.44 shows measured building energy use and various temperatures under operational conditions during December–January 1978–1979. The rock bed did not seem to be very involved in heating the home according to the data, compared to the mass wall and natural convection contributions.

A small speculatively built home located in Prescott, AZ, uses a similar approach to passive/hybrid solar heating. The "Hullco" home uses a 12-in.-thick concrete block and sand-filled thermal storage wall between interior spaces and a greenhouse that covers the entire southside of the home. A rock bin, supplied by excess greenhouse heat (figure 4.45) uses 76 tons of rock that is actively charged, and then discharges heat passively through the floor slab into the space. The home's thermal protection levels are adequate for mild, sunny Arizona, but might not be appropriate elsewhere (Howard and Pollock, 1982). The mass wall moderated interior temperature swings to 8°–12°F (4.5°–6.7°C) depending on outside temperature and solar radiation levels. Wood stove operation in the the evenings following cool, cloudy days was commonly observed. Figure 4.46 shows three consecutive days during a "charging cycle" of increasing available sun each day. At night, the storage temperature, mass wall and floor, is usually slightly higher than the building air temperature, improving comfort. During the sunlit portion of the day (8:30–2:30 PM) on bright days, the indoor temperature floats above the mass temperature. For example, on February 13, 1981, some venting occurred after 2:00 PM, according to the data plots, showing the mass could not accept all the energy provided it, and caused some overheating.

David Wright designed a variant on sunspace passive systems, constructed in White Rock, NM. The large 3,350-ft² home uses a 600-ft² sloped "greenhouse" roof and three mass walls. One mass wall supports the roof glazing structure, which has lid-type shutters to control solar gains to the indoor space. Other solar apertures consist of clerestory and double-glazed south windows. Two fans, insulating shutters, greenhouse roof vents, and shading devices (added later to reduce overheating) were used to control

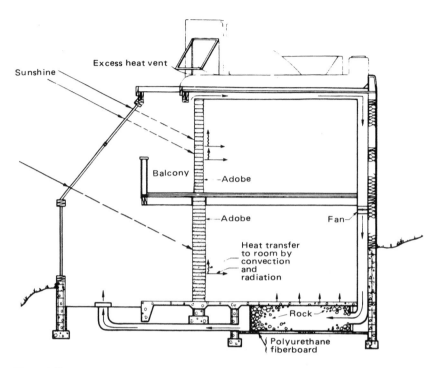

Figure 4.42
Unit 1—First Village cross section and floor plans for first and second floors.

the space. The house was estimated to have a 95% solar contribution, but is an obvious example of potential overkill in passive design. Current trends indicat that small attached sunspaces on well insulated buildings provide better performance at lower cost, plus offer additional usable floor space.

Two of the sunspace designs monitored by the SERI Class B program are of note. Despite a lack of specific monitoring of mass function, the sunspace designs used significant mass to control temperature swings. Their construction costs tended to be higher than for other passive system types, however. The Ferguson House (figure 4.47) employs a large solarium with 365 ft^2 of single-glazed windows with movable insulation. A composite mass wall of face brick and concrete block supports the upper floor structure, provides thermal storage, and separation on the lower level, which is a living area, not a "basement." The solarium temperatures swing 10°–20°F on very sunny days, but the indoor air temperature swings are

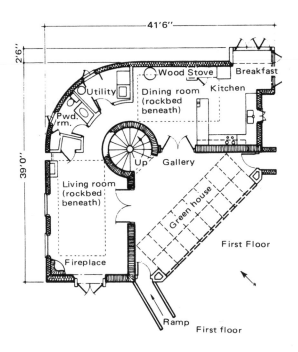

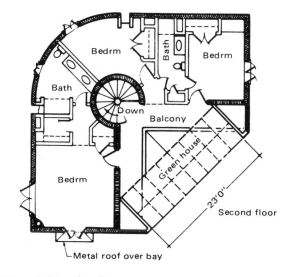

Figure 4.42 (continued)

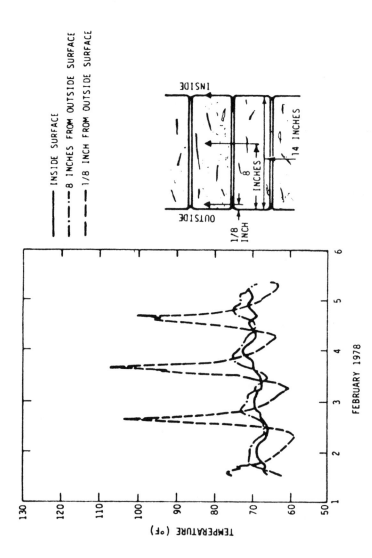

Figure 4.43
Temperatures monitored in the adobe: temperatures within adobe wall (top) on first floor and (bottom) on second floor.

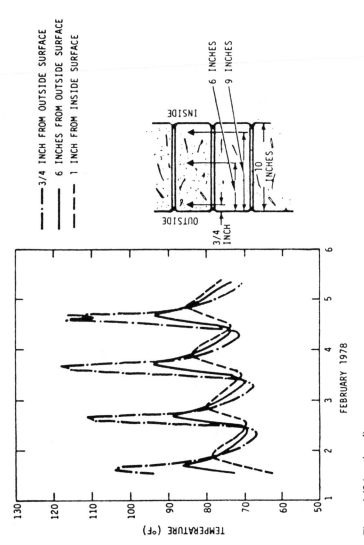

Figure 4.43 (continued)

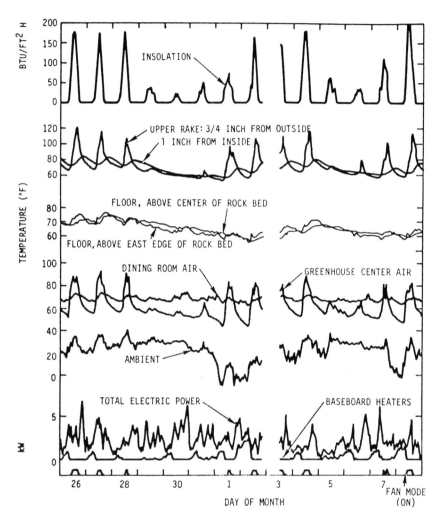

Figure 4.44
Two-week whole house performance profile Of Unit 1–First Village.

moderated by the mass of the walls and interior contents (figure 4.48). The rooms located away from the sunspace seem to be thermally well coupled to it via natural convection heat flow. Observe the apparent coupling on the very sunny last day plotted in figure 4.48. This home was 46% passive solar heated according to an analysis of SERI data.

Another Class B home monitored was the Unique Home, in Arvada, CO. Its sunspace is separated from the main living area by patio doors. Brick veneer mass walls distributed elsewhere indoors store the solar heat that is introduced to the home using a thermostatically controlled fan. The sunspace heat is also distributed via the homes HVAC ductwork. There is a quantity of distributed mass in floors and veneer walls—such as in the master bedroom, which gains added passive heat via its clerestory "loft." Figure 4.49 shows floor plans and cross section drawings.

The sunspace, which does not have much mass, can reach 100°F (38°C) on sunny days, and also dips below 50°F (10°C) at night. The living room adjacent to the sunspace has 10°–14°F temperature swings when the sunspace patio doors are open (figure 4.50). The occupants seemed to have difficulty determining whether or not to open the patio doors. Also, some auxiliary heat leaks back into the sunspace when the furnace is running. It is not generally appropriate to heat sunspaces since proper mass design can limit temperature swings, and separation or other forms of control can be used to minimize the effects of cool sunspace temperatures on the living space. On days when the patio doors were opened, much less auxiliary heat for the home was required because the passive heat was stored in the well distributed mass in the house (see days 2 and 3 in figure 4.50).

The measured data on sunspace performance indicate several key design issues needing careful integration by architects and builders. First, the sunspace should not be coupled to the auxiliary heating and cooling plant. Second, sloped glazing may provide limited thermal benefits compared to the numerous problems with its use like overheating, water leaks, code requirements for tempered glass, etc. (Spears, 1983). Vertical glazing with operable skylights in an insulated roof section may provide more manageable comfort. Sunspace design should generally provide useful floor space because most data shows that they produce minimal energy gains (marginal economics). Separation walls can be either masonry or insulated in construction. The choice depends on whether collected solar heat is to be used in the attached building or whether it is used to condition the sunspace itself.

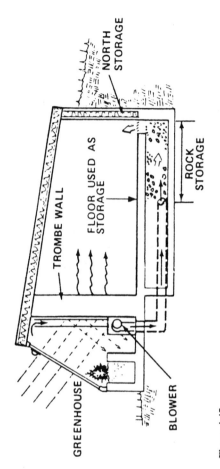

Figure 4.45
Cross section (top) and floor plan (bottom) Hullco. Source: Howard and Pollock (1982).

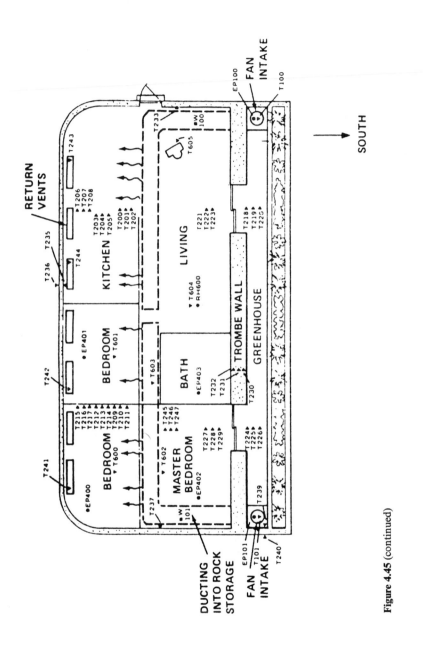

Figure 4.45 (continued)

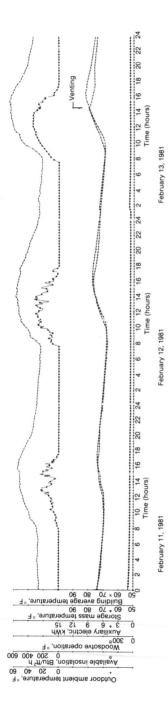

Figure 4.46
Three-day "charge cycle" of performance data at Hullco.

More mass in the sunspace means lower temperature swings and higher average sunspace temperature as well as less "excess" heat for interior use. The opposite is true of sunspaces with less mass, except where the highest performance glazings are utilized.

4.5 Thermosyphon and Hybrid Remote Heat Storage

The thermosyphon collector has been mated to underfloor heat storage in a number of unique passive solar homes. However, the approach has not caught on with speculative builders. In 1972, Steve Baer's Davis House in Albuquerque used a thermosyphon system to heat a rock bed placed in parallel to air flow from the collectors to the house (figure 4.51). One problem of such systems is that the air flow when the sun is not shining must be controlled to limit back flow. Also, the top (concrete) cover of the rock bed/bin must be radiative floor space to the building conditioned zone to be effective.

W. Scott Morris (1982) has taken the thermosyphon system a step further by the use of air-core concrete block topped by pebbles and concrete. A residential heat storage system of ten block beds (figure 4.52), which are heated by a sloped thermosyphon air panel, is used in an 1,800-ft^2 (165-m^2) house in Santa Fe. The collector uses a single pane of low-iron glass for a cover plate. Results indicate good natural air flow occurs on sunny days, eliminating the parasitic electric energy load of a fan. Morris reported 45% collection efficiency based on air velocity and temperature readings near midday. Thermocouples were installed in the block bed to read mass temperatures. A 40°–50°F temperature differential was measured across the collector. The natural flow of solar-warmed air did develop some large differences in heat transfer into the beds due to balancing of pressure drops in the complex system. A zone located to the west of the collector away from the main "beds" had 3 to 4 times lower heat flow (Morris, 1982).

One method for improving circulation through isolated storage elements—rock beds, block beds, air-core, or cavity wall systems—is to use hybrid fan-forcing of air from source zones indoors, or collectors to the storage. With simple dampers, cool outdoor night air can also be forced through such systems to directly cool the mass in summer. Control over the mass temperature is better achieved in this manner, especially in the summer months. Summer temperature control can be achieved in thermosyphon

Solar collection:
A Solarium (Total south-glazing area: 365 ft²)
B Clerestory (provides limited direct-gain to living room)
C Active solar domestic hot-water system

Thermal storage:
D Mass wall (brick veneer on concrete)
E Slab floor with tile surface
F Concrete foundation walls

Heat distribution:
G Paddle fans
H Louvered power-exhaust vent
J Furnace return-air duct from solarium

Auxiliary heat:
K Woodstoves (2)
L Gas forced-air furnace
M Partial earth berm
N Air-lock entryway

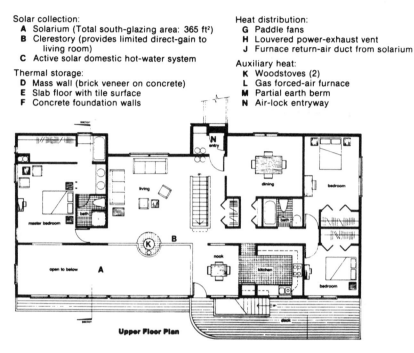

Figure 4.47
Cross section and floor plan, Ferguson House.

systems only through careful design of external shading devices, and ventilation.

Such a system, a hybrid, was instrumented and monitored by the DOE-NSDN. Known as the Roberts Home (Howard, 1983, 1986), this 2,300-ft² (215-m²) architect-designed residence uses a large vented thermal storage wall protected by a multilayer thermal curtain that is automatically controlled. Excess heat from the thermal storage well (figure 4.53) is gathered at the home's top level and moved through a concrete masonry block wall toward the north of the home via small "muffin" fans located in air plenums atop the walls. Complete temperature and heat flux measurements were made in the building, by VITRO Corporation. Analysis software compared indoor and outdoor temperatures with the ASHRAE comfort "envelope" (ANSI/ASHRAE, 1981) for summer months. A total building energy balance was computed based on detailed, 320-second data points for over seven months of monitoring. The instrumented results indicated

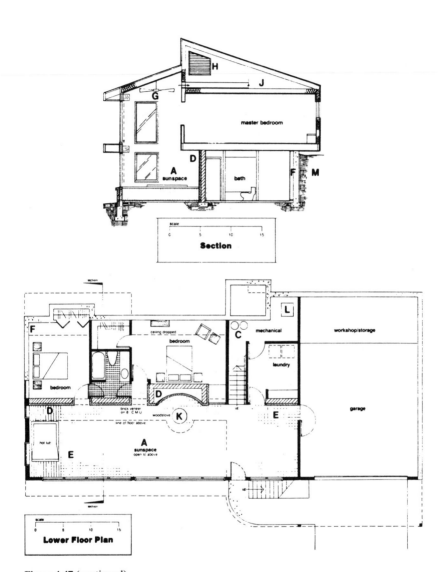

Figure 4.47 (continued)

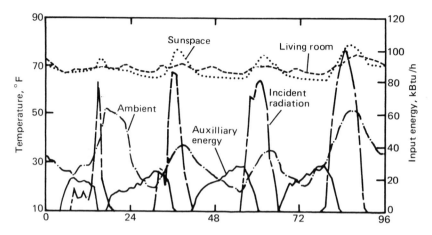

Figure 4.48
Four days of performance data, Ferguson House. Key (time in hours, from February 22, 1982, midnight): auxiliary energy (———); incident radiation (—-—); ambient (—·—); northeast bedroom (- - -); low solarium (. . .).

that the heating solar fraction of the house was 82% (February–April 1982), and that 99% of the cooling demand was satisfied by natural architectural methods (May–August 1982) (Howard, 1983).

The surrounding of interior spaces by solar warmed masonry walls protected by a well insulated envelope provided superior comfort levels. Occupants indicated they were comfortable at lower than expected air temperatures. Figure 4.54 illustrates how the storage effectively "discharges" to heat the indoor space on a cold cloudy day following a day of good sun. The storage system responds the following sunny mild day by fully "recharging" to a temperature above that of building air. Total electric power use in the home is shown, along with both vertical south-facing and horizontal insuation readings. The thermal storage is night flushed in summer, and the thermal curtain operates to reduce daytime gains (open at night) to the mass storage. Temperature readings show the mass is cooler than building air temperatures about 90% of the time in summer.

4.6 Ceiling Systems

The ceiling systems in passive solar buildings are of three basic types. These are roof ponds, phase change tiles and concrete slabs that are directly or indirectly irradiated by solar energy and protected from uncontrolled heat loss in some manner.

The roof pond system dates back to the mid-1960s in its development. More recent work on the roof pond approach has attempted to demonstrate its effectiveness in climates other than the desert Southwest. Figure 4.55 shows typical solar system operation of the roof pond in winter. A movable insulation system protects the pond or water bags from night heat loss, and directs the heat downward toward the conditioned space. In summer, the movable insulation is placed over the collector/storage mass during the day to avoid unwanted gains, while the pond is exposed to nocturnal sky radiation on summer nights. Monitored results from several prototype roof pond buildings have been encouraging. Indoor temperature fluctuations of 5°F are typical in winter, and similar thermal stability is observed for cooling season weather. Very little auxiliary heating or cooling is needed in most cases, in mild climates.

The Skytherm system has been transported to other climates (and significantly modified), such as New Hampshire and Minnesota, in an effort to verify its wider feasibility. Relatively poor performance was generally achieved, on the order of 45% solar fractions. However, 45% is not "poor" compared to other designs. The approach used was that of a roof pond/solar attic configuration where sloped glazing admitted sunlight into an insulated space in which the roof water bags were laid. Either pivoting movable insulating panels or a polystyrene-bead insulation blown into the space between double glazing panels was used. Distribution of heat from the roof pond in a two-story house typical of the north proved troublesome. The systems tend to add to stratification of indoor temperatures. This helps absorb and reject unwanted heat for cooling but is not advantageous for heating.

Los Alamos National Lab measured the performance provided by a roof pond system built into a mobile home (Hasking and Stromberg, 1979). The system was designed by Architects Taos of New Mexico and built by the Navajo Nation (native American tribe). The system consists of four rows of south-facing roof apertures providing sunlight to roof water bag panels resting on the ceiling beneath (figure 4.56). A movable insulating panel system controls admission of solar energy and heat loss from the "pond." The solar mobile home was

Solar collection:
  A Attached greenhouse-style sunspace
  B Clerestory glazing
  C Additional south-facing glass
Thermal storage:
  D Mass walls — brick veneer on frame
  E Brick paved flooring
  F Basement slab and 9" concrete walls
Heat distribution:
  G Warm-air duct from sunspace to bedrooms and basement mass
  H Thermostatically controlled fan
  J Powered destratification units (circulate heat from loft, ceilings)
Auxiliary heat:
  K Gas forced-air furnace
  M Brickalator fireplace
Thermal buffers:
  N North-zoned garage,
       bedrooms
  P Air-lock entryway

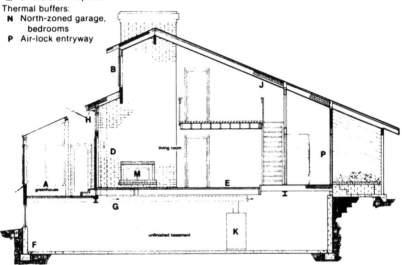

Figure 4.49
Cross section and floor plan, Unique.

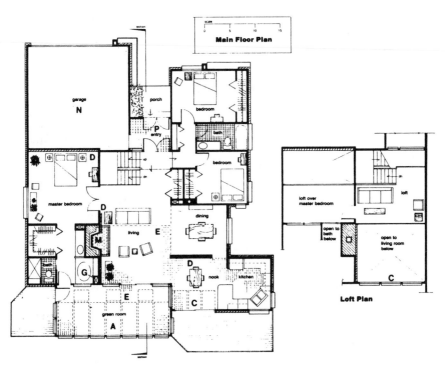

Figure 4.49 (continued)

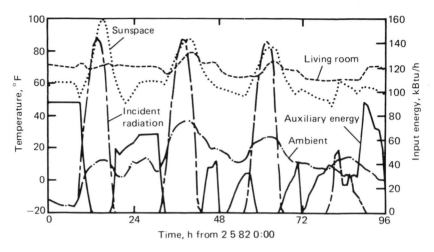

Figure 4.50
Four days of performance data, Unique. Key (time, in hours, from February 4, 1982, midnight): auxiliary energy (———); incident radiation (——–); ambient (———); living room (- - -); sunspace (. . .).

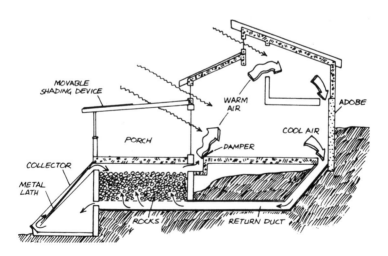

Figure 4.51
Davis thermosyphon house, 1972. Source: LANL (1979).

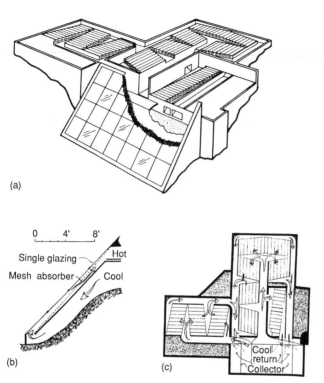

(a)

(b)

(c)

Figure 4.52
W. Scott Morris block bed system, 1981: (a) perspective of collector/block bed system; (b) section through collector; (c) plan of block beds. Source: Morris (1982).

completed in 1977 and monitored during the winter and spring of 1978.

Data show that this system of clerestories, insulated shutter controls, and water bags could operate quite effectively. Shutter operation was motorized and controlled by a photoelectric sensor to reduce loss under poor sun conditions. On a sunny day, the water temperature responds fairly evenly following shutter opening, but the room air temperatures below vary over a wider range, indicating that the roof pond systems provide only part of the total passive gains (figure 4.57). The control system for the insulating shutters allowed excess heat loss in the late afternoon by remaining open too long. The building tended to overheat due to its high solar fraction (89%) and very low air leakage rate. Also, the light frame construction meant that the roof pond was the only mass available for heat storage.

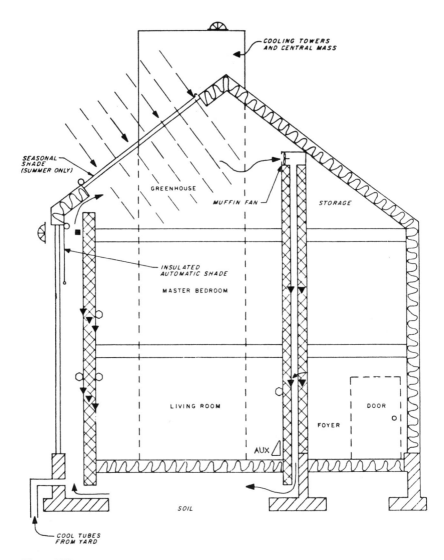

Figure 4.53
Cross section, Roberts House. Source: Howard (1983).

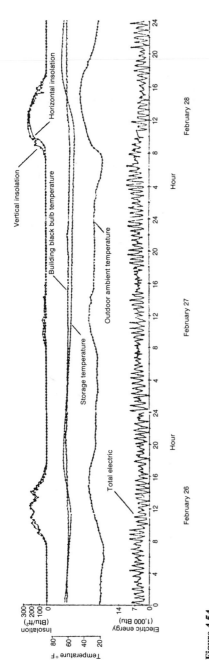

Figure 4.54
Roberts House performance data, February 1982. Source: Howard (1983).

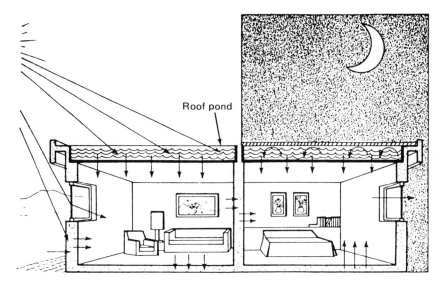

Figure 4.55
Roof pond system winter operation. Source: Hasking and Stromberg (1979).

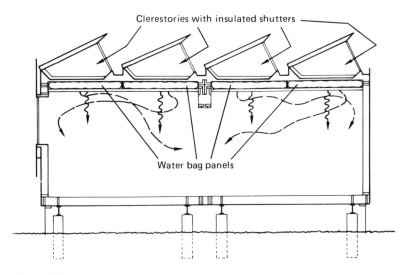

Figure 4.56
Mobile modular home with roof pond clerestory system. Source: Hasking and Stromberg (1979).

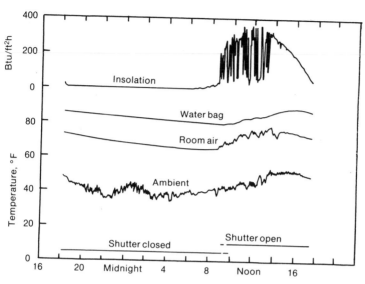

Figure 4.57
One-day performance plot, mobile modular house.

The use of phase ceiling heat storage tiles was pioneered at MIT (Johnson, 1978, 1979) and later demonstrated in a production home located in Frederick, MD, monitored by the NSDN (Spears, 1982). The MIT Solar Building 5 was constructed in late 1977 using advanced passive components (Johnson, 1978). Its heat storage system is comprised of phase change materials (PCM) contained in tile form placed on the ceiling and on the upper surface of window "settees." Foil bags sealed inside the tiles contained the PCM, which proved capable of sustaining 4000+ thermal cycles. Other features of MIT Solar Building 5 included the use of low emissivity windows, specifically Heat Mirror™ and prototype oxide coated glass. Also, louvers inside the windows were used to direct transmitted solar radiation to the ceiling panel surfaces (figure 4.58). The building performed well according to MIT measurements, having a 75.9% solar fraction. About 14.4% of the heat needs came from internal gains. The tiles contain a PCM designed to melt at 73°F, and remained 6°–10°F warmer than air temperature during typical days during the monitored heating season (figure 4.59).

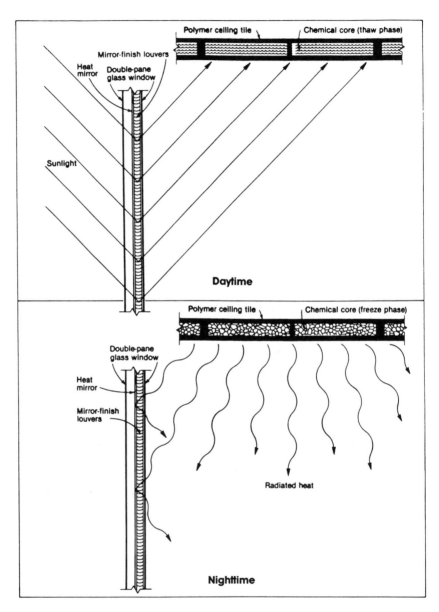

Figure 4.58
Cross section MIT PCM ceiling system design. Source: Johnson (1978).

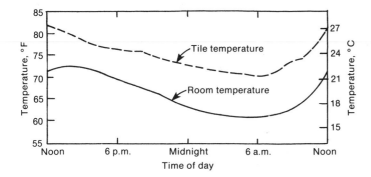

Figure 4.59
One-day temperature comparison, storage tile temperature versus room air, MIT House 5.
Source: *Passive Solar Journal.*

4.7   Advanced Concepts

This section discusses new developments in the thermal storage area, which is under investigation by U.S. DOE and its contractors.

The Transwall concept, developed by AMES Laboratory–Iowa State University, offers qualities similar to Trombe walls while avoiding significant reductions in daylighting behind mass wall common to early masonry types. Using water sandwiched between glazings to absorb a quantity of solar radiation transmitted through an outer glazing, the Transwall heats up like a Trombe wall. The visual clarity through the system is roughly similar to tinted glazings used on commercial buildings and residential structures in the sunbelt (McClelland, 1981). The thermal performance of Transwall has been tested in Iowa State's Passive Test Facility under both winter and summer conditions. Results indicated that winter heating performance is similar to that of masonry Trombe walls. Summer loads are moderated by the water mass and lower overall solar transmission of the assembly.

Los Alamos Laboratories has studied massive wall elements, called liquid convective diodes (LCD), which promise an efficient, modular approach to mass wall construction (figure 4.60). Mathematical models were developed to analyze flow and heat transfer in these modules. Measured data from the Los Alamos test cells indicated that a Trombe wall constructed of LCD modules could expect 50% passive collection efficiency or higher.

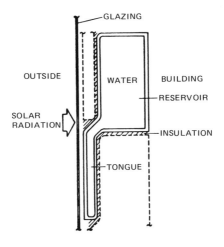

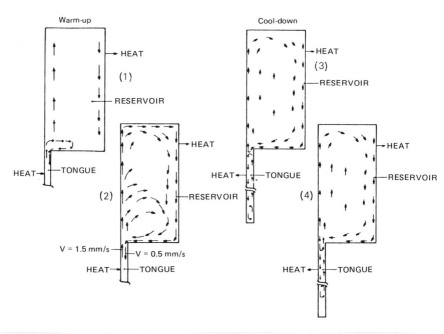

Figure 4.60
Liquid convection diode system cross section and heat transfer schematics: (top) liquid convective diode; (bottom) fluid behavior. Source: Jones (1984).

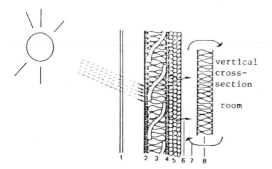

Figure 4.61
Heat pipe storage wall concept. Source: Van Dilk and de Wit (1983).

Several "tongue" type arrangements were evaluated, and results indicated that offsets cause elevated tongue temperatures and high heat loss. The in-line tongue configuration was found to have less flow interference between return (heated) fluid and supply (dense-cooled fluid) The tongue only obtains flow with the main storage vessel during times of good solar radiation. At night, heat loss from the tongue cools its contents and isolates the water from water in the storage vessel by a density gradient. The tongue hanging in front of the storage vessel below it would require back insulation to control heat loss from the vessel when the tongue is cooled down. Conclusions indicated that the thermal diode modules may attain 60–65% system efficiency when fully developed (Jones, 1984).

Researchers from the Institute of Applied Physics of the Netherlands have explored combinations of heat pipes and phase change material (PCM) in wall panels (Van Dilk and de Wit, 1983). The system consists of "S-shaped" heat pipes that are arranged to transmit collected solar heat through an insulation layer (figure 4.61) to a back plate of conductive material. PCM elements in contact with the conductive heat pipe material pick up and store the heat for later release to the conditioned space. The outer layer of glass and a selective coating on the absorber panel complete the system. Heat is distributed to the room by natural radiation and convection from the inner PCM layer surface. Thermal analysis indicates that such a system could produce nearly double the net energy gains (accounting for losses) of a conventional masonry thermal storage wall (Van Dilk and de Wit, 1983). The authors measured the performance of various heat pipes in a special calorimeter device. Copper pipes were used

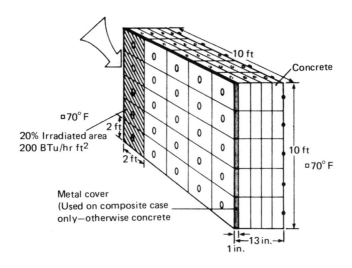

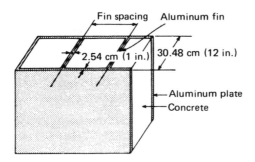

Figure 4.62
Transfer wall concept (SERI): (top) composite wall with highly conductive surface; (bottom) representative section of transfer wall. Source: Ortega (1981).

and both water and alcohol-water mixtures were evaluated. The PCM materials evaluated were both paraffin wax and salt hydrate types. The researchers have planned to construct a prototype of the system.

As a subtask for Innovative Building Systems, the Solar Energy Research Institute (SERI) has investigated thermal storage modules fabricated with highly conductive metal facings and "fins" (figure 4.62) in the hope of improving heat transfer into the heat storage mass (Ortega, 1981). Improved diffusion of heat into concrete storage modules, similar in size to conventional concrete blocks, could help improve performance of structural thermal storage walls. Both solar absorbance and through wall heat flow are targeted for enhancement. The concrete itself could be mix designed to include encapsulated or solid-solid phase change materials in finished modules. Lightweight concrete could keep overall U-values from being too high in completed thermal storage walls, and could also help conventional masonry technique overcome problems of excess unit weight per unit of effective heat storage capacity. Potentially, such a composite metal-concrete wall can save up to 30% of incident solar radiation by better thermal diffusion, 10% of which can be stored in the wall with the remainder discharged to the conditioned space. SERI has received statements of interest from several companies on this system (Ortega, 1981).

Darby and Wright (1983) have suggested a hybrid PCM system designed for retrofit construction, but also adaptable to new construction, which shows great promise. Figure 4.63 illustrates three generic applications tied to alternative sources of solar heat: a sunspace, a preheat chamber, and a wall panel. The authors suggested that due to the light weight per unit heat capacity of PCMs, such a system could be integrated easily into typical ceiling construction. Such systems would be served by either natural convection air flow or small fans. The use of fans would enable the system also to reject stratified heat scavenged from the interior during summer months.

4.8   Ramifications of Thermal Storage Systems

Over the last ten years trends in the use of thermal storage inside passive buildings have diverged from some of the original guidance, which tended to be weak on quantification and long on imagination. Today, architects plan spaces with comfort lighting, environmental interaction, and humanistic scale related to movement of natural energy to sources and sinks inside

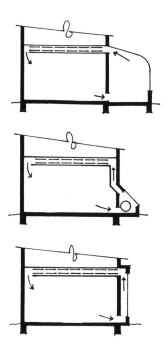

Figure 4.63
Three alternatives for hybrid charge passive discharge PCM ceiling systems: (top)
greenhouse source: (middle) preheat chamber source: (bottom) wall collector source.
Source: Darby and Wright (1983).

the building envelope. Society is gradually accepting climate responsive
building designs as a cultural norm, where as in the past two decades, the
envelope had become intertwined with a mechanistic view of the HVAC
system as doing battle with, rather than embracing, the environment.

Research has discovered important physical and thermal relationships
among the level of envelope insulation, the size of solar aperture, and heat
storage requirements. If the mass of exterior envelope is elevated, then a
change in the amount of internal and transmitted solar gains must be
carefully reconciled. As more energy using (heat generating) equipment
and persons are added to the interior, the requirements for solar heat are
decreased, and the need for cooling increases and becomes less "seasonal."
Addition of thermal mass can help control transient thermal discomfort if
coupled with controlled ventilation. In the case of commercial buildings,
cooling may be required on an annual basis if too much solar gain is
permitted, and the role of mass is left to chance.

If a very highly insulated envelope is designed, with little thermal mass inside, care must be used to avoid using too much glass as passive solar collective area. Research at Los Alamos, confirmed by monitored results, indicated that about 8% of floor area in south-facing windows was the limit for low-mass well insulated houses. For direct gain systems, south-facing window areas greater than about 10–12% of floor area require thermal mass, well distributed over floors, walls, and ceilings, to reduce temperature swings. The designer should first provide adequate view and natural lighting with moderate direct gain glass areas; then if more heat is needed from passive solar, the designer should consider indirect heating such as thermal storage walls, sunspaces, or isolated gains systems. With proper levels of thermal protection for the climate, and "optional mix" of conservation and solar representing a most economical solution can be found for each design through sound analysis techniques. These analysis techniques have resulted in simplified guidelines for builders.

Mechanical systems can be controlled to take advantage of thermal mass effects to reduce building energy use. However, evidence from detailed studies of thermal mass indicates that steady state methods should still be used for equipment design sizing, unless full year simulations are run for the building that incorporate mass responsive algorithms. The existence of interior and/or envelope thermal mass results in longer building time—constants that can reduce the need for costly and inefficient oversizing. Building heat capacity has been demonstrated to reduce equipment cycling, thereby boosting net efficiency. Research by SERI has shown that use of "traditional" oversizing of furnaces in passive solar homes leads to inefficient operations of equipment with otherwise excellent combustion efficiency (Frey, Swisher, and Holtz, 1982). One reason for this problem also may be undermassing of passive buildings where glazed areas have about 10 times more heat loss than walls and 15–25 times more heat loss than ceilings. Under fluctuating weather conditions, passive buildings with low mass tend to change indoor temperature rapidly—to which HVAC system controls quickly respond. In buildings of very high mass, thermostat setback has been shown to deliver minimal benefits. Morning reheat in winter or afternoon recool in summer for residential buildings can change peak utility demands and requires more detailed investigation. The high-mass building should be well insulated, and control using minimal night setback should be carefully evaluated. However, given identical envelope heat loss, low-mass and high-mass designs with the same solar gains and internal load will use fairly similar quantities of energy over long time periods under similar weather conditions unless specific passive solar and ventilation is provided. The high-mass building is likely to have its peaks shifted in time and reduced amplitudes of cyclical patterns of conditioning energy use. The designer's job is to analyze the impact of these patterns for the specific building use, weather, and utility interface to the best advantage in designing thermal energy storage.

References

ANSI/ASHRAE, "Standard 55-1981, Thermal Conditions for Human Occupancy," January 1981.

ASHRAE, *Fundamentals Handbook*, Atlanta, GA: American Society of Heating, Refrigerating and Air-Conditioning Engineers, 30329, 1989.

Balcomb, J. D. and R. Jones, *The Passive Solar Design Handbook*, Vol. 1 and 2. 1980. Vol. 3, 1982, U.S. DOE #CS-0127/1.2.3.

Balcomb, J. D., "Heat Storage and Distribution in Passive Solar Buildings," LA-9694-MS, 1983, Los Alamos National Laboratory, New Mexico, 87545.

Balcomb, J. D., and K. Yamagichi, "Heat Distribution by Natural Convection," Proc. 8th National Passive Solar Conference, Santa Fe, New Mexico, 1983, 289–294.

Balcomb, J. D., "Conservation and Solar: Working Together," Proc. 5th National Passive Solar Conference, 1980, 44–50.

Balcomb, J. D., "Conservation and Solar Guidelines," Proc. 8th National Passive Solar Conference, 1983, 117–122.

Beir, J. "Performance of a Low Cost Owner-Built Home Using Vertical Solar Louvers," Proc. 3rd National Passive Solar Conference, 1979, 643–647.

Benson, D. K., et al., "Materials Research for Passive Solar Systems: Solid State Phase Change Materials," SERI/TR-255-1828 (NTIS #DE85008779)., 1984.

Burch, D. M., K. L. Davis, and S. A. Malcomb, "The Effect of Wall Mass on the Summer Space Cooling of Six Test Buildings," ASHRAE Transactions 90.2, 1984.

Butti, K., and J. Perine, *A Golden Thread*, 1981.

Chapman, H. L., "A Rock Pile Thermal Storage Heating and Cooling System," ISES Annual Conference, 1970, Melbourne, Australia, 5.

Childs, K., G. E. Courville, and E. L. Bales, "Thermal Mass Assessment," Oak Ridge Laboratories, 1983, U.S. DOE Building Systems Division.

Darby, R., and D. Wright, AIA, "An Integrated Phase Change Heating and Cooling System for Retrofit and New Construction," Proc. 8th National Passive Solar Conference, Santa Fe, New Mexico, 1983.

Davies, M. G., "Model Studies of St. Georges School: Wallasey, " *Journal. Inst. of Heating and Ventilating Engineers*, (U.K.), #39, 1968.

Franta, G., et al., *Solar Design Workbook*, 1981, #SERI/SP-62-308, U.S. DOE Solar Energy Research Institute.

Franta, G., and S. Hogg, "Creative Interior Design for Thermal Storage Walls," 1983, Proc. 8th National Passive Solar Conference, 519–522.

Frey, D. J., J. N. Swisher, and M. J. Holtz, "Class B Performance Monitoring of Passive and Hybrid Solar Buildings," Proc. ASME Solar Division Conference, 1982, Albuquerque, New Mexico, 571–577.

Givoni, B., *Man, Climate and Architecture* (2nd edition), London: Applied Science Publishers, 1976.

Hasking, D., and R. P. Stromberg, "Passive Solar Buildings," U.S. DOE/Sandia Laboratory, #SAND-79-0824, 1979.

Howard, B. D., and E. O. Pollock, "Comparative Report: Performance of Passive Solar Space Heating Systems," Vitro Corp./U.S. DOE National Solar Data Network, 1982, #DE82108506, NTIS, Springfield, Virginia.

Howard, B. D., "The *Air Core* System for Thermal Storage," *Passive Solar Journal*, 3, No. 3, 1986 ASES.

Howard, B. D., "Monitored Total Performance of a Solar Home Using Concrete Masonry," Proc. 8th National Passive Solar Conference, 1983. ASES, Boulder, CO, 283–288.

Johnson, T. E., "Second Generation Architectural Finish Materials for Passive Space Heating," Proc. 4th National Passive Solar Conference, 358–360, 1979.

Johnson, T. E., "Preliminary Performance of the MIT Solar Building 5," *Passive Solar Design: A Survey of Monitored Buildings*, 1978, AIA Research Corp., 29–35, U.S. DOE, #HCP/CS-4113-2.

Jones, G. F., "Liquid Convective Diodes," Proc. 1984, Passive and Hybrid Solar Energy Update.

Jones, R., et al., *Passive Solar Design and Analysis Handbook*, ASHRAE, Atlanta, GA, 1984.

Kelbaugh, D., "A Thermal History of the Kelbaugh House," 1983, Proc. 8th National Passive Solar Conference.

Lang, M., "Phase Change Thermal Storage Materials in Masonry Construction," Proc. U.S. DOE Passive and Hybrid Solar Energy Program Update, August 9–12, 1981, Washington, DC, CONF-810832 (Contract DE-FC02-80CS30586).

Langa, F. S., "Sunshine at Night," *New Shelter*, Emmaus, PA: Rodale Press, 1981.

Mazria, E., *The Passive Solar Energy Book*, Emmaus, PA: Rodale Press, 1979.

McClelland, J. F., "Transwall Research," U.S. DOE Passive and Hybrid Solar Energy Program Update, August 9–12, 1981.

Morris, W. S., "From Balloons to Blockbeds," *Solar Age*, August 1982, 16–20.

Morris, W. S., "Performance Evaluation of a Thermosyphon Blockbed System," Proc. 8th National Passive Solar Conference, 1983, 265–269.

National Concrete Masonry Association (NCMA), "Pitkin City Airport," *Pictorial*, 33 no. 11, 1977.

National Concrete Masonry Association (NCMA), TEK Note 122, McLean, VA, 1982.

Neeper, D. A., and R. D. McFarland, "Some Potential Benefits of Fundamental Research for the Passive Solar Heating and Cooling of Buildings," LA-9425-MS, 1982, Los Alamos National Laboratory, New Mexico.

Olgyay, V., *Design With Climate*, Princeton, NJ: Princeton University Press, 1963.

Ortega, K., "Innovative Building Systems", Proc. 1981 Passive and Hybrid Update, 3–55.

Passive Solar Construction Handbook, (Steven Winter Associates, editors), 1981, revised 1984, NCMA/U.S. DOE #DE82030748 (Also available from Rodale Press, Emmaus, PA).

Perry, J. E., "The Wallasey School," Proc. 1st Passive Solar Conference, Albuquerque, New Mexico, 1976, 223–237 (Los Alamos Laboratories, LA-6637-C).

Rhodes, F., et al., "Ceiling Fans as Extenders of the Summer Comfort Envelope," Kansas State University Institute for Environmental Research.

(Anon.) SERI, "Solar Design Briefs 1–11," (Denver Metro Class B Houses), 1984.

Sliwkowski, Joseph, "The Application of Phase Change Materials in Passive Solar Systems," in Proc. U.S. DOE Passive and Hybrid Solar Energy Program Update, September 21–24, 1980, Washington, D.C., CONF-800972 (Contract DE-FG-04-79GS 34146).

Spears, J. W., "Comparison of Vertical High Performance Glazing to Sloped Double Glazing with Movable Insulation," Proc. 8th National Passive Solar Conference, 1983, 253–258.

Spears, J. W., "Seasonal Energy System Performance Evaluation: Rymark I, II and III, " Vitro Corp., DOE—National Solar Data Network, 1982, #Solar/1106, 1110, 1107-82/14.

Swet, C. J., "Phase Change Storage in Passive Solar Architecture," in Proc. 5th National Passive Solar Conference, 1980, Amherst, MA.

Trombe, F., et al., "Some Performance Characteristics of the CNRS Solar House Collectors," Proc. 1st Passive Solar Conference, 1976.

Van Dilk and de Wit, "High Performance Passive Solar Heating System with Heat Pipe Energy Transfer and Patent Heat Storage," Proc. 8th Passive Solar Conference, 1983, ASES.

Yanda, W., "Considerations for Retrofitting an Attached Solar Greenhouse," Proc. 1st Passive Solar Conference, 1976, 160–164.

5 Thermal Energy Distribution in Building Interiors

Gregory Franta

5.1 Introduction

Building interiors provide an important element of thermal energy distribution for the effective use of solar energy. The thermal energy distribution in buildings is the final process that provides the common end-use goal of human comfort and safety. By no means are issues of human comfort and safety simple as they relate to the thermal energy distribution in building interiors. Even in the simplest interior environments, consideration should be given to air temperature, mean radiant temperature, air movement, humidity, building function, visual quality, and indoor air quality. These considerations will have a direct or indirect impact on the effective distribution of thermal energy in building interiors.

Analyzing internal factors of both small and large buildings can be a difficult task. The internal factors related to thermal energy transfer in building interiors include solar heat gain, internal heat gain, occupancy, lighting, and equipment. The awareness of the interactions among these factors is important when attempting to understand the thermal energy transfers in building interiors.

Many of the issues presented in this chapter are often overlooked or are poorly understood by building designers and engineers. This chapter presents the major related research and development as of 1982 on the thermal energy distribution in building interiors. The chapter is divided into two major sections: a background of the topic and a review of research and development between 1972 and 1982.

5.2 Background

As background information, the key mechanisms and opportunities related to thermal energy distribution in building interiors are summarized in the following text. This chapter is intended to augment the information presented in volume 4 in this series, *Fundamentals of Building (Energy) Dynamics*. The thermal energy distribution in building interiors can have a significant impact on the effectiveness of solar utilization and thus energy use. The thermal energy transfer within buildings has an effect on the energy use and thermal comfort of the occupants. The primary mechanisms relative to thermal transfer for both heating and cooling include conduction, convection (natural and forced), direct radiation, reflected and diffused radiation, and evaporation. The control of the thermal distribution within building interiors is primarily through building design and mechanical/ electrical systems.

The primary goal of thermal distribution in building interiors is to provide human comfort, health, and safety. The distribution issues related to this goal include

1. air temperature and stratification,

2. mean radiant temperature,

3. air movement,

4. humidity,

5. building interior function (occupants' activity rate and clothing),

6. visual quality, and

7. indoor air quality (indoor pollution related to inadequate air distribution and the emittance of pollutants from building materials, occupants, machines, and equipment).

Most of the fundamental heat transfer processes (conduction, convection, and radiation) are relatively well understood. One-dimensional steady conduction through building materials and radiative exchange between building surfaces are two examples. However, there are a significant number of heat transfer topics that are more complex and therefore of great research interest since they are not yet fully understood.

The current understanding of convective heat transfer in buildings is poor for several reasons. First of all, most building geometries are more complex than the geometries of building interiors that have been investigated and reported prior to 1972. These early studies involve simple shapes and surfaces such as flat, vertical, or horizontal plates, cylinders, or cones in a large body of fluid or inside simple two-dimensional enclosures (i.e., space between a double-glazed window). Further, most of the previous research involved small-scale objects with low Rayleigh numbers (Rayleigh numbers are derived from the Rayleigh dimensional analysis method using algebra to determine interrelationships among variables—in this case, the Rayleigh number describes the driving force for natural convection heat transfer). However, most building convection involves high Rayleigh numbers that are two or three orders of magnitude larger than most earlier studies. The transfer of thermal energy from a centralized system may create problems in distribution and control of the heat.

In 1972, there were available several technical research studies conducted generally on small-scale heat transfer systems that might be related to larger scale multizoned buildings. However, most work was not oriented toward larger applications. To complicate the issues of thermal distribution even further, the architectural elements sometimes interfere with the proper distribution of thermal energy in building interiors. These concerns may relate to aesthetic factors, air quality issues, thermal comfort, functional requirements, desired building materials, etc.

The thermal energy distribution problems vary significantly from small single-zone buildings to large multizone and multistory buildings. The type and use of building also has a significant impact on the thermal energy distribution in building interiors. Small buildings with small internal loads have energy requirements that are generally dominated by climate. But buildings with large internal loads have energy use patterns that are significantly less impacted by climate.

The perimeter zones of building interiors are often affected by solar orientation. Figures 5.1 and 5.2 illustrate horizontal zoning of building interiors resulting from orientation.

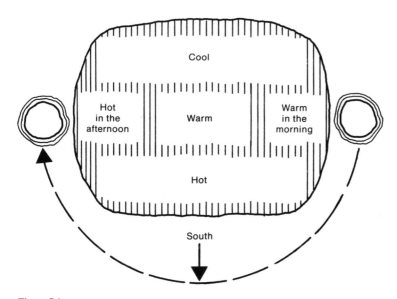

Figure 5.1
Horizontal temperature zones of building interiors. Source: American Institute of Architects (1981).

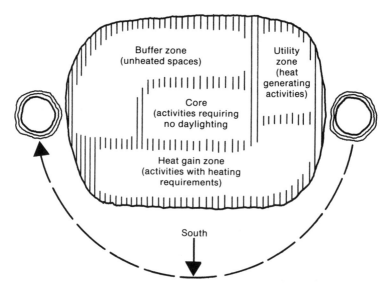

Figure 5.2
Potential design response to horizontal zones of building interiors. Source: American Institute of Architects (1981).

Of course, building interiors are also impacted by vertical zoning. In general, the higher the zone, the potentially warmer the zone. Figure 5.3 illustrates the concepts for both winter and summer for vertical zoning.

Natural distribution of thermal energy in buildings with climate-responsive architecture was common prior to the extensive use of mechanical systems for heating, cooling, and ventilating. Practical mechanical systems with both temperature and humidity control were developed during the 1920s. Fluorescent lighting, a more efficient and therefore less heat-producing alternative to incandescent light, became commercially available in the 1930s. These technological advances did not become common applications for total internal environmental control for several years. Climate-responsive commercial buildings using daylight strategies and natural ventilation were common until the 1950s. At that time, the increased reliability of the mechanical equipment, reduced capital cost of the equipment, and the low operating costs of fuel and electricity allowed the internal environmental control approach of the "climate-rejecting" building to become the standard solution (Ternoey et al., 1984).

In the years directly prior to 1972, most energy distribution in large modern buildings was through forced means and little attention was given

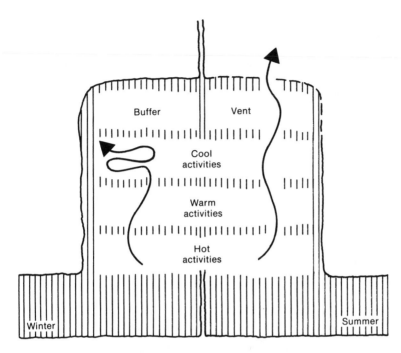

Figure 5.3
Potential design response to vertical zones of building interiors. Source: American Institute of Architects (1981).

to natural distribution within building interiors. The technology of thermal energy distribution within building interiors through forced means was fairly well understood. The architectural community had to become more aware of natural energy distribution within buildings as a result of a need to lower energy operating costs in buildings following the 1973 oil embargo. The following documentation guides the reader through selective, significant research projects related to the thermal energy distribution in building interiors. In some cases the reader is referred to other volumes in this series to avoid major redundancies.

5.3 Review of Research and Development (1972–1982)

Several issues complicate the discussions of thermal energy distribution in building interiors. To clarify the discussion, the primary issues that affect the thermal energy distribution in building interiors are summarized as follows:

1. energy flows within rooms and buildings (heating, cooling, lighting),

2. room geometry (length, width, height, shapes) and building form,

3. room and building function (activity use, activity rates, furniture placement),

4. building materials (walls, floors, and ceilings; room-to-room differences; massive versus light construction),

5. single-zone or multizone building interiors,

6. room relationships to thermal storage, exterior openings, interior openings, and adjacent rooms,

7. ambient conditions affecting building interiors (orientation, siding, adjacent buildings, exterior openings),

8. control strategies,

9. strategy optimization and design integration, and

10. energy performance.

For several years prior to 1972 thermal energy within buildings was distributed in an acceptable manner by the use of mechanical systems. The engineering for proper use of mechanical systems in regard to low initial system cost and basic human comfort was well understood. As energy became more of a concern through the use of conservation and solar applications, there was a desire to distribute thermal energy within buildings using as little power as possible. This resulted in designers attempting to distribute energy within buildings by natural rather than mechanical means. However, this effort was crusaded by relatively few designers on mostly small buildings. Since 1972, the significant research that has been conducted on thermal energy distribution in building interiors relates to natural convection, conduction, interzone convection, natural ventilation, infiltration, radiation, daylighting, and forced convection/ controls.

5.3.1 Convection

Natural convection within building interiors can be a very effective process for the distribution of heat. Los Alamos National Laboratory, the Solar Energy Research Institute, and other federally funded institutions have investigated natural convection within buildings. The following summarizes the research results.

5.3.1.1 Project: Heat Storage and Distribution Inside Passive Solar Buildings   Institution: Los Alamos National Laboratory; principal investigator: J. Douglas Balcomb.

Project Description   Los Alamos National Laboratory has characterized the heat exchange within buildings to verify work done by the various investigators on the development of heat transfer correlations. Full-scale experiments and numerical experiments were conducted corresponding to work done by Brown and Solvason (1962) that describe natural convective heat transfer through a doorway in terms of the Nusselt (Nu), Grashof (Gr), and Prandtl (Pr) similarity numbers. These experiments result in the following conclusions (Wray and Weber, 1979; Weber, Wray, and Kearney, 1979):

1. It was confirmed that convection through doorways is a very effective way of heating remote rooms. Quite reasonable temperature differences between the driving room and the remote room can be maintained.

2. The steady state solutions given in figure 5.4 and in the following equation gives good indication of the temperature differences that can be expected under most conditions:

$$\Delta t = t_d - t_r = \{[\text{LDR}(t_r - t_a)/4.6]^2/d\}^{1/3}, \tag{1}$$

where,

Δt = temperature difference (°F),

t_d = driving temperature (°F),

t_r = room temperature (°F),

LDR = load-door ratio, loss coefficient (Btu/°F h), divided by the doorway width (ft) × the doorway height (ft),

T_a = ambient temperature (°F),

d = doorway height (ft).

3. The effect of large variations in the driving temperature is advantageous, generally decreasing the difference between the average temperature in the driving room and in the remote room. Temperature swings in the remote room were always less than those in the driving room.

4. If the temperature swing in the driving room is quite large as in the case of an unattached sunspace, a diode door control strategy, where the door

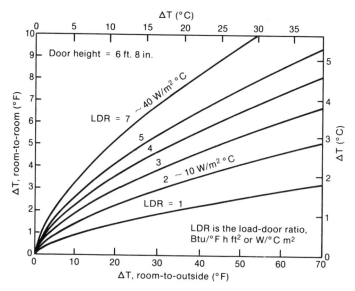

Figure 5.4
Steady-state results from Los Alamos National Laboratory illustrating air flow through a doorway to a remote room. [The curve shows the average temperature difference between the driving room and the remote room as a function of the average temperature difference between the remote room and the outside and the load-door ratio (LDR). The LDR is the ratio of the heat-loss coefficient of the room to the door area. The curves are drawn for a standard height door.] Source: Balcomb (1983a).

between zones is open during the day and closed at night, can improve the situation by decreasing the temperature difference.

5. Heat storage in the remote room is quite important if the driving temperatures swing is large. Insufficient mass will lead to excessive temperature swings.

In addition to the simple doorway experimentations, Los Alamos investigated two-story buildings with sunspaces and reported on the results. Figure 5.5 illustrates the typical convective loop in a two-story home with a sunspace. Figure 5.6 illustrates the air-flow pattern near the floor of a test home measured by Los Alamos. The return air from the kitchen-dining area stays very close to the floor.

As a result of their experimentation, Los Alamos has made recommendations as design guidelines in regard to the distribution of thermal energy from solar gain areas into small yet multizoned buildings. Although the

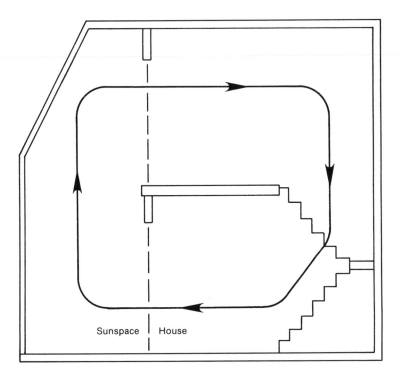

Figure 5.5
Typical convective loop in a two-story house with a sunspace and stairway.

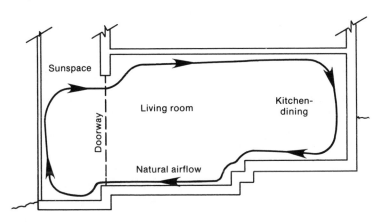

Figure 5.6
Air-flow pattern near the floor of a test home observed by Los Alamos National Laboratory. (The return air from the kitchen-dining area stays very close to the floor and cascades down the stairs similar to water flow.)

work described by Los Alamos is still in progress and is far from complete, certain initial guidelines have been developed (Bohn, 1983).

In the current studies, it is evident that there is a major amount of thermal storage inside the test house due to convection from the sunspace. The major driving mechanism for this convection is the heat engine, driven by the sun on one side and by walls absorbing heat on the opposite side. If the designer is fully aware of the principles involved, Los Alamos suggests that building designs can benefit significantly from effective convective exchange.

Los Alamos reports that the key design factor is to lay out the building so that the convective loops can operate effectively. The designer should be able to accomplish this without architectural compromise. In the examples reported by Los Alamos, convective loops were due to the architectural considerations.

This research by Los Alamos National Laboratory was intended to provide assistance for architects and engineers while designing for the thermal energy distribution within building interiors. The resulting guidelines are published in a Los Alamos document (Balcomb, 1983a) that gives clear recommendations to building designers.

5.3.1.2 Project: 3-Dimensional Natural Convection at High Rayleigh Number Institution: Solar Energy Research Institute; principal investigator: Mark S. Bohn.

Project Description The Solar Energy Research Institute (SERI) has identified two convective processes that are particularly important in the building sciences: (1) the heat transfer rate between building surfaces and adjacent air (i.e., internal and external surface convection coefficients) and (2) the heat transfer rate through openings in the building surfaces (i.e., interzone conduction, natural ventilation, and infiltration). Previous work has focused on the first process, heat transfer between interior surfaces and air in a single zone. Several empirical heat transfer correlations were developed from data in a cubical water-filled enclosure test cell. These correlations describe heat transfer from the vertical and horizontal surfaces for several configurations of heated and cooled surfaces. In addition, the importance of the boundary layer flow on the vertical surface in transferring heat was demonstrated. This research represents some of the first conducted for high Rayleigh number, 3-dimensional enclosure flows.

The importance of the boundary layer in heat transfer was exploited to enhance heat transfer from building interior surfaces. SERI reports (Bohn, 1983) that by roughening the surface texture, the boundary layer could be forced to undergo transition to turbulence sooner, thereby increasing natural convection heat transfer. A thorough investigation indicated that it should be possible to double the heat transfer by this technique. The validity of testing in a water-filled enclosure (to predict full-scale heat transfer in air) was confirmed by SERI. Detailed temperature profiles and heat transfer measurements were made in the cubical test cell in water.

Natural convection in buildings is characterized by a full 3-dimensional flow at high Rayleigh numbers (Ra ~ 10^{10}). At present little is known about heat transfer in this regime, although a better understanding of it would allow for the design of more energy-efficient buildings. A SERI report (Bohn, 1983) documents the problems of 3-dimensional natural convection in enclosures with differentially heated walls and top and bottom surfaces at high Rayleigh numbers. The application of interest is passive solar heating and cooling of buildings. The objective of the research was to determine the natural convection heat transfer between heated and cooled surfaces in a cubical enclosure. This problem involved 3-dimensional flow between perpendicular walls and across parallel walls.

Flow visualization experiments and heat transfer measurements were completed with the test cell in two orientations. The first orientation consisted of adiabatic top and bottom surfaces and isothermal vertical walls. Four combinations of heating and cooling the isothermal walls were tested. The second orientation consisted of two facing adiabatic walls and isothermal floor and ceiling and two isothermal walls. Three combinations of heating and cooling the isothermal surfaces were tested.

The adiabatic floor/ceiling test verified the existence of a relatively inactive core surrounded by boundary layers on each of the four vertical walls. Heat is transported from heated walls to the cooled walls by flow in the boundary layers. The layer around the boundary turns the corner at the top of the cell and the heated fluid moves across the bottom to the cooled wall, where heat is given up in the reverse process.

The key finding of the research was in the definition of temperature to be used in the correlative equation for the Nusselt number (the dimensionless heat transfer coefficient that scales the heat transfer to what would exist if pure conduction took place). As a result of the experimentation, the significant correlations as recommended by SERI for high Rayleigh number range application to building interiors are as follows. The first equation for each configuration is the dimensionless equation. The second equation gives the heat transfer coefficient in watts per square meter per degree Celsius when the temperature difference is in degrees Celsius and the length is given in meters. Property values are for air at an average temperature of 20°C (68°F).

I. Adiabatic floor, ceiling with isothermal walls, any combination of heating and cooling

$$Nu = 0.620\,Ra^{0.250} \tag{2}$$
$$h = 1.64(\Delta T/L)^{0.250} \tag{3}$$

II. Heated floor with two facing adiabatic walls

  A. Cooled walls and ceiling (walls, floor, and ceiling)

$$Nu = 0.346\,Ra^{0.285} \tag{4}$$
$$h = 1.75\,\Delta T^{0.285}\,L^{-0.145} \tag{5}$$

  B. One cooled wall, one heated wall, cooled ceiling

    1. Walls

$$Nu = 0.141\,Ra^{0.313} \tag{6}$$
$$h = 1.20\,\Delta T^{0.313}\,L^{-0.061} \tag{7}$$

    2. Floor and ceiling

$$Nu = 1.10\,Ra^{0.236} \tag{8}$$
$$h = 2.25\,\Delta T^{0.236}\,L^{-0.292} \tag{9}$$

  C. One cooled wall, one heated wall, heated ceiling

    1. Walls

$$Nu = 0.233\,Ra^{0.286} \tag{10}$$
$$h = 1.20\,\Delta T^{0.286}\,L^{-0.142} \tag{11}$$

    2. Floor

$$Nu = 2.544\,Ra^{0.212} \tag{12}$$
$$h = 3.34\,\Delta T^{0.212}\,L^{-0.364} \tag{13}$$

    3. Ceiling

$$Nu = 0.233\,Ra^{0.207} \tag{14}$$
$$h = 0.267\,\Delta T^{0.207}\,L^{-0.379} \tag{15}$$

where

Nu = Nusselt number (dimensionless heat transfer coefficient),

Ra = Rayleigh number (describing the driving force for natural convection heat transfer),

h = height (meters),

ΔT = temperature difference in °C,

L = length (meters).

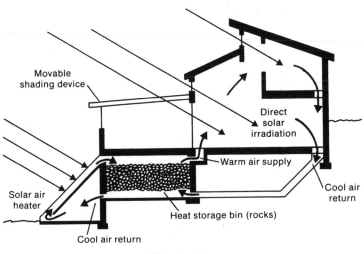

Movable shading device

Direct solar irradiation

Warm air supply

Solar air heater

Cool air return

Heat storage bin (rocks)

Cool air return

Winter heating

Figure 5.7
Davis residence system diagram. Source: Yellott (1975).

5.3.1.3 Project: Davis Residence Location: Corrales, NM; energy designer: Steve Baer.

In 1972, the Paul Davis residence demonstrated energy distribution in a building through the use of natural convection. Flat-plate solar air collectors produce hot air that rises to the rockbed thermal storage, where heat is transferred to the rocks. The cooler air drops to the bottom of the rockbed and then back to the collector.

In a similar manner, the warm air is distributed in the building as shown in figure 5.7. When desired, warm air is allowed to rise in the residence on the south side. As the air cools when it reaches the north wall and roof, the heavier air drops to the floor and sinks back to the rockbed, where the process is repeated.

5.3.1.4 Evaluation: Convection Most of the research and development on thermal distribution in buildings has been on convection. These research and development projects have greatly improved the understanding of convection flows in buildings. However, a significant portion of the research is very scientific and is currently not useful to architects and engineers when designing buildings. Selected research needs to continue, but this work must be converted to usable forms for use in building design, occupancy, and energy management. Therefore, technology transfer activities are important to utilize properly the pertinent research and development.

5.3.2 Natural Ventilation

The use of natural ventilation in building design can distribute thermal energy in a manner that would keep the occupants comfortable during much of a cooling season. Natural ventilation in especially small buildings has been investigated through a variety of research since 1972. One example of natural ventilation is demonstrated in section 5.3.2.1. The impacts of natural ventilation on the thermal energy distribution in building interiors is covered in chapter 14 of volume 4 in this series, *Fundamentals of Building Energy Dynamics*. The reader is referred to that chapter for further information on ventilation.

5.3.2.1 Project: Princeton Professional Park Location: Princeton, NJ; energy designers: Princeton Energy Group.

As part of the U.S. Department of Energy's Passive Commercial Buildings program, the design process of the Princeton Professional Park was documented (Ternoey et al., 1984). This project demonstrates many of the energy transfer techniques presented in this chapter.

Natural ventilation provides cooling through the use of an atrium in between the office zones as illustrated in figure 5.8. The stack effect aids natural ventilation and pulls air from the offices into and out of the atrium. Other strategies used in the Princeton Professional Park, such as daylighting, cooling, and heating, are shown in figures 5.9, 5.10, and 5.11.

5.3.2.2 Evaluation: Natural Ventilation The work done on the Princeton Professional Park is typical of much applied research and development on natural ventilation applications. Simplified methods of accurately predicting effects of natural ventilation need to be developed. Natural ventilation as related to multizone and multilevel buildings has only been lightly researched, and several components of the topic still need to be researched for a better understanding of their implications for thermal performance.

5.3.3 Infiltration

One of the most significant unknown factors in analyzing or predicting the energy use in buildings relates to the infiltration rate of the building. Infiltration can often be the largest single heat loss element in small

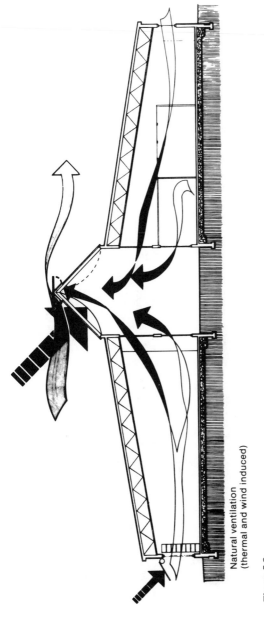

Natural ventilation
(thermal and wind induced)

Figure 5.8
Natural ventilation section of the Princeton Professional Park. Source: Ternoey, Bickle, Robbins, Busch, and McCord (1984).

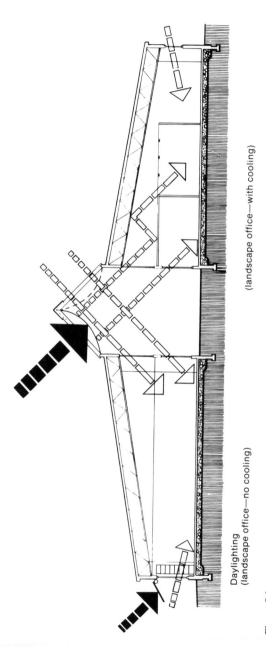

Daylighting
(landscape office—no cooling)

(landscape office—with cooling)

Figure 5.9
Daylighting section of the Princeton Professional Park. Source: Ternoey, Bickle, Robbins,
Busch, and McCord (1984).

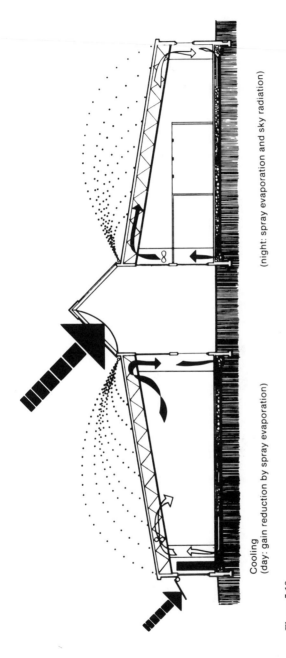

Figure 5.10
Cooling section of the Princeton Professional Park. Source: Ternoey, Bickle, Robbins, Busch, and McCord (1984).

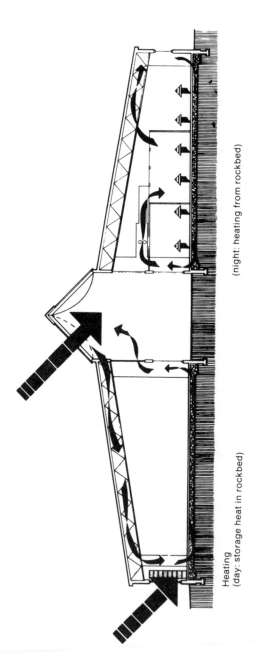

Heating
(day: storage heat in rockbed)

(night: heating from rockbed)

Figure 5.11
Heating section of the Princeton Professional Park. Source: Ternoey, Bickle, Robbins, Busch, and McCord (1984).

buildings. Infiltration is somewhat less of a concern in very large buildings, although the control of infiltration at any building scale is of importance in order to reduce energy operating costs properly. Some research since 1972 has focused on infiltration implications in buildings.

5.3.3.1 Project: A Multizone Infiltration Monitoring System Institution: Solar Energy Research Institute; principal investigators: David N. Wortman, Jay Birch, and Ronald Judkoff.

Project Description In order to understand infiltration impacts on multizone building interiors better, the Solar Energy Research Institute developed a multizone infiltration monitroing system (MIMS) using a simple tracer gas (Wortman, Burch, and Judkoff, 1982). MIMS measures zonal infiltration and exfiltration as well as interzonal air movement rates. The system has been used in a SERI multizone test building. The system can determine zonal infiltration rates, and the SERI results show significant differences in infiltration rates for various zones.

Several methods and variations thereof exist that directly or indirectly measure infiltration rates in buildings. Generally, these techniques are classified as tracer gas methods or blower door methods. SERI's work in this area is conducted using tracer gas. The resulting information from the SERI tests is directly related to thermal energy distribution of building interiors.

Analysis of the data (Wortman, Burch, and Judkoff, 1982) illustrated that several of the hourly air flow rates could be consistently determined when the regression search technique was started from different points in the 18-parameter test space (see figure 5.12). These results were developed by using two starting points on ten sets of consecutive hourly data. These flow rates were, in general, associated with the greatest difference in the tracer gas (sulfurhexafluoride) concentrations between the zones. It should be noted that these paths were also the most important from a thermal aspect. Depending upon the starting point for the regression search, other flow rates could vary greatly.

Other research at SERI is involved in the instrumentation of multizone residential buildings (Judkoff et al., 1983) and variations in the testing (Frey, McKinstry, and Swisher, 1982) of the multizone tracer gas tests. Work is proceeding to determine interzonal rates better. This will allow for the better study of natural convection from high insolation zones such as sunspaces and direct-gain spaces.

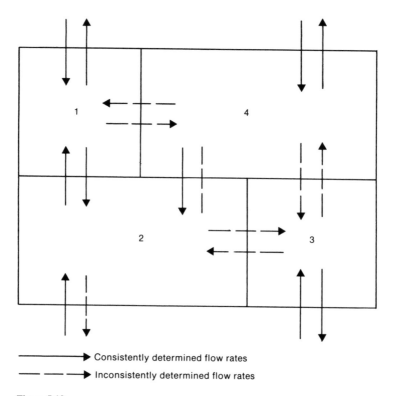

→ Consistently determined flow rates

---→ Inconsistently determined flow rates

Figure 5.12
Air flow rates that can be determined using current experimental and analysis schemes as presented by SERI.

5.3.3.2 Project: Infiltration Monitoring Institution: Lawrence Berkeley Laboratory; principal investigators: P. C. Strong, M. Sherman, and D. Grimsrud.

Project Description In addition to the tracer gas method described in the above project, blower door tests can also be used. The blower method uses a fan usually mounted in a frame that replaces an exterior door to pressurize or depressurize a building. Lawrence Berkeley Laboratory (LBL) has done a variety of tests related to infiltration.

The air flow rates in the LBL tests were determined by using fan curves and rpm measurements or a calibrated nozzle at the inlet to the fan. The indoor/outdoor pressure difference in the air flow rates are compared and a measure of the building's tightness (i.e., the effective crack area) is calculated by using a simple mathematical model (Sherman and Grimsrud,

1980). These results could be used to calcuate air infiltration rates if indoor/outdoor pressure differences are either assumed at some nominal value or determined from measured weather data. These blower door tests have been shown to be relatively simple to conduct and the data from them can be used to predict whole building infiltration rates to about 15–30% as a function of time and weather conditions. This information is extremely useful to architects and engineers in understanding infiltration implications on thermal energy distribution in building interiors.

The Lawrence Berkeley Laboratory has developed a continuous infiltration monitoring system, which is another tracer gas method (Strong, 1981). The equipment and software used in this technique continuously monitor the tracer gas concentration in a building volume and constantly inject enough tracer gas to keep the concentration relatively low. This method has microprocessor-controlled hardware and can be used to obtain single-zone infiltration data over a relatively long period of time (Strong, 1981).

5.3.3.3 Evaluation: Infiltration Significant and quality research has been conducted on the aspects of infiltration. The infiltration monitoring research has led to a better understanding of the thermal distribution issues. This work is partially well documented, but technology transfer activities, up until now very limited, are needed.

5.3.4 Radiation

Radiation can also be an effective means of thermal energy distribution in building interiors. A relatively uniform distribution of energy can be achieved, as well as good thermal comfort conditions for the occupant. John Yellott, Harold Hay, and others tested the radiation effects for both heating and cooling prior to 1972. A variety of radiation distribution studies have been conducted since 1972. The results of these are included in the section on passive solar heating and on passive cooling and in volumes 7 and 8 in this series.

5.3.5 Lighting/Daylighting Implications

The use of electric light and/or daylight can have an important impact on the thermal energy distribution in building interiors. Electric light gives off heat and therefore has a impact on the heating and cooling distribution in the space. By using daylight the internal heat gains in the building are often reduced, therefore requiring less cooling. The effective distribution of daylight in the spaces is also an issue related to this chapter. Through the

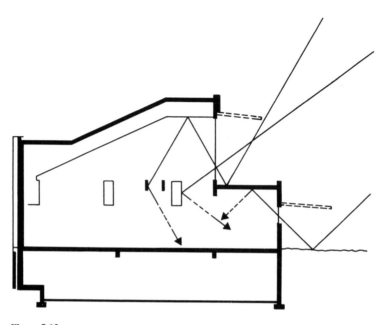

Figure 5.13
Security State Bank building in Wells, MN.

1970s, much work has been conducted on the use of daylighting in buildings intended to reduce the use of electric lights and cooling loads in buildings.

5.3.5.1 Project: Security State Bank Building Location: Wells, MN; energy architect: John Weidt, AIA.

Project Description This project is typical of many small commerical buildings constructed in the late 1970s and early 1980s that are intended to integrate properly the use of daylighting, passive solar heating, and reduced cooling load measures. The design process was in part funded and documented by the U.S. Department of Energy's Passive Commercial Buildings program (1979–1982).

Figure 5.13 illustrates the penetration of daylight into the building so that electric light is not required in most of the building during daylight hours. During the winter months, passive solar heat gain is collected in the upper part of the space and the resulting warm air is drawn into the mechanical heating and ventilating system and is distributed elsewhere in the building. The cooling loads associated with the heat given off

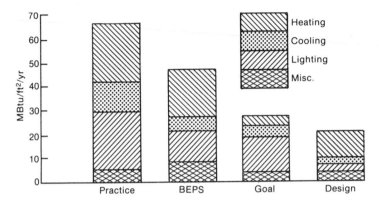

Figure 5.14
Energy-use breakdown of a base case (practice) building compared to the Building Energy Performance Standards (BEPS), design team goal, and final design of the Security State Bank building in Wells, MN.

by electric lights have been significantly reduced due to the daylighting design.

Figure 5.14 shows the projected energy use breakdown of a base case compared to the building energy performance standards, goal, and final design.

The Princeton Professional Park in section 5.3.2.1 also illustrates an example of daylighting combined with thermal energy distribution techniques.

5.3.5.2 Evaluation: Lighting/Daylighting   Daylighting research at the Solar Energy Research Institute and the Lawrence Berkeley Laboratory, in addition to numerous projects in the private sector similar to the Security State Bank Building, have provided several opportunities to evaluate the thermal distribution implications of daylight and electric light in buildings. However, this work is poorly understood, incomplete, and will need more specific research, development, and a full technology transfer program on thermal distribution related to daylighting and lighting techniques.

5.3.6 Forced Convection and Controls

By forcing convection through the use of mechanical and electrical systems, the thermal energy distribution in building interiors can be accurately controlled. Since the general design technology for forced convection was known prior to the 1970s, little research needed to be conducted to understand the relevant principles. Simple systems that destratify warm air into cooler parts of the building became very popular in the 1970s. Solar-generated heat in sunspaces and other solar-gain rooms is often transported from the overheated spaces to the cooler spaces of buildings or into thermal storage, for an example, see section 5.3.6.1.

Often the solar-generated heat gains are transferred by forced convection into a storage medium for distribution into the building interiors. These concepts are reported on in the previous chapter on the thermal energy storage for building interiors.

Los Alamos National Laboratory has conducted research in the area of forced convection and thermal storage in buildings. This work (Balcomb, 1983b) is reported in the passive solar heating section of the passive solar buildings book of volume 7 in this series. A variety of research was conducted on the control of solar energy systems for the heating and cooling of buildings in the 1970s.

Most of the work is covered in volumes 7 and 8 in this series. Further information is found in the proceedings of the Conference on the Control of Solar Energy Systems for Heating and Cooling of Buildings at Boston University in September 1978. Honeywell in Minneapolis also has conducted research in solar energy management systems, and this work will appear in volume 7 in this series.

Controlling moisture in buildings is also important for the proper thermal energy distribution in building interiors. Natural ventilation, forced ventilation, and vapor barriers are the key elements in regard to controlling moisture in buildings. Rick Schwolsky (1980–1981) has documented the major issues related to moisture in buildings.

The Solar Energy Research Institute has compiled key design strategy information on various laboratories related to thermal distribution in buildings—especially forced convection. This information is documented in the *Solar Design Workbook* (Franta et al., 1981), which is a result of the Solar in Federal Buildings Program.

5.3.6.1 Project: Franta Residence   Location: Lakewood, CO; energy architect: Gregory Franta, AIA.

Project Description   Typical of many passive hybrid systems of the 1970s and early 1980s, the Franta residence (Franta, Connolly, and Winn, 1981) combines the use of forced destratification with thermal storage and distribution. Figure 5.15 is a building section illustrating that warm air from

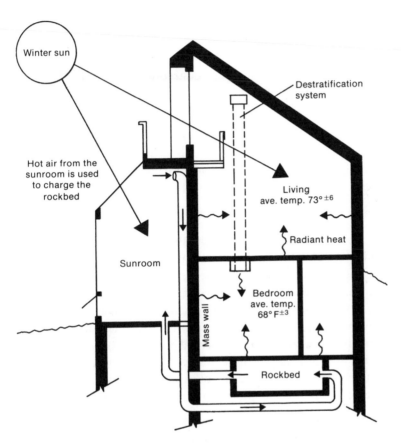

Winter sun

Destratification system

Hot air from the sunroom is used to charge the rockbed

Living
ave. temp. 73° ±6

Radiant heat

Sunroom

Mass wall

Bedroom
ave. temp.
68° F±3

Rockbed

Figure 5.15
Building section of Franta residence showing the forced convection system.

high in the sun room is transported to thermal storage under the floor on the lower level. The heat conducts through the floor and radiates into the rooms on the lower level.

High in the upper level are inlets to a destratification system. The warm air is drawn through the inlets into ducts with fans and is redistributed in the lower level.

5.3.6.2 Evaluation: Forced Convection and Controls The research and development on forced convection and controls has been very comprehensive. The design information has been very well documented. Technology dissemination has been initiated, but is still inadequate.

5.3.7 Analysis Methods of Energy Flows

A main focus of research related to the thermal energy distribution in buildings has been on the performance evaluation of buildings. Experience gained through the understanding of the behavior of existing buildings can be used both to predict the performance of future buildings and to devise strategies to make them more effective. Therefore, the major emphasis of passive solar research has been (1) on devising mathematical models that characterize heat flow and therefore thermal behavior, (2) the validation of these models by comparison with test results, and (3) the subsequent use of the models to investigate the influence of various design parameters. Significant research in this area is summarized in the following.

5.3.7.1 Project: Mathematical Models of Heat Flow Institution: Los Alamos National Laboratory; principal investigator: J. Douglas Balcomb.

Project Description The relationship of analytical modeling is indicated in the schematic diagram of figure 5.16. The logical progression of activity flows from left to right in this schematic beginning with the experimental results obtained in test models, special experiments, or monitored buildings. Based on these results and known physical principles, analytical models are developed and validated. The models can be used for sensitivity analysis, to develop simplified prediction methods, and to explore the relationship between passive solar and conservation strategies (Balcomb, 1983c).

As reported by the Los Alamos National Laboratory, the response of a building to any type of heat input is simulated by solving a set of differential equations that describe heat flow from point to point within the building. It is suggested that one first select a reasonably small set of elements within

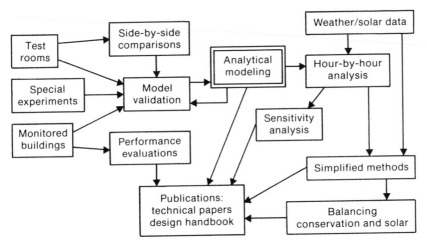

Figure 5.16
Schematic design of key elements fo the analytical modeling at the Los Alamos National
Laboratory.

the building whose temperatures will be calculated. Elements that can be
expected to be at about the same temperature can be lumped together in
one element. Massive portions expected to be at rather different temperatures should be characterized with different elements.

After making this selection, the energy analyst or designer can then write
an ordinary differential equation that describes the heat balance for each
element. This heat balance includes heat flow to neighboring elements by
radiation, conduction or convection, solar energy input, and other heat
inputs. This set of differential equations can then be solved as an initial
value problem with several independent variables including solar gain,
outside temperature, and thermostat setting. Auxiliary heat input is adjusted
to maintain a desired temperature of one or more of the elements.

Los Alamos has illustrated that the simulation of the energy use in
building interiors can be a powerful tool due to the tremendous amount of
information of thermal behavior that is revealed. The information that can
be learned is limited primarily by the time and patience of the analyst. As
a research tool, the simulation of the energy use in buildings is superb.
However, as a design tool, simulation has had very serious drawbacks.
It has been time consuming and requires a computer and computer opera-
tors—often not part of a normal architectural office. However, with the

rapidly accelerating use of microcomputers, architectural practice is changing and computers are and will continue to be used more in architectural offices.

Los Alamos also concludes that another difficulty with simulation is the sheer mass of output information. Of course, the output can be limited if desired. However, it appears unnecessary to perform extensive calculations in pursuit of one number, perhaps the annual auxiliary heat, before repeating the calculations.

Los Alamos has conducted a validation program of the simulation activities. The primary puropse of the validation has been to assure that the algorithms contained in the simulations models are in reasonable conformance with the physics of what is occurring in the building. A straightforward method is to compare simulation results point by point with measured values in a structure. Los Alamos has conducted the validation procedure with very favorable results (Reisfeld and Neeper, 1980).

The Los Alamos report concludes that the basic physics of energy flows in buildings is well understood and that the behavior of the basic passive solar heating types is very predictable given the knowledge of the relevant climatic conditions and other factors influencing the building load. Therefore, Los Alamos suggests that it is unlikely that further refinements and accuracy are warranted by the inherent uncertainties of weather and occupancy characteristics. These remarks apply to direct gain thermal storage walls and sunspaces geometry and are indirectly related to the thermal energy distribution in building interiors.

5.3.7.2 Project: Single-Room Heat Balance for Building Heat Transfer
Institution: National Bureau of Standards; principal investigator: B. A. Peavy.

Project Description A single-room heat balance was developed by the National Bureau of Standards (NBS) to provide a more precise computational tool than what was currently available. The primary purpose for this tool is to evaluate the effects of the approximations presently used in computer programs on the determination of building, heating, and cooling loads. Specific algorithms to be incorporated in the room balance concern radiation-shape factors, temperature differences, dependent convection heat transfer coefficients, simulated room masses, and an interactive methodology for the determination of room temperatures.

Heat transfer algorithms were published by the National Bureau of Standards (Peavy, 1981) and are intended to be used in part or whole for the purpose of determining heat exchange within a room. For comparing different analytical techniques dealing with heat exchange in a room, the effects of external and internal heat balance algorithms on the results should be distinguished. To perform such comparisons the NBS recommends a simple model be used that simulated four wall surfaces, a flat roof, and a floor raised from the ground level so that all six envelope surfaces are exposed to the environment. With this model, comparisons of the method proposed by NBS can be made with other methods.

NBS concludes its research by suggesting that the iterative solution for the surface and air temperatures offers a method by which the more exact algorithms may be used whereby a computation time savings is evident when compared to other methods of solution. A computer program using this feature is possible.

5.3.7.3 Project: Calculation of Interroom Air Movement   Institution: National Bureau of Standards; principal investigator: George N. Walton.

Project Description   This model, calculation of interroom air movement, has been incorporated into a comprehensive loads-predicting computer program (Walton, 1981). Air flows, room temperatures, and heating loads for a typical building under different conditions of environment and with various construction features were computed.

The calculations show the feasibility of detailed multiroom air movement analysis. They also indicate that when the interroom openings of a low-rise structure are large compared to the envelope openings, the infiltration and total load can be accurately and more quickly computed by assuming no resistance to air flow between rooms. This property will also allow simplified calculations for high-rise buildings with many rooms. Methods are proposed for handling more complex air-flow phenomena.

The primary objective of the work by NBS is to develop a research-oriented building loads analysis computer program. The program is to include a sufficient variety of building features to allow parametric studies of the interactions of any proposed algorithms with the many complex features present in real buildings.

This computer program is of significant value to a design community. However, validation of the program needs to continue and is planned by NBS.

5.3.7.4   Project: Effects of Internal Gains   Institution: Solar Energy Research Institute; principal investigators: Craig Christensen and Robert Perkins.

Project Description   The Solar Energy Research Institute (SERI) has investigated the effects of internal gain assumptions in building energy calculations (Christensen and Perkins, 1981). The utilizations of direct solar gains in building interiors can be affected by operational profiles such as schedules for internal gains, thermostat controls, and ventilation rates. Building energy analysis methods use various assumptions for these profiles. The research by SERI describes the effects of typical internal gain assumptions in energy calculations.

Heating and cooling loads from simulations using the DOE 2.1 computer code are compared to various internal gain inputs: typical hourly profiles, constant average profiles, and zero gain profiles. Prototype single-family detached and multifamily attached residential units are studied for various levels of insulation and infiltration. Small detached commercial buildings and attached zones in large commercial buildings are studied with various levels of internal gains.

The results of the SERI study indicate that calculations of annual heating and cooling loads are sensitive to internal gains but in most cases are relatively insensitive to hourly variations in internal gains.

5.3.7.5   Evaluation: Analysis Methods of Energy Flows   The research and development of analysis methods of energy flows has been extensive in small test buildings. Several methods are available in the private sector. The work on analysis methods, especially simple-to-use and relatively accurate tools, regarding multizone, multilevel large buildings has just begun. Further, the validation of the developing programs needs to be completed.

Analysis methods that are design tools are needed. This activity is very important for the proper design of thermal distribution in buildings.

5.3.8   Thermal Comfort Conditions

The primary reason for distributing thermal energy in building interiors is to achieve thermal comfort conditions for the occupants. Therefore, most of the discussions presented in this section are indirectly related to thermal comfort. Much work on thermal comfort preceded 1972. Work in the thermal comfort research conducted in the 1970s is still continuing.

5.3.8.1   Project: Analysis of Thermal Comfort   Institution: National Bureau of Standards; principal investigator: S. Liu.

Project Description   An analytical investigation was conducted by the National Bureau of Standards on the thermal comfort conditions in a passive solar heated residence. The National Bureau of Standards load determination program was used to simulate the indoor thermal environment of an actual passive solar residence. The relevant thermal comfort parameters such as the space air temperature, mean radiant temperatures, operative temperatures, radiant temperature asymmetry, and temperature drifts of the occupied zone were computed for a prime heating month.

These parameters were analyzed (Liu, 1981) in accordance with the criteria specified in ASHRAE 55–81. It was found that for the specific passive solar residence analyzed, the upper boundary of the comfort envelope can be exceeded (overheating) during a typical clear day in the transition month of April. The upper boundary will be exceeded during a typical clear day in the prime cooling month of August for a person in typical summer clothing, unless the average air movement in the occupied zone is increased above the natural circulation or the thermostat setting is reduced to a lower level.

The information found in this research as well as follow-up research (Liu, 1982) is typical of findings related to thermal comfort conditions. The information obtained by NBS and other federally funded work has progressed steadily and will be useful to the design community when designing solar buildings.

5.3.8.2   Evaluation: Thermal Comfort Conditions   Much of the basic research for thermal comfort has been conducted. But it is often difficult to convert this work to useful design information. The fundamentals of thermal comfort are well understood by several researchers and some building designers. Much information is available for use in the design process. Other research that deals with the variety of issues of thermal comfort in complex spaces is almost impossible to convert to simple and quickly usable design information. Therefore, it is concluded that extensive research in this area is not needed and that any future activities be oriented toward the development and technology transfer activities regarding the fundamentals of thermal comfort usable in the design process.

5.3.9   Indoor Air Pollution

The quality of indoor air has become a major issue in recent years. The source of the problem is not so much the distribution of energy through building interiors but rather building materials and other internal factors that cause pollution of the indoor air quality. As a result, there is a concern to assure the proper ventilation and provision of adequate fresh air into building interiors. This obviously has an indirect relationship to the thermal energy distribution in building interiors and the resulting energy performance. Since this is an indirect issue with respect to the main topic, a thorough discussion of indoor air pollution will not be presented, but only mentioned as an important concern.

Research on the health implications of pollutants emitted from new materials in building interiors and the reduction in ventilation rates in order to conserve energy has only just begun. The American Society of Heating, Refrigerating and Air Conditioning Engineers (ASHRAE) has taken a strong position (ASHRAE, 1982) on the federal role in regard to indoor air quality. ASHRAE believes that private interest alone cannot perform the research to identify problems and develop their general solutions. ASHRAE suggests that public policy options for improving and maintaining the quality of air in indoor environments must be developed. Once the research has identified needs for better solution for improving health, ASHRAE believes the private sector will respond to these needs with improved innovative and cost-effective solutions.

The quality of indoor air is influenced by outdoor air quality, building structure, consumer products, appliances, building materials, occupant activities, and other factors. The government, industry, professional societies, and individuals all share in the responsibility for the quality of indoor environments. ASHRAE has issued a position statement on indoor air quality and suggests a strong federal role in the research and development of solutions to improve our indoor air quality and to improve understanding of the health impacts.

In the late 1970s and early 1980s a variety of technical papers was presented at federally sponsored conferences in regard to indoor air pollution in energy-conserving and solar buildings (Scott and Scott, 1980). The American Institute of Architects has also sponsored major conferences on this topic (Guerin and Butler, 1982). One of the major issues of indoor air pollution in energy-conserving and solar buildings is the buildup of radon gas. Radon gas, often produced from stone, concrete, and other materials used as thermal storage, has the potential to accumulate to unhealthy levels in tight buildings with low infiltration rates. It is anticipated that research on this issue will be continued by the federal sector and will produce informative results.

5.3.9.1 Evaluation: Indoor Air Pollution The minimizing of indoor air pollution is of the utmost importance. The issues are extremely complex and of great importance. Much is understood about basic pollution problems, but a significant amount of research will need to be continued as new materials produce more pollutants and as energy costs rise, forcing a desire to minimize the conditioning (heating and cooling) of fresh outside air into buildings. New methods of addressing these issues are being developed by both public and private sources. More effective and economically feasible solutions need to be developed in the near term if solar technology and conservation measures are going to have a major impact on reducing fossil fuel energy use in new buildings.

5.3.10 Furnishings

The types, size, and characteristics of furnishings for interior environments have an effect on the thermal distributions within buildings. Again, this may have a direct or indirect impact on the thermal energy distribution. Small amounts of research have been conducted on this topic.

5.3.10.1 Project: Thermal Conductivity of Upholstery Textiles Institution: Miami University; principal investigators: Denise Guerin and Sarah Butler.

Project Description The Department of Home Economics and Consumer Sciences of Miami University in Ohio identified upholstery textiles that are commercially available to residents of passive solar homes to be tested in order to determine their sunlight resistance and thermal conductivity properties. Those textiles with the highest rating for sunlight resistance could then be suggested for use in direct-gain passive solar buildings. The project (Guerin and Butler, 1982) was designed to investigate the effects of exposure to daylight on currently available upholstery textiles.

Two specific objectives were

1. to determine which currently available upholstery textiles are most resistant to exposure to the daylight received in the Ohio climate, and

2. to determine which currently available upholstery textiles are reflective and conductive of heat.

The results of the investigation were published through the American Solar Energy Society. It was concluded that further implications for future research could include more statistical analysis to provide data leading to highly developed results.

5.3.10.2   Evaluation: Furnishings   The work in this field has been important, but is less significant than many of the other categories presented in this chapter. In a way, furnishings are addressed in the research of most categories above, with some projects specifically addressing the impact of furnishings on thermal distribution related to a specific topic (i.e., convection or indoor pollution). Therefore, it is anticipated that minor research and development will continue but that any major funding specifically for such activities will need to be federally supported.

5.4   Summary

Obviously, important research has been conducted on the thermal energy distribution within building interiors. But there is far less research in this area than in many other areas in solar energy technology. However, the research that has been conducted will serve a vital role in the enhancement of our understanding of thermal energy transfer in building interiors. It is evident that much of the research has been conducted in the heat transfer or heat flow within buildings on a small scale. Currently, much is understood about the energy distribution within one zone or small multizone buildings. Further research is planned to improve our understanding of these simple applications and to study the implications for larger multizone buildings. Since most larger buildings require forced convection through mechanical and electrical systems, the energy distribution is fairly well understood by conventional engineering practices.

This topic is obviously directly connected to the previous chapter on thermal energy storage in building interiors. It is understood that the reader will review both chapters to understand better the impact of thermal energy storage and distribution in building interiors.

Some items, such as daylighting and natural ventilation, are thoroughly discussed in other chapters and were mentioned in this chapter to identify their importance. These items are not intentionally being downplayed, rather, readers have been referred to the other chapters for consideration of these items to avoid redundancies.

It is apparent that there is a scarcity of quantitative information in the field of thermal energy distribution that is useful for designers of building interiors. The continuation of significant research that was identified in this chapter is very important in order that building designers may improve their understanding of the implications of thermal energy distribution in building interiors.

References

American Institute of Architects, *Energy in Architecture: Level 3a, Applications*, Washington, DC: AIA, 1981.

ASHRAE Committee on Indoor Air Quality, "Position Statement on Indoor Air Quality," *ASHRAE Journal*, American Society of Heating, Refrigerating, and Air Conditioning Engineers, Atlanta, GA, Aug. 1982, pp. 46–47.

Balcomb, J. D., "Heating Remote Rooms in Passive Solar Buildings," *Proceedings of the International Solar Energy Society Solar World Forum*, Brighton, England, Aug. 23–28, Oxford: Pergamon Press, 1982, pp. 1835–1839.

Balcomb, J. D., *Heat Storage and Distribution Inside Passive Solar Buildings*, LA-9694-MS, Los Alamos National Laboratory, 1983a.

Balcomb, J. D., "Heat Storage and Distribution inside Passive Solar Buildings," *Proceedings of the International Conference on Passive and Low-Energy Architecture, Crete, Greece*, LA-UR-83-1114, Los Alamos National Laboratory, July 1983.

Balcomb, J. D., "Passive Research and Practice," *Proceedings of the International Congress on Building Energy Management—II*, May 30–June 3, 1983, Ames, Iowa.

Balcomb, J. D., "Passive Solar Heating Research," *Advances in Solar Energy*, Boulder, CO: American Solar Energy Society, 1983b, TP265–303.

Balcomb, J. D., and Kenjiro Yamaguchi, "Heat Distribution by Natural Convection," *Proceedings of the 8th National Passive Solar Conference*, Boulder, CO: American Solar Energy Society, 1983.

Bohn, M. S., *Experimental Study of 3-Dimensional Natural Convection at High Rayleigh Number*, SERI/TR-252-1912, Golden, CO: Solar Energy Research Institute, June 1983.

Bohn, M. S., D. A. Olson, and A. T. Kirkpatrick, "Experimental Study of Three-Dimensional Natural Convection at High Rayleigh Number," ASME 83-H-12, 1983 ASME-JSME Thermal Engineering Joint Conference, Honolulu, Hawaii.

Boyack, B. E., and D. W. Kearney, "Heat Transfer by Laminar Natural Convection in Low Aspect Ratio Cavities," ASME 72-HT-52, 1972.

Brown, W. G., and K. R. Solvason, "Natural Convection through Rectangular Openings in Partitions Part I: Vertical Partitions," *International Journal of Heat and Mass Transfer*, Vol. 5, 1962, pp. 859–868.

Carroll, J. A., "An MRT Method of Computing Radiant Energy Exchange in Rooms," *Proceedings of Systems Simulation and Economic Analysis*, San Diego, CA: Jan. 23–25, 1980, Solar Energy Research Institute Report SERI/TP-351-431, 1980, pp. 343–348.

Catton, I., and D. K. Edwards, "Effect of Side Walls on Natural Convection between Horizontal Plates Heated from Below," *Journal of Heat Transfer*. Vol. 89, 1967, pp. 295–299.

Chao, B. T., and G. L. Wedekind, "Similarity Criteria for Thermal Modeling of Spacecraft," *Journal of Spacecraft*, Vol. 2, 1975.

Christensen, Craig and Robert Perkins, *Effects of Internal Gain Assumptions in Building Energy Calculations*, Report No. SERI/TP-721-1031, Golden, CO: Solar Energy Research Institute, Jan. 1981.

Conference on the Control of Solar Energy Systems for the Heating and Cooling of Buildings, Boston University, Boston, MA, Sept. 1978.

El Sherbiny, S. M., G. D. Raithby, and K. G. T. Hollands, "Heat Transfer by Natural Convection across Vertical and Inclined Air Layers," *Journal of Heat Transfer*, Vol. 104, 1982, pp. 96–102.

Emergy, A., and N. C. Chu, "Heat Transfer across Vertical Layers," *Journal of Heat Transfer*, Vol. 87, 1965, pp. 110–116.

Franta, G., et al., *Solar Design Workbook*, Golden, CO: Solar Energy Research Institute, 1981.

Franta, G., M. Connolly, and B. Winn, "Utility Impact and Thermal Performance of the Franta Residence," *Proceedings of the Sixth National Passive Solar Conference*, Boulder, CO: American Solar Energy Society, 1981.

Fujii, T. and H. Imura, "Natural Convection Heat Transfer from a Plate with Arbitrary Inclination," *International Journal of Heat and Mass Transfer*, Vol. 15, 1972, pp. 755–767.

Frey, D., M. McKinstry, and J. Swisher, *Installation Manual: SERI Class B Passive Solar Data Acquisition System*, Golden, CO: Solar Energy Research Institute, Feb. 1982.

Gadgil, A., "On Convective Heat Transfer in Building Energy Analysis," Ph. D. Thesis, Department of Physics, University of California, Berkeley, 1979 (also Lawrence Berkeley Laboratory Report LBL-10900).

Gadgil, A., F. Bauman, and R. Kammerud, "Natural Convection in Passive Solar Buildings: Experiments, Analysis, and Results," *Passive Solar Journal*, Vol. 1, 1982, pp. 28–40.

Gill, A. E., "The Boundary-Layer Regime for Convection in a Rectangular Cavity," *Journal of Fluid Mechanics*, Vol. 26, 1966, pp. 515–536.

Globe, S., and D. Dropkin, "Natural-Convection Heat Transfer in Liquids Confined by Two Horizontal Plates and Heated from Below," *Journal of Heat Transfer*, Vol. 81, No. 24, 1959.

Goldstein, R. J., and T. Y. Chu, "Thermal Convection in a Horizontal Layer of Air, *Progress in Heat and Mass Transfer*, Vol. 2, 1969, pp. 55–75.

Guerin, Denise A., and Sarah L. Butler, "Thermal Conductivity of Upholstery Textiles Following Exposure to Daylight," *Progress in Passive Solar Energy Systems*, Boulder, CO: American Solar Energy Society, 1982, pp. 623–626.

Haggard, K. L., et al., *Research Evaluation of a System of Natural Air Conditioning*, California Polytechnic State University, HUD Contract No. H 2026R, Jan. 1975.

Hay, H. R. and J. I. Yellott, "A Naturally Air Conditioned Building," *Mechanical Engineering*, Vol. 92, No. 1, Jan. 1970, pp. 19–23.

Hjertager, B. H., and B. F. Magnussen, "Numerical Prediction of Three Dimensional Turbulent Buoyant Flow in a Ventilated Room," *Heat Transfer and Turbulent Buoyant Convection*, Vol. II, edited by D. B. Spalding and N. Afgan, Hemisphere Publishing Corporation, 1977, pp. 429–441.

Hollands, K. G. T., G. D. Raithby, and L. Konicek, "Correlation Equations for Free Convection Heat Transfer of Horizontal Layers of Air and Water," *International Journal of Heat and Mass Transfer*, Vol. 18, 1975, pp. 879–884.

Inaba, H., N. Seki, S. Fukusaka, and K. Kanayama, "Natural Convective Heat Transfer in a Shallow Rectangular Cavity with Different End Temperatures," *Numerical Heat Transfer*, Vol. 4, 1981, pp. 459–468.

Jones, R. F., G. Dennehy, H. T. Ghaffari, and G. E. Munson, *Case Study of the Mastin Double-Envelope House*, Brookhaven National Laboratory Report BNL 51460, May 1981.

Judkoff, R., D. Wortman, R. O'Dougherty, and J. Burch, *A Methodology for Validating Building Energy Analysis Simulations*, Report No. SERI/TR-254-150, Golden, CO: Solar Energy Research Institute, August 1983.

Katzoff, S., *Similitude in Thermal Models of Spacecraft*, NASA, TND–1631, 1963.

Kirkpatrick, A. T., and M. S. Bohn, "High Rayleigh Number Natural Convection in an Enclosure Heated from Below and from the Sides," presented at the *ASME-AIChE National Heat Transfer Conference*, Seattle, WA, July 1983. SERI/TP-252-1907, Solar Energy Research Institute, Golden, CO: May 1983.

Kirkpatrick, A. T., and C. B. Winn, "A Frequency Response Technique for the Analysis of the Enclosure Temperature in Passive Solar Buildings," *Proceedings of the 1982 Annual Meeting of the American Solar Energy Society*, 1982, pp. 773–777.

Liu, S., *Analysis of Thermal Comfort in a Passive Solar Heated Residence*, Report No. NBSIR81-2393, U.S. Department of Commerce, National Bureau of Standards, Washington, DC, Nov. 1981.

Liu, S., *Thermal Comfort Conditions in the NBS/DOE Direct-Gain Passive Solar Test Facility*, Report No. NBSIR82-2621, U.S. Department of Commerce, National Bureau of Standards, Washington, DC, Dec. 1982.

Mallinson, G. D., and G. deVahl Davis, "Three Dimensional Natural Convection in a Box: A Numerical Study," *Journal of Fluid Mechanics*, Vol. 83, 1977, pp. 1–31.

Muncey, R. W. R., *Heat Transfer Calculations for Buildings*, London: Applied Science Publishers Ltd., 1979.

Nansteel, M., and R. Greif, "Natural Convection in Undivided and Partially Divided Rectangular Enclosures," *Journal of Heat Transfer*, Vol. 103, 1981, pp. 623–629.

Newell, M. E., and F. W. Schmidt, "Heat Transfer by Laminar Natural Convection within Rectangular Enclosures," *Journal of Heat Transfer*, Vol. 92, 1970, pp. 159–165.

Ostrach, S., "Natural Convection in Enclosures," *Advanced Heat Transfer*, Vol. 8, 1972.

Parczewski, K. I., and P. N. Renzi, "Scale Model Studies of Temperature Distributions in Internally Heated Enclosures," ASHRAE Paper No. 1854, June 1983.

Peavy, B. A., *Single Room Heat Balance for Building Heat Transfer*, Report No. NBSIR81-2321, U.S. Department of Commerce, National Bureau of Standards, Washington, DC, Nov. 1981.

Raithby, G. D., and K. G. T. Hollands, "A General Method of Obtaining Approximate Solutions for Laminar and Turbulent Free Convection Problems," *Advances in Heat Transfer*, Academic Press, Vol. 11, 1975, pp. 265–315.

Raithby, G. D., K. G. T. Hollands, and T. E. Unny, "Analysis of Heat Transfer by Natural Convection across Vertical Fluid Layers," *Journal of Heat Transfer*, Vol. 99, 1977, pp. 287–293.

Reisfeld, S. K., and D. A. Neeper, *Solar Energy Research at Los Alamos Scientific Laboratory: Oct. 1, 1979, to Mar. 31, 1980*, Los Alamos Scientific Laboratory, Report No. LA-8450-PR, Nov. 1980, pp. 20–23.

Richardson, R. W., and S. M. Berman, "Dynamic Similitude in Scale Models of Buildings," LBL-13262, funded by the U.S. Department of Energy, Aug. 1981.

Schwolsky, R., "Moisture in Buildings," *Solar Age Magazine*, 3-part series, Nov. 1980, Dec. 1980, Jan. 1981.

Scott, L. A., and M. G. Scott, "Indoor Air Pollution in Passive Structures," *Proceedings of the 5th National Passive Solar Conference*, Boulder, CO: American Solar Energy Society, 1980.

Shannon, R. L., "Thermal Scale Modeling of Radiation-Conduction-Convection Systems," *Journal of Spacecraft*, Vol. 10, No. 8, 1973.

Sherman, M., and D. Grimsrud, *Measurement of Infiltration Using Fan Pressurization and Other Data*, Berkeley, CA: Lawrence Barkeley Laboratory, Oct. 1980.

Shiralkar, G., A. Gadgil, and C. L. Tien, "High Rayleigh Number Convection in Shallow Enclosures with Different End Temperatures," *International Journal of Heat and Mass Transfer*, Vol. 24, 1981, pp. 1621–1629.

Simpkins, P. G., and T. D. Dudderar, "Convection in Rectangular Cavities with Differentially Heated End Walls," *Journal of Fluid Mechanics*, Vol. 110, 1981, pp. 433–456.

Strong, P. C., *Continuous Infiltration Monitoring System*, Berkeley, CA: Lawrence Berkeley Laboratory, 1981.

Ternoey, S., L. Bickle, C. Robbins, R. Busch, and K. McCord, *The Design of Energy-Responsive Commercial Buildings*, funded by Solar Energy Research Institute, New York: John Wiley and Sons, Inc., 1984.

Tichy, J., and A. Gadgil, "High Rayleigh Number Laminar Convection in Low Aspect Ratio Enclosures with Adiabatic Horizontal Walls and Differentially Heated Vertical Walls," *Journal of Heat Transfer*, Vol. 104, 1982, pp. 103–110.

Walton, G. N., *Calculation of Inter-room Air Movement for Multi-Room Building Energy Analysis*, Report No. NBSIR81-2404, U.S. Department of Commerce, National Bureau of Standards, Washington, DC, Nov. 1981.

Weber, D. D., "Similitude Modeling of Natural Convection Heat Transfer through an Aperture in Passive Solar Heated Buildings," Ph. D. Thesis, University of Idaho, LA-8385-T, 1980.

Weber, D. D., and R. J. Kearney, "Natural Convective Heat Transfer through an Aperture in Passive Solar Heated Buildings," *Proceedings of the Fifth National Passive Solar Conference*, Amherst, MA, Oct. 19–26, 1980 (Publication Office of the AS/ISES, Newark, DE), pp. 1037–1041.

Weber, D. D., W. O. Wray, and R. Kearney, "LASL Similarity Studies: Part II. Similitude Modeling of Interzone Heat Transfer by Natural Convection," *Proceedings of the Fourth National Passive Solar Conference*, Kansas City, MO, Oct. 3–5, 1979 (Publication Office of the AS/ISES, Newark, DE), pp. 231–234.

Wortman, D. N., J. Burch, and R. Judkoff, "A Multi-Zone Infiltration Monitoring System," *Progress in Passive Solar Energy Systems*, Boulder, CO: American Solar Energy Society, 1982, pp. 767–711.

Wray, W. O., and D. D. Weber, "LASL Similarity Studies: Part I. Hot Zone/Cold Zone: A Quantitative Study of Natural Heat Distribution Mechanisms in Passive Solar Buildings," *Proceedings of the Fourth National Passive Solar Conference*, Kansas City, MO, Oct. 3–5, 1979 (Publication Office of the AS/ISES, Newark, DE), pp. 226–230.

Yellott, J., *Solar Oriented Architecture*, Arizona State University, Washington, DC: AIA Research Corporation, 1975, pp. 111–114.

6 Architectural Integration: Residential and Light Commercial Buildings

Edward Mazria

6.1 Introduction

This chapter shows the progression of solar architectural integration from ancient to modern times and discusses advances in the state of the art. Sixteen figures illustrate the varying levels of architectural integration, from solar system components mounted on the roof to solar systems comprised of architectural building elements, i.e., walls, floor, roof, finish materials, and fenestrations (figure 6.1).

The architectural integration of most active solar energy systems is analogous to the integration of mechanical and electrical equipment in the building design process. As with other applied building technologies, active solar systems integration either falls within the specific expertise of the mechanical and electrical engineer or is practiced as an entirely separate discipline. However, solar and other natural energy systems need not be considered solely as separate mechanical systems, but can be approached as part of the architectural design itself, with solar energy strategies considered throughout the design process and influencing many design decisions. In many instances a combination of both approaches is appropriate in the design of a building.

Most of the modern buildings discussed in this chapter use solar energy systems designed as part of the buildings' architectural components, and are skin-load dominated; i.e., exterior climate conditions determine energy consumption for heating and cooling. Internal heat gains from occupants, lights, and equipment do not significantly affect the energy consumption of these buildings. Architectural integration of solar systems in predominantly internally load-dominated, and larger commercial buildings are covered in chapter 7.

6.2 An Overview of Early Solar Integration

Early architectural expressions incorporating solar concepts appear to have been spiritual rather than thermal in nature. However, the archeoastronomical structures of ancient peoples provide us with amazingly accurate examples of the architectural incorporation of sun-earth geometries. One well-known example shown in figure 6.2 is Stonehenge, which

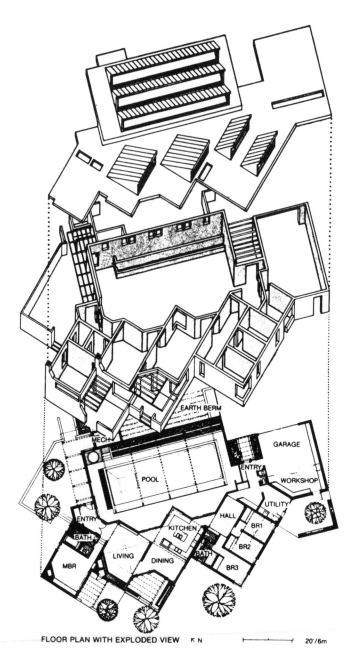

FLOOR PLAN WITH EXPLODED VIEW ⤢ N ├──────┤ 20′/6m

Figure 6.1
Isometric of Stockebrand residence. Source: Mazria (1979).

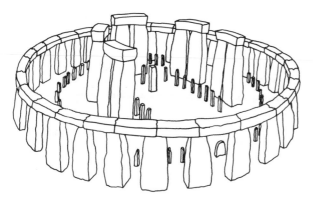

Figure 6.2
Stonehenge. Source: Franta and Olsen (1978).

dates back to 2700 B.C. and is located in central southern England. Stonehenge consists of stone monoliths each weighing up to 50 tons (907.2 kg) and placed in a circle 98 ft (29.6 m) in diameter. Additional stone monoliths are precisely located inside the circular structure to facilitate astronomical observations of the sun and moon. Stonehenge thus architecturally integrated the diverse alignments of the sun and moon within a symmetrical structure.

Archeological excavations in ancient Egypt similarly reveal deliberate solar and lunar architectural alignments. The Temple of Rameses II at Abu Simbel was situated so that on October 21, 1260 B.C. (the 30-year jubilee of Rameses II's reign), the rising sun penetrated the axis of the temple and illuminated three pharaoh god effigies located 180 ft (55 m) inside. The ancient Egyptians also architecturally integrated solar thermal and daylighting principles in building design. Masonry construction buffered interior spaces against the fierce heat and intense sunlight characteristic of a hot climate with little rainfall. Homes constructed of mud and wood-beamed roofs, and thick mud brick walls with few openings, effectively delayed and reduced the impact of the sun and heat until evening when outdoor temperatures were cooler. Small rooms in these houses typically centered around a central hall or living room. The high living room roof contained a clerestory that both daylit the space and facilitated air movement, thereby cooling the house. In evening, when outdoor temperatures dropped, the temperature difference between warm indoor room air and

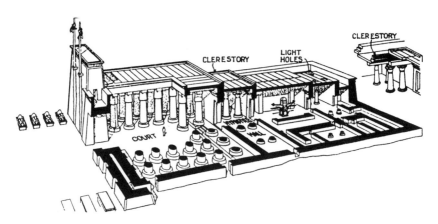

Figure 6.3
Temple of Khons, Karnak. Source: Fletcher (1963).

cooler outdoor air caused a "stack effect": warm air escaped through the clerestory openings in the living room while cooler outdoor air entered simultaneously through openings located low in the building. Similar thermal and daylighting strategies were employed in temple design. Temples constructed of stone with massive unbroken exterior walls admitted sufficient light to interior spaces through clerestory openings or small light holes (unglazed skylights) in the roof (figure 6.3). The clerestory openings, fitted with stone grilles, kept most direct sunlight from entering the building (Fletcher, 1963).

Solar design principles are also evident in ancient Greek architecture. Firewood was scarce in many parts of Greece by the fifth century B.C., so homes were built to take advantage of the sun for winter heating. Houses made of stone located main rooms opening onto south-facing courtyards. The masonry walls and floors stored a portion of the solar energy entering these rooms through the south facade, thermally tempering the interior environment into the evening. In summer, overhanging roofs shaded the south-facing interior spaces from the less-welcome high sun.

Wood was also scarce for first-century B.C. Romans. This undoubtedly encouraged them to adopt the Greek techniques of integrating solar energy into building design and then advancing the state of the art by using glass and other transparent window coverings to trap heat more effectively in homes, baths, and greenhouses. The importance of the integration of solar energy into early Roman architecture is underscored by the fact that, for the first time in recorded history, laws were enacted protecting a building's access to sunlight (Butti and Perlin, 1980).

Despite heavy Roman inroads into solar architecture, for nearly 1,000 years after the fall of Rome, solar principles were largely ignored in developing European cities. However, folk architecture throughout the world continued to demonstrate an ingenuity for climate control through building design. For example, in the predominantly overheated arid regions of the Middle East, settlements of compact groupings of buildings were formed to lessen the thermal impact of the sun and to block sand-laden winds and undesirable airborne dust. Buildings shaded each other to minimize exposure to solar radiation. Houses in this region were constructed of stone and mud, and had thick walls with small exterior openings, and domed or vaulted roofs. Most rooms opened to a shaded outdoor court-yard where many day-to-day family activities took place. The courtyard offered privacy and shelter from the wind and, when landscaped with trees, plants, and water elements, offered a cool shaded refuge from the heat of the day. In many courtyard houses throughout the middle East, unique wind towers, or "badgirs" as they are called in Iran, assisted in cooling interior spaces by natural convection. Airflow was either through the wind tower into the house or from the house and exhausted through the tower depending upon which windows in the house were opened. Today in the town of Hyderabad, India, the wind tower remains the prominent archi-tectural feature that dominates the town's skyline.

Traditional building design elsewhere in the world illustrates the utiliza-tion of air movement for cooling. In the warm, humid regions of Thailand, houses of wood and thatch have steeply pitched roofs and raised floors to facilitate natural ventilation. Similarly, in the warm, humid region sur-rounding Maracaibo Lake in Venezuela, Indian buildings, or "Churuatas," have used air movement for cooling for hundreds of years. These wood-framed structures with nonload-bearing walls have large and pointed thatched conical roofs. The roof, the dominant visual and structural ele-ment, protects against heavy rain while facilitating air movement between the entry doors and vents located high in the roof (Hutchinson, 1981).

In the United States, the building and community design of the ruins of southwestern pueblo villages demonstrates a sophisticated understanding of the sun's daily and seasonal movement. For example, the builders of Pueblo Bonito, an archaeological site in northwestern New Mexico, inte-

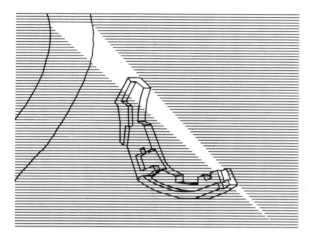

Figure 6.4
Pueblo Bonito. Source: Franta and Olsen (1978).

grated both astronomical solar alignments and solar thermal concepts into the design of the pueblo. The multileveled pueblo was oriented to the south with upper floor levels terraced back to the north. Daytime work and family activities took place on these warm southern terraces in winter. The interior climate of the building was tempered by heat stored during the daytime in the south-facing masonry walls and roof. As illustrated in figure 6.4 Pueblo Bonito was also designed to record the sunrise of the summer solstice (Franta and Olsen, 1978).

Early settlers in the United States also incorporated many solar and energy conservation techniques in their building designs. New England colonists developed a unique house type, "the salt box," derived from traditional English sources but adapted to the local climate. The typical salt box design consisted of two stories along the front (south facade) and one story to the rear of the building (north facade), with the roof sloping steeply to the rear, providing protection from the winter winds. The front of the building contained the main rooms, with a large north-facing kitchen and pantry in the back. As was customary with this house type, the upper floor projected beyond the lower floor, shading the south-facing first floor windows in summer.

Later, from the time of the Industrial Revolution to 1973, technological advances such as the introduction of mass production, iron, electricity, the elevator, mechanical heating, ventilating, and air conditioning significantly affected American building design. During this period, interior space could be inexpensively and adequately conditioned by mechanical means. Commercial and industrial buildings increased in size and enclosed more interior space with less building perimeter and exterior surface area. Housing design broke with traditional regional responses to climate in favor of standardized plans and materials for use in all locations.

The role of the architect similarly changed with the establishment of the engineering profession in France in the early 1800s. In 1840, John Ruskin, a prominent English architectural critic, stated that the profession should concern itself with "only those characters of edifice which are above and beyond its common use." Since then, the engineer has progressively assumed more design control over both the building's structure and mechanical environmental control systems.

This period also produced a number of individuals who either researched solar design principles or designed and constructed actual buildings integrating solar design concepts. For example, in the early 1900s, architect William Atkinson of Boston conducted a series of experiments confirming his theory on the passive solar heating potential of south glazing, which later formed the basis for his book *The Orientation of Buildings or Planning for Sunlight*. Consequently, a number of "solar houses" were actually constructed in the Chicago area in the late 1930s and 1940s, incorporating large south-facing windows protected by deep overhangs for summer shading. The Sloan House, a solar house designed by architect George Fred Kick in 1941, was such a success that its owner, Chicago real estate developer Howard Sloan, built a 30-unit housing development in Glenview, IL, the first solar-oriented community in the modern United States. In 1947, Libby Owens Ford Glass Company published a book entitled *Your Solar House* in which 48 prominent architects prepared designs for direct-gain solar houses for each state in the country. Most of the designs incorporated south-facing double glazing, but few recognized the importance of building mass as a means of providing heat storage.

Among those in the early twentieth-century building design community, only part of the thermodynamics of what we now call "passive" solar heating was understood. Although the principles of orientation and solar heat gain were reasonably well-grasped, the importance of heat storage and distribution was not generally known. By the late 1940s energy became cheaper and mechanical heating and ventilating systems became increasingly popular. As a result, interest in solar architecture declined.

6.3 Solar Experimentation

By 1965, interest in solar architectural integration began to emerge. Inventor Harold Hay and engineer John Yellott of Arizona State University constructed a prototype passively heated and cooled test building using a roof pond of water bags. Felix Trombe and Jacques Michel, the French engineer and architect team, constructed buildings in the Pyrenees to investigate solar heat gain, storage, and distribution (AS/ISES, 1976). These examples, however, were not well-known within the American architectural community (figure 6.5).

Finally, in the early 1970s with the onset of the oil embargo, interest in solar and alternative energy technology virtually exploded. This interest was strongly encouraged by large-scale federal energy research and development programs. Many buildings were constructed incorporating solar and other energy-conserving strategies. These experiments and prototypes represented a large variety of building styles and sizes, construction techniques, and energy schemes. However, only a small part of the American architectural community participated in these endeavors. Homeowners, do-it-yourselfers, tinkerers, academics, grassroots community organiza-

Figure 6.5
Attached housing units with thermal storage walls, Odeillo, France. Source: AIA Research Corp. (1976).

tions, and students were the primary participants. In many cases, these efforts were part of a widespread philosophy aimed at a democratization of energy production in the United States through some measure of self-sufficiency. These thoughts also closely followed contemporaneous environmental and ecological movements. The state of passive solar heating knowledge resulted from determined efforts of this group of dedicated designers and builders. Relatively little scientific research included passive solar heating and cooling projects. In the absence of such research, most learning occurred through experiences with various existing private projects. Finding a client or benefactor and designing and constructing a building enabled one to learn from one's mistakes. Such an experimental process yielded the available information on passive solar building and design concepts up to that time. Sorely lacking in the early 1970s was a thorough understanding of how solar buildings and systems worked, with only limited guidelines existing for sizing active solar collectors and water storage tanks. Unfortunately, there were no simple guidelines or consistent rules for sizing, glazing, and heat storage materials in passive solar buildings. Understandably, this resulted in hesitation on the part of the building and design community to adopt this solar technology.

6.4 Federal Solar Programs

In 1976 the Energy Research and Development Administration held the first National Passive Solar Heating and Cooling Conference in Albuquerque, NM. This conference focused on the state of the art of passive solar building design with presentations covering virtually every then-known passive solar project in the United States and abroad (AS/ISES, 1976). At the Fourth National Passive Solar Conference in 1979, the importance of passive solar integration as a design issue was recognized, and a section of the conference devoted to emerging architecture was established (ISES, 1979).

By the late 1970s and early 1980s, federal solar programs were oriented toward studies of passive solar building and test cells, development of passive solar products, performance monitoring, and the development of passive solar heating, cooling, and daylighting design guidelines, rules of thumb, and evaluation techniques. Guidelines were developed for sizing various systems or system elements, e.g., the thickness of a masonry thermal storage wall and glazing areas for direct-gain spaces (Rush, 1980,

1981). New products such as insulating curtains, water tubes, sun control devices, transparent insulation, and exterior insulation systems were being tested and marketed. In 1980 the Los Alamos National Laboratory in New Mexico published volume II of *The Passive Solar Design Handbook* containing both guidelines for designing passive solar systems and techniques for evaluating system performance. In 1982, volume III of the same book was published and included 94 different passive solar system configurations, including 28 solar sunspace configurations. In 1981, the first International Passive and Hybrid Cooling Conference was held in Miami Beach, FL, and in 1984 the First Daylighting Conference was held in Phoenix, AZ. The federal solar program helped to advance the state of the art in passive solar design and product development; it also introduced these new concepts and products to the architectural profession and the general public.

6.5 Architectural Integration

In the late 1970s the architectural profession followed the public's shift from broad environmental concerns toward the more urgent matters of energy conservation. This rekindled an awareness that energy and resource conservation were the prime generators of architectural form prior to the modern movement. During this time energy conservation became a consideration in the design process. Energy implications also had some impact on the exterior building envelope, HVAC (heating, ventilating, and air conditioning) systems, lighting, and many other building components. Today, architectural firms are now likely to include at least some mention of energy design strategies in a client presentation. An information and methodology base has resulted from the wealth of energy research, innovation, and design produced over the last decade.

Until recently, the architectural profession emphasized the aesthetic aspects of the design process while largely ignoring energy concerns. However, the larger architectural community now acknowledges energy issues while the energy-conscious community has broadened its aesthetic aspirations (Balcomb, Hedstrom, and Moore, 1979).

In 1979, for example, *Progressive Architecture* magazine devoted its April issue to energy concerns in architecture and continue to publish an energy issue every year. In 1972 the Owens-Corning Fiberglass Company instituted its well-publicized annual Energy Conservation Awards program, and over the past years many prominent architects have participated.

Also during this period the American Institute of Architects recognized energy as a major design issue in architecture and developed a series of workshops in energy-conscious design as part of its architecture professional development program.

In early passive solar buildings, solar system integration dominated building design to the exclusion of more traditional architectural concerns. For example, buildings incorporating direct gain and thermal storage wall systems were designed as simple three-dimensional configurations of system diagrams. In most direct-gain buildings the entire south wall was glazed, with little or no glazing incorporated into the roof, east, west, or north walls. Because the glass-to-mass surface area ratio was usually very high, these early buildings experienced large interior diurnal temperature fluctuations and daytime overheating. With the entire south wall glazed, interior spaces became intolerably bright and visually, as well as thermally, uncomfortable. Fortunately, many of the problems associated with early passive solar buildings disappeared as designers experimented with various systems and building configurations, and as researchers published more extensive and reliable technical information.

Buildings became more responsive to both thermal and traditional architectural criteria. Systems were chosen, and at times combined, with specific design criteria. In residential design, for example, thermal storage walls incorporating direct-gain glazing provided more balanced heating over the day, i.e., direct gain for early morning warm-up and the thermal storage wall for nighttime heating.

In 1979, after extensive monitoring of his own home, J. Douglas Balcomb discovered that heat collected in the sunspace of his home was transferred to the rest of the house primarily by convection. In 1981, he published a paper titled "Performance Summary of the Balcomb Solar Home" (Balcomb, 1983). This paper dispelled the popular belief that heating from a mass-backed sunspace with a convective building connection, such as a door or window, was accomplished primarily by radiation from the mass wall. In fact, the mass wall served primarily to dampen daily temperature fluctuations in the greenhouse. This discovery led to numerous studies published by Los Alamos National Laboratories regarding the movement of heat within buildings by natural convection (Vonier, 1983).

Since 1973 many new design tools have been developed and integrated into the architectural design process. Both simplified and computerized energy analysis tools originally developed under federal research initiatives are now used in the private sector. These tools also include traditional design techniques such as three-dimensional scale models and calculation procedures to predict, for example, the effects of daylighting in a particular design. Strategies for wall and roof aperture design evaluated and publicized under federal solar programs are now widely used (Balcomb et al., 1980). These include the "light shelf" for enhanced daylighting of perimeter spaces and various clerestory configurations for distributing sunlight to interior spaces (figure 6.6).

The development of new products in response to passive solar design strategies is affecting residential and small commercial/institutional buildings. For example, stucco and stuccolike finish systems are gaining popularity again in this country as an inexpensive method for insulating and finishing the exterior surface of masonry construction.

Exterior sunscreens and shading devices, at one time unnecessary because of the availability of cheap energy, are also experiencing a rebirth. They are being integrated into building facades for shading and daylighting. They can also be used to redirect sunlight deep into interior spaces.

New research concerning the effect of mass distribution and surface area in passive solar applications has also led to a wider use of masonry in both residential and small commercial/institutional buildings. In the late 1970s, as more reliable information about the effects of various mass configurations became available, the design of interior mass distribution and surface color changed in passive solar buildings. For example, it was initially believed that masonry mass in a direct-gain space should be at least one foot thick, located in direct sunlight, and painted a dark color. In contrast, recent studies show that uniformly distributed masonry only a few inches thick functions more effectively. There is a certain depth of mass that the heat can penetrate during the daytime and then return to the surface in the evening. Beyond this depth additional mass is not very useful. The surface area and thickness of masonry mass is also directly tied to the amount of south glazing used. In some locations, where only a small amount of south glazing is necessary for passive heating, such as in southern California, masonry one inch thick (e.g., plaster) is sufficient. The selection of interior surface colors in passive solar applications has likewise changed. Distributing sunlight over masonry interior surfaces by reflecting it from light-colored walls and ceilings can effectively further reduce diurnal temperature swings in direct gain spaces.

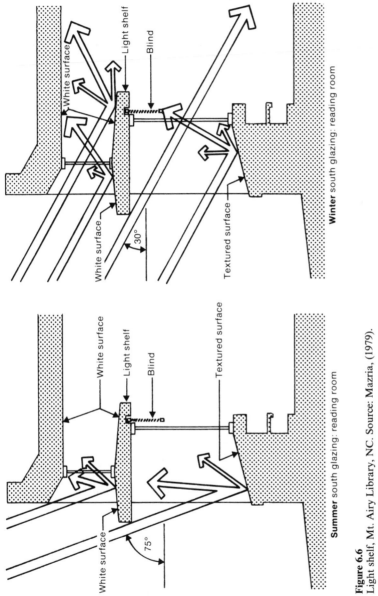

Figure 6.6
Light shelf, Mt. Airy Library, NC. Source: Mazria, (1979).

Until recently, masonry thermal storage (Trombe) walls were usually designed with thermocirculation vents located in rows at the top and bottom of the wall. This was believed to be the principal method of heat distribution from the wall. However, in 1979 a study published by Los Alamos Scientific Laboratory indicated that masonry thermal storage walls without vents were as effective as vented walls. As a result of that study, most walls are currently designed without vents and are therefore easier to maintain and less expensive to build.

The movement to energy-consciousness and solar design has also affected mechanical and electrical system design. In small houses and buildings HVAC systems are designed to conserve energy, and mechanical systems are less likely to be oversized. Architectural and engineering firms increasingly emphasize and inspect for the proper installation of equipment and systems during construction and choose equipment and systems based upon life-cycle costing methods. The professional responsible for HVAC design is often responsible for supplying projections of annual energy consumption and cost.

Since passive solar systems are designed space by space, HVAC systems with quick response times and capable of being zoned are the most compatible. For example, electric or hot-water baseboard systems are easily zoned and respond quickly to demand, whereas a zoned radiant electric or hot-water system located in a concrete floor slab has a slow response time. Forced air systems with a quick response time can be zoned, but must be perfectly balanced to perform effectively unless individual units are designed for each zone. In many parts of the country where air pollution is not a problem, wood-burning stoves and fireplaces are effective as backup heating systems.

Building construction has been greatly affected by energy conservation concerns. Residential buildings now often include interior use of masonry materials. For some speculative housing builders, solar features are used as a marketing strategy to lure potential buyers to their properties. Again, considerably more care and quality control is required by supervisory personnel and subcontractors to ensure the thermal and energy integrity of completed structures.

The financial community has generally supported reasonable building investments in solar design because of market acceptance and consumer interest. Passive solar design has been well-supported because it can be easily integrated into architecturally conventional buildings; and increased glass areas and masonry are often viewed as marketable features by builders, lenders, and consumers.

6.6 Conclusion

A return to regional aesthetics appears to be emerging as part of recent passive-solar and energy-conscious design. This often includes the preferred use of local resources and materials to reduce transportation and embedded energy costs in built form. Future developments are even more likely to stress the most effective use of our limited physical resources. Consumers wishing to optimize their resources are buying more intelligently manufactured products and buildings. The federal solar programs initiated in the past 12 years have contributed immeasurably to consumer education and professional advancements in the architectural integration of solar heating, cooling, and daylighting concepts.

References

AIA Research Corp., 1976. *Solar Dwelling Design Concepts*. Washington, DC: HUD.

AS/ISES, 1976. *Proc. Passive Solar Heating and Cooling Conference*. Albuquerque, NM: American Section of the International Solar Energy Society.

Balcomb, J. D., 1983. Heat storage and distribution inside passive solar buildings. Presented at the International Conference of Passive and Low Energy Architecture (Greece), Los Alamos National Laboratory.

Balcomb, J. D., C. D. Barley, R. D. McFarland, J. E. Perry, Jr., W. O. Wray, and S. Noll, 1980. Passive Solar Design Handbook, Vol. II. Washington, DC: U.S. Department of Energy.

Balcomb, J. D., J. C. Hedstrom, and S. W. Moore, 1979. Performance data evaluation of the Balcomb solar home (SI units). In *Proc. Second Annual Heating and Cooling Systems Operational Results Conference*, Colorado Springs, CO.

Butti, K., and J. Perlin, 1980. *A Golden Thread*. New York: Cheshire Books, Van Nostrand Reinhold Co.

Dixon, J. M., 1983. Glass under glass. *Progressive Architecture*.

Ertug, 1980. Indigenous settlements. *Progressive Architecture*. Tokyo.

Fletcher, B., 1963. *A History of Architecture*. New York: Charles Scribner's Sons.

Franta, G., and K. R. Olsen, 1978. Solar architecture. In *Proc. Aspen Energy Forum 1977*. Ann Arbor, MI: Arbor Science Publishers Inc.

Gideon, S., 1967. *Space, Time and Architecture*. Cambridge, MA: Harvard University Press.

Hutchinson, F. W., 1981. The solar house. *Progressive Architecture*, May 1947. *International Passive and Hybrid Cooling Conference*. Miami Beach: American Section of the International Solar Energy Society.

ISES, 1979. *Proc. 4th National Passive Solar Conference*. Kansas City, MO: International Solar Energy Society.

Lam, W. M. C., 1977. *Perception and Lighting as Formgivers for Architecture*. New York: McGraw-Hill.

Mayer, E., 1981. Passive cooling in Venezuela. *International Passive and Hybrid Cooling Conference*. Miami Beach.

Mazria, E., 1979. *The Passive Solar Energy Book*. Emmaus, PA: Rodale Press.

McAlester, V., and L. McAlester, 1984. *A Field Guide to American Houses*. New York: Alfred A. Knopf.

Rush, R., 1980. Energy: An expanding force for change. In *Progressive Architecture*.

Rush, R., 1981. The assimilation of energy. In *Progressive Architecture*.

Vonier, T., 1983. Presented at the *1983 International Daylighting Conferences*. Washington, DC: A.I.A. Service Corporation.

Watson, D., 1977. *Designing and Building a Solar House*. Charlotte, VT: Garden Way Publishing.

7 Nonresidential Buildings

Harry T. Gordon, John K. Holton, N. Scott Jones, Justin Estoque,
Donald L. Anderson, and William J. Fisher

7.1 Background on Architectural Integration of Solar Strategies

Energy consumption and costs of nonresidential buildings became public issues with the 1973 Arab oil embargo. The roots of this problem go back to the growing gap between growth rates in consumption and domestic production of energy. Total energy use in the United States had doubled since 1950, while the population had grown only one-third. In addition, imported fuel, primarily oil, had closed the gap between U.S. production and consumption. In just two decades, the United States changed from a net exporter of energy to an importer of about 15% of its energy. While our use of energy had been rising at slightly more than 4% annually, only 5% of the world's population was consuming 33% of the world's energy.

Nonresidential building energy use was rising at 5.4% per year since 1960. Much of this growth was reported in the energy consumption needed for space heating and cooling, lighting, and office equipment. Office buildings built in recent years use more energy on the average than do older buildings with an equivalent amount of space (see figure 7.1). The difference can be traced to higher lighting levels, sealed windows (requiring mechanical ventilation), glass curtain walls (allowing high levels of heat loss and gain), and the proliferation of computers, elevators, escalators, electric type-writers, and duplicating machines. For example, a typical pre-1973 office building would consume about 3,000 MJ/m² yr (250,000 Btu/ft² yr) while current guidelines recommend approximately 850 MJ/m² yr (75,000 Btu/ft² yr) (Johnson and Pierce, 1980). By 1972, this resulted in 9 out of 72 quads (1 quad = 10^{15} Btu) total energy consumed for commercial purposes.

Up to 1973, builders of large commercial buildings tended to ignore the climatic environment, including solar resources. Speed of design and construction processes (primarily to reduce initial costs) was desirable and made possible by producing typical building components (standard equipment, catalog systems, etc.) that did not take advantage of the building's specific use, site, and orientation. A need to maximize the use of interior space resulted in more space not adjacent to exterior glass areas, which increased lighting requirements. Furthermore, the advent of curtain wall technology made possible by the development of lightweight building skins (structural glass is an important example) and advances in synthetic caulk-

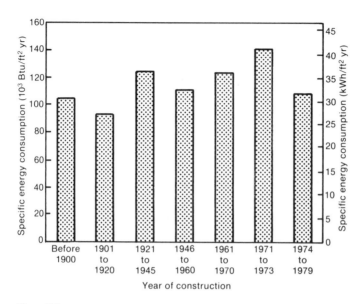

Figure 7.1
Specific energy consumption in commercial buildings by age distribution graph. Source:
EIA (1979).

ing compounds produced a sealed building that was totally dependent on mechanical systems. This reliance on internal environmental control was reinforced by the availability of cheap fuel.

The technology of environmental control had a significant impact on the formal expression of many important buildings. As Reyner Banham has explained, the elegant abstraction and detailing of the Seagram Building (figure 7.2) would not have been possible without advances in heating, ventilating, and air conditioning (HVAC) technology, which provide comfort through the use of "concealed power." Documenting a change in the attitude of designers about the importance of mechanical equipment, Banham cites Kahn's Richards Medical Building as a seminal expression of "exposed power" (Banham, 1969).

Passive solar design is an obvious reaction to positions of both concealed and exposed power. Rather than relying on HVAC equipment and the consumption of hidden energy to provide comfort, passive design seeks to use the form and envelope of a building to act as mediator between climate and people, providing comfort by natural energy flows. Although there are many successful technical examples of this approach, the integration of

Figure 7.2
Seagram Building. Source: SERI (1985, p. 25).

passive design concepts into the formal language and aesthetics of architecture has been limited at best. The causes are complex and reveal in part the extent to which our reliance on HVAC systems and artificial lighting have cut us off from experiencing thermal and luminous phenomena (Fraker, 1984).

The St. George's School in Wallasey is one of the best early examples of a direct gain and mass wall application. Built in 1962 in Liverpool, England, it was the first use of a direct gain system in a school. The construction consists of 7–10 in. (18–25 cm) of concrete in the roof, floor, and three walls, with 5 in. (13 cm) of expanded polystyrene exterior insulation. The south-facing solar wall is an expanse of glass 27 ft (8 m) tall and approximately 230 ft (70 m) long. There are two panes of glass: one clear pane on the outside and one diffusing pane 2 ft (0.6 m) inside that provides uniform distribution over the ceiling and floor. About 50% of the heat is supplied by the sun, the remaining heating energy coming from the artificial lights and occupants. The auxiliary heating system has not been needed (Banham, 1969).

On the other hand, active system solar collectors have been used in the United States since the turn of the century, though primarily for solar water heating. In 1939, the first of many experiments with solar space heating began at the Massachusetts Institute of Technology. In the late 1950s, a handful of solar houses were built in various parts of the country. In 1956, one of the first significant solar nonresidential buildings, the Bridgers and Paxton Solar Office Building, was constructed. The 4,300-ft^2 (399-m^2) Albuquerque, NM, building includes a south sloping wall with 790 ft^2 (73 m^2) of solar water heating panels and a 6,000-gal (22,880-L) underground storage water tank. Enough heat could be stored for three days of cloudy weather. The solar-powered unit netted a 53% savings in operational costs as compared to natural gas.

Early solar designers were provided scarce research and no empirical basis for decision making. One of the earliest solar classics is Olgyay's *Design with Climate* (1963), which made significant inroads in solar control, an important determinant of building form. *Man, Climate and Architecture* by Baruch Givoni (1969) also represented a seminal piece of research that guided early adapters. His method is based on the psychrometric chart, which gives the designer an accurate representation of the potential effect of the building envelope, as well as other environmental control strategies, on achieving human comfort in buildings.

By the early 1970s the federal government had started to become involved in solar building design by constructing several solar office buildings. The 1972 GSA Energy Conservation Demonstration Program sought to demonstrate innovative techniques through the construction of the Manchester Federal Office Building and the Saginaw Federal Office Building in Michigan. The purpose of these endeavors was (a) to dramatize the commitment of GSA to the conservation of energy in the design, construction, and operation of federal buildings; (b) to provide a laboratory for the installation of techniques/equipment; and (c) to inspire others in the building construction industry to pursue energy conservation as a goal.

Other federal government agencies also became involved in solar research and applications for buildings. The National Science Foundation Phase Zero Report, begun in 1973, was a comprehensive assessment of the state of the art of solar energy. In 1974 the passage of the Solar Heating and Cooling Demonstration Act signaled the involvement of several federal agencies in solar research and development. The Energy Research and Development Administration (ERDA) was formed to administer the program; subsequently, ERDA was replaced by the Department of Energy (DOE), which raised energy R&D to the status of presidential cabinet level importance.

Much of the early effort in nonresidential buildings was directed to active space heating and service water heating; later, absorption space cooling systems powered by solar energy were constructed and tested. Late in the 1970s, experimental work in the use of passive solar systems for heating, cooling, and lighting of nonresidential buildings increased in importance.

The research and development of active and passive solar techniques required attention to many different aspects of nonresidential buildings. This chapter focuses on five of the most important of these integration areas:

1. integration of active and passive solar systems with architectural, structural, mechanical, and electrical systems,

2. characteristics of solar systems that affect occupants of buildings,

3. economic considerations of active and passive systems for nonresidential buildings owners and developers,

4. integration of solar system controls with conventional system controls, and

5. regulatory developments in building codes and standards.

7.2 Integration with Building Systems

7.2.1 General Considerations of Solar Design Integration

Fundamental to the successful application of either active or passive solar systems in nonresidential buildings is an understanding of building energy requirements by end-use systems during the design process. Unlike residential applications of solar energy, in which the space conditioning requirements are largely a function of climate, and domestic water heating is a significant energy use, nonresidential building energy requirements are significantly influenced by the activities the building will accommodate.

Buildings with minimal or highly intermittent occupancy, such as warehouses, will have energy requirements that are—like residences—largely climatically influenced. However, buildings such as offices, schools, community centers, retail establishments, and restaurants are different because of the presence of people, lights, and appliances, all of which generate significant amounts of heat. When occupied, many nonresidential buildings do not need heat until the outside temperature is quite low, typically $20°–40°F$ ($-7°–4°C$). Many of these buildings require substantial amounts of lighting, and hence electricity, to function for their intended purposes.

Because combustible fossil fuels, especially natural gas, are commonly used for space heating and some service heating applications, while the more expensive electricity is almost always used for lighting and space cooling, it is important to consider the type and cost of purchased energy when evaluating building operating costs and energy priorities. In the last decade, a significant difference has existed in the cost of natural gas and electricity. On the average, electricity is about two to three times as expensive as natural gas for equivalent amounts of delivered energy. Hence, the value of a solar energy collection system that displaces natural gas is less in present-day economic terms than a system that displaces electricity. Fuel oil, once commonly used for building heating purposes, has been much less widely used in the last decade, because of the limited quantities domestically available and the volatility of international prices.

Recognition of these facts has caused substantial differences in the design process for nonresidential buildings in the last decade. In the early 1970s the most commonly performed calculations were for equipment sizing. The calculations were made under peak heating, cooling, and lighting conditions and were intended to determine the maximum number of Btus (or kilowatts in the case of electricity) that the mechanical and lighting equipment must provide (usually during a 1-hour period) to maintain desired conditions within the building. The efficiency of the equipment, especially at part-load conditions, in converting purchased energy to delivered lighting or space conditioning was seldom considered; similarly, the cost of the purchased energy was seldom a factor in decision making, since energy costs were low.

As energy costs started to rise, designers and owners began to consider the total amount of energy that must be purchased to maintain comfort and building operations. Over time, this led to annual energy calculations that considered equipment efficiency and energy costs. Conservation of energy was an immediate response, and alternative energy sources began to be considered to supplement purchased energy. Some people spoke of total independence from nonrenewable energy sources, but this seldom proved to be a practical or economic alternative. Instead, designers sought ways of combining conventional techniques for space conditioning and lighting with alternative energy techniques. Solar energy, initially through active solar collection systems and later through passive techniques, became one of the most widely used forms of alternative (that is, renewable) energy.

7.2.1.1 Active Solar Design Considerations In many ways, active solar collection systems were an easy extension of conventional design thinking. Solar collectors, placed on or near a building and linked to the mechancial systems, are fundamentally an alternative means of generating heat; they reduce the load on the conventional space heating or service water heating systems by providing heat that would otherwise come from purchased energy. Although displacing natural gas (the most common heating fuel) was economically questionable, many solar heating systems were constructed because they were readily understood and could be made to work reasonably well with the conventional heating systems in the building. Uncertainty about future costs and availability of natural gas also induced people to consider adding solar. Some of these active heating systems, especially those in buildings that used electricity for heating, provide an attractive economic return to the building owners. Service water heating systems were generally more economically viable than space heating systems, since the output of the solar collector array could be used throughout the whole year.

Active solar systems have also been used for space cooling applications, usually by means of the absorption refrigeration cycle. Although solar space cooling systems have the advantage of displacing electricity, a more expensive fuel, the inherent inefficiencies in converting solar heat to space cooling usually made the overall economics unattractive and severely limited the number of nonresidential solar cooling applications that were constructed.

The incorporation of active solar collection systems in nonresidential buildings posed some important challenges to designers. Since the quantity of collectors needed to significantly reduce conventional energy requirements is usually large, architects had to find ways of dealing with a major visual element (see figures 7.3–7.6). The most common approach was to place the collectors on the roof of the building, making a frank statement of their presence; many owners accepted this because it "announced" that the building was solar. Some architects attempted to integrate the collectors with the overall form of the building either by creating bold sloping planes that accommodated the collectors or by separating the collectors from the building and using them as part of another functional element, such as a covered walkway.

Structural engineers designed supports for the large collector arrays, either by extending the main structural system for the building or by creating an independent structural framework. Although the collectors are not heavy, they present a large surface to the wind, and engineers who did not recognize the potential wind or snow loading were occasionally faced with embarrassing situations.

The major challenges in incorporating active solar energy systems are in the area of mechanical engineering. First of all, the collectors and piping must be designed to collect heat reliably and efficiently. Since more heat is commonly available from the solar collectors than is needed during the period of collection, thermal storage is an important element in making the system work. This in turn means that controls are needed that sense when the solar collectors are sufficiently warmer than the storage containers, so that heat can be collected; the controls then initiate the operation of the pumps and fans needed to transport water or air to collect the energy. Liquid circulating collectors must be prevented from freezing during periods of noncollection. The most commonly used approaches to freeze protection are to use an antifreeze mixture (similar to an automobile radiator) or to drain the collector and piping contents when freezing conditions occur. In addition, the mechanical equipment within the building must be selected and controlled to use collected solar heat first, and conventional energy second, to maximize energy savings.

Figure 7.3
Richards Laboratories. Source: Banham (1969, p. 250).

Figure 7.4
St. George's School. Source: Banham (1969, p. 280).

Figure 7.5
Bridger-Paxton Building. Source: Shurcliff (1978, p. 158).

Figure 7.6
Manchester Building. Source: NBS (1975).

These design considerations, while not onerous, have required that engineers adjust their thinking and design approaches to accommodate the characteristics of available solar energy. In the early 1970s, designers either overlooked or inadequately responded to many of these considerations; some systems saved much less energy than predicted or failed to work at all. By the end of the decade, active solar design was much better understood, and more reliable systems resulted; however, the material-intensive nature of the systems, and the fact that they were always an additional cost to the project, has limited the number of applications that have been constructed. Currently, the most common use of active solar systems in nonresidential buildings is for service water heating where water use is high; hotels, dormitories, restaurants, hospitals, and laundries are typical examples.

7.2.1.2 Passive Solar Design Considerations Unlike active solar systems, which are typically an obvious addition to the building with no purpose other than to collect energy, passive systems usually make use of the elements of the building itself to collect and store energy. This has often allowed the passive systems to address multiple elements of building energy requirements, such as lighting and heating, without significantly adding to the building cost. From a design standpoint, the integration of the passive elements with the conventional architectural (building form, skin, structure), mechanical space conditioning, and lighting systems has required distinctly different approaches by architects and by engineers.

Conceptually, passive systems are often thought of as load modifiers (rather than load suppliers, as is the case with active systems). That is, they change the building's fundamental need for heating, cooling, and lighting, rather than merely provide an alternative supply of heat. While this greatly extends their potential to achieve significant energy savings, it also requires that the design team work closely together to create a successful design. The role of the architect is more central in passive design than in active, but the importance of careful decisions on the part of the engineers remains significant.

By 1979, active solar systems had been installed on nonresidential buildings throughout the United States. Churches, offices, schools, retail facilities, community/recreation centers, and warehouses had all been the subject of these efforts. However, little experimentation in the role of passive systems had taken place, except in residences. DOE issued a major Program Opportunity Notice in 1979 that signaled the beginning of an experimental application of passive solar techniques to reduce nonrenewable energy requirements for heating, cooling, and lighting of nonresidential buildings. Unlike participants in previous DOE active solar efforts, who received funding only for construction and some performance monitoring, the participants in this passive program also received design assistance from recognized experts.

In the DOE Nonresidential Experimental Buildings Program, design considerations were well documented for the 20 passive solar buildings that were designed, constructed, and monitored. By virtue of their load-reducing characteristics, passive systems had to be considered by the architect very early in the design process, much more so than in conventional buildings whose design process often leaves the details of the mechanical system to the later stages. For example, in the programming phase, the teams of architects and engineers found it important to establish the nature, timing, and quantity of building energy requirements. How important were heating, cooling, and lighting energy requirements? How do they rank in importance? Did those requirements occur during occupied or unoccupied periods? Did the timing of those energy requirements coincide with the availability of solar or other environmental resources? Invariably, it was useful to establish the nonsolar "base case" building for answering some of these questions.

Analysis of a conventional (nonsolar) building helped determine the building energy problems identified above. It was used to quantify the magnitude and timing of heating, cooling, and lighting energy requirements. Internal heat generators, such as computers, or unusual ventilation requirements, such as those for an indoor swimming pool or gymnasium, were an important part of this analysis. The anticipated use patterns of the building, including timing and number of people, were estimated and the probability of changes in these patterns assessed.

Design tools became an important part of the design process. The Building Design Tool Development Council, a national consortium of building industry representatives formed to provide guidance for energy design tool research, defines a design tool as "any device which assists in the formulation and/or evaluation of energy efficient strategies for a new or existing building." This broad definition comprises a number of procedures varying in accuracy, cost, and ease of use, including workbooks, nomographs, calculator routines, physical models, microcomputer software, and mainframe computer programs. The problem for the solar building designer is to choose the right tool for his or her needs.

Designers participating in the Nonresidential Experimental Buildings Program learned quickly which tools were appropriate. The best tools at early design stages were those that accepted simple input. A tool that required mechanical equipment part-load curves was too cumbersome for predesign and schematic design. Consequently, the design tool had to incorporate reasonable default values if it did not require detailed input. For example, if hour-by-hour building operating schedules were not required as input for an office building, the design tool assumed an 8-to-5 schedule, five days per week, not the 24-hour occupancy that characterizes a residence.

In addition, the design tool had to be comprehensive, integrating the various energy end uses. Output that told the designer that a proposed clerestory reduced artificial lighting needs by 30%, but neglected the effects on heating and cooling, left him or her the additional work of calculating these effects.

Finally, the process of optimizing energy performance required that the designer make assumptions about the expected building use and operation in order to project energy use. Some of these assumptions had room for change; others did not without compromising energy performance. When the actual building occupant behavior deviated from these assumptions, energy performance did not meet expectations. At the outset, the design team settled issues such as whether atria would be strictly used as such for circulation and, therefore, could tolerate more extreme temperatures; whether meeting rooms would never have to accommodate slide presentations and therefore could be daylighted; and whether schools would only be used during the daytime, thereby minimizing the need for thermal storage.

The buildings that were the products of this intensive design effort demonstrate the importance of attention to detail. Those that have been constructed and monitored (for both energy use and occupant reaction) have achieved impressive reductions in heating, cooling, and lighting energy compared to equivalent nonsolar buildings. The average reduction in energy use for the new buildings in the Nonresidential Experimental Buildings Program was almost 50%.

Since the design efforts were focused on integration of the solar features, few of the buildings look as if solar has been added to a conventional design (see figures 7.7–7.15). This characteristic enabled such elements as atria, clerestories, and roof monitors to function for multiple purposes. Although this makes it difficult to isolate the costs of individual passive

Figure 7.7
Towns Elementary.

Figure 7.8
St. Charles.

Figure 7.9
Troy-Miami County Library. Source: Shurcliff (1978, p. 213).

Figure 7.10
Friendship Federal Savings & Loan.

features, it is significant that 70% of the buildings in the program were constructed within typical industry ranges for the building type, location, and time of construction.

An additional benefit was the response of building occupants, who indicated a high degree of satisfaction with the interior environment of these buildings. The fact that the buildings were typically bright and visually connected to the outside enhanced this reaction. Some owners report higher levels of productivity from those who use the building, although this is difficult to measure scientifically.

7.2.2 Effects on Occupants

Although active systems have a minimum effect on the occupants of buildings unless they seriously malfunction, passive solar systems are normally integral elements of the building and can directly affect occupants. Four of the most important factors from the viewpoint of design integration are temperature, visual comfort, acoustics, and indoor air quality.

7.2.2.1 Temperature Architectural integration suggests the consideration of all forces contributing to the built environment. For this reason,

Figure 7.11
Saratoga.

much research addressing human temperature requirements has not taken place within closely controlled laboratory conditions. In general, assessment of these requirements is based on rigorous questionnaire methodologies using real occupants of solar buildings, occupants whose environmental perceptions are simultaneously influenced by all parts of the built environment.

Several comfort surveys have been conducted in solar nonresidential buildings, many of which were built with public monies to demonstrate the feasibility of passive solar technologies. Balcomb (1981) documented the perceptions of faculty and students at grade schools in Santa Fe, NM, some of the first solar nonresidential buildings. In some cases, they reported conditions too cool, and in others, too warm. Those for whom this was their first solar experience expressed doubts that solar energy technology could perform as well as conventional HVAC systems. Later, however, Kantrowitz (1984) studied the occupancy effects of 23 passive solar nonresidential buildings whose design, construction, and evaluation

Figure 7.12
Christian Reform Church Center of Hope. Source: Shurcliff (1978, p. 45).

Figure 7.13
Federal Building. Source: Shurcliff (1978, p. 133).

Figure 7.14
Macomb County Building. Source: *Progressive Architecture*, April 1979, p. 145.

Figure 7.15
Shelley Ridge Girl Scout Center—interior.

were funded by the U.S. Department of Energy. Questionnaires were completed by full-time and part-time users every month. Most users were thermally comfortable, confirming the success of these solar buildings. Those who had complaints revealed a pattern of too cool mornings and warm afternoons. Perceptions of cool mornings seemed to be related to (1) setback strategies that were too deep and/or too long, (2) incorrect thermal mass, or (3) changed schedule of building use, including earlier and later than predicted occupancy, thus rendering the planned timing of heat release inappropriate. Perceived warm afternoons may be related to (1) increased building use and (2) ventilation problems such as solar shading strategies that conflicted with natural ventilation.

7.2.2.2 Visual Comfort The same researchers also reported on the building occupants' visual comfort, since most of the buildings studied employed daylighting to offset electric lighting energy. Balcomb (1981) reported nearly universal satisfaction with the natural daylighting. Glare was not a serious problem. Minor complaints revolved around the difficulty of darkening rooms for slide presentations. Kantrowitz reported similar results, with users expressing their acclimatization to the variable qualities and quantities of light, which sometimes dropped to 10 footcandles. This last observation was studied in more depth and confirmed by Andersson et al. (1984) in two specific buildings. They compared manual lighting controls to simulated daylighting dimming and on/off controls that maintained 50 fc and concluded that the manual controls yielded energy performance as good as or better than the automatic controls.

Other research bears out psychological amenities of solar technologies relative to view and sunlight (Heerwagen and Dean, 1984). Such research stems from other research analyzing human emotional responses to the environment from a biological perspective that address qualities such as visual access ("prospect") and places to hide ("refuge") (Appleton, 1975). Theories proposing that contact with the outside world through windows satisfy these basic biological needs point to benefits of solar apertures other than energy conservation. A few studies have attempted to measure the effects of daylight on people's psychological state (Wells, 1965). Although subjects expressed a preference for natural over artificial lighting, they were not good at distinguishing the difference. More research is needed in this area to draw definitive conclusions.

The design implications of such biological research have been explored, again primarily through questionnaires. Using scale models, McLain (1983) determined that building occupants prefer a combination of direct and indirect gain versus gain only, which offers no privacy, or Trombe walls, which offer no view.

7.2.2.3 Acoustics Passive solar has been found to have both positive and negative acoustic effects. Positive effects include decreased transmission of sound from outside sources. Ruegg (1982) suggests that the dollar value of decreased sound transmission of highway and aircraft noise through mass walls and sunspaces can be quantified and included in net present value calculations. Some evidence, however, is presented to the contrary. Kantrowitz (1984) reports complaints from the occupants of the DOE-sponsored passive nonresidential buildings that the hard wall and floor surfaces reflect sound excessively. Furthermore, the open floor plans designed to enhance air convection prevent sound isolation. There was no evidence of increased sound transmission through solar apertures, though in nonresidential buildings whose primary load is often lighting, entering sound can be baffled by the same building elements that baffle direct beam radiation. More work is necessary to establish how and to what degree acoustics is affected by passive solar building designs.

7.2.2.4 Air Quality The integration of active or passive solar techniques is normally preceded by energy conservation techniques, including tightening of the building envelope to minimize the unintentional infiltration of outside air, which then must be heated or cooled. Since most nonresidential buildings are required by building codes to supply outside air to the interior mechanically, the potential for indoor air pollution is different from that in residences. Nevertheless, the issues associated with air quality in low-energy buildings are very similar for both building categories.

Most of the research on indoor air pollution is based on residential-scale buildings, but it can be extrapolated to nonresidential buildings if the pollution sources remain the same. These sources are building construction materials, especially concrete, stone, particleboard, insulation, adhesives, and paint; water service; natural gas; and occupants, particularly metabolic activity and smoking.

Major research developments in this building integration issue were presented in the International Symposium on Indoor Air Pollution, Health and Energy Conservation in Amherst, MA (October 13–16, 1981), the Conference on Indoor Air Quality in Stockholm, Sweden (August 20–24, 1984), and the EPRI Indoor Air Quality Seminars in Denver, CO (May

1–2, 1984). In Denver, the U.S. Department of Energy identified primary areas of research being addressed by the Lawrence Berkeley Laboratory (Milhone and Fowler, 1984). These include the following: characterization of indoor air pollutants, identification of pollutant sources, determination of pollutant transport mechanisms, examination of health effects, development of control technologies, development of testing and monitoring instruments, and conducting laboratory and field studies.

Research conducted before the U.S. Department of Energy's Residential Conservation Service (RCS) program shows that in the vast majority of existing homes, indoor air quality appears satisfactory down to 0.24 air changes per hour (ach). In a very small percentage of existing homes, radon from soil gas is disturbingly high. Finally, indoor air in new homes where the ach is between 0.1 and 0.3 is more likely to be unacceptable. DOE recognizes the need to identify when and where air quality deteriorates and thus is continuing research to identify organic emissions from building materials in commercial office buildings; explore strategies for controlling formaldehyde and nitrogen dioxide; survey key pollutants and their dependence on building features, geographic location, and use patterns; and assess radon sources and building entry.

Much of the results of current research have not yet been transferred to the construction industry. Commercial building construction will probably respond more slowly to this research than residential building construction for several reasons:

1. Commercial buildings have areas of potential energy savings other than decreasing ventilation—areas such as lighting and solar shading.

2. Cooling construction strategies for commercial buildings often depend on *increasing* ventilation (economizers).

3. Health and building codes regulate minimum ventilation rates for commercial buildings. Changing such regulations is an added institutional barrier to reducing ventilation.

7.2.3 Economic Considerations

Building owners may have diverse reasons for incorporating active or passive solar features in nonresidential buildings. Improved public image, enhanced amenity, better employee morale, and protection from fuel shortages are some of the most common reasons.

Few owners, however, exclude economic considerations from this decision-making process; whether simple payback, discounted cash flow/net present worth, savings to investment ratio, or other valuing techniques are used, the principles are the same—the benefits associated with an investment in solar should outweigh the costs over some period of time. In nonresidential buildings, institutional factors among various kinds of building owners may vary significantly, and these differences directly affect the integration of solar in the design process.

The attractiveness of energy savings is significantly influenced by the building owner's profile as well as the building design characteristics. DOE-funded research has indicated that building owners are most interested in the bottom line that directly relates to their initial outlay and subsequent cash flow. Therefore, building designers must be cognizant of the various ownership types, which can be divided into four categories depending on the owner's financial interests. The first group, government owners, tends to judge investments on a 30–40-year building life. Financing depends on legislation that authorizes bond issues. Not-for-profit organizations, like the previous category of government, engage in a one-time fund-raising effort before the building is designed and constructed. Ongoing financing charges may not be as much of a concern as regular utility costs, which can overwhelm limited operating budgets. The third category is owner-occupied buildings. Their owners compare building investments with other investment opportunities. The ability to deduct debt service and other operational costs such as business expenses makes an energy-savings investment less attractive to a building owner than it is for the first two categories of building owners. Finally, the most demanding building owner is the speculative builder who seeks to lease space to others and hence is looking for opportunities to keep initial costs at a minimum. Less incentive exists for reducing monthly utility bills, since these expenses are generally passed on to the lessee.

Active solar systems, which are a hardware addition to a building, have always increased the construction cost of the building. They are, in effect, an alternative means of producing space heating, cooling, or service water heating and are usually accompanied by counterpart conventional systems, which use purchased nonrenewable energy when insufficient solar energy is available. Designers can make value-based decisions to minimize costs of construction and maintenance, and maximize benefits produced, but the issue of financial return remains paramount since active solar systems generate few nonenergy benefits.

Since passive systems are frequently integrated with the overall building and serve multiple purposes, it is often difficult to identify precisely the cost of implementation or the benefits received. It is common for well-conceived passive solar techniques such as daylighting to reduce the size and, therefore, the cost of conventional building components. For example, a reduction in the peak cooling load reduces the size of the chiller, as well as the ducts and fans used for distribution. These cost trade-offs are a key element that reduces the effective cost of the solar elements. Somewhat less quantifiable, but clearly evident in good passive designs, are increases in amenity as perceived by building users. These have resulted in higher building leasing rates and reports of higher worker productivity in some instances.

Achieving low construction costs in passive buildings is highly dependent on the effect of the interaction of disciplines on the design team. If a more expensive building envelope significantly reduces the size of the mechanical heating and cooling system required, no construction cost savings will occur unless the mechanical engineer recognizes the reduced building load.

The federal government has passed legislation that encourages energy conservation investments. Two instances of such legislation worthy of note are the Economic Recovery Act of 1981 and Solar Equipment Tax Credits.

The Economic Recovery Act of 1981 offered energy conservation and solar tax incentives, which were added to the standard investment tax credit of 10%. Specifically, the act authorized 15% additional energy equipment investment tax credit for solar equipment through the end of 1985; it was also applicable to wind energy equipment. Conservation equipment carried a 10% energy equipment tax credit that expired in 1982.

Retrofits may have had even greater benefits. A certified historical structure would get an additional benefit of 25% in the first year. For retrofits of other, significantly older, buildings, tax credits ranged from 15% for buildings that are 30 years old to 20% for buildings that are 40 years old. These applied to the buildng whether the owner was making a solar or conventional rehabilitation.

In addition, depreciation laws encouraged investment in solar equipment for buildings. The 1981 depreciation schedule set a baseline 15-year depreciable life (since modified). "Solar equipment" was eligible for an accelerated 5-year life. This tended to favor active solar buildings, since only about 10% of the passive system cost was viewed as equipment. It was difficult to classify mass walls and other integrated passive elements as depreciable solar equipment. Passive buildings could depreciate clearly defined elements such as fans and movable insulation over the 5 years, but the remainder of the passive solar system investment had to follow the normal depreciation schedule. On the other hand, active solar buildings could depreciate a greater fraction of solar equipment over 5 years.

These tax incentives spawned various creative financing structures for investors desiring tax shelters. Third-party financing enabled a building user to reduce energy costs with capital furnished by investors seeking tax relief. The arrangement usually involved three parties: the energy user, the equipment supplier, and the equipment investor. The user was a building operator, owner, or tenant with an ongoing need for large quantities of hot water, steam, or other energy. The equipment supplier usually designed, engineered, installed, and maintained the solar equipment on the user's premises.

The investor was a person, or group of persons, eligible for an investment tax credit, energy tax credit, and the depreciation allowed on the system. These incentives allowed investors to install solar technologies and take advantage of tax incentives that may not have been attractive to the users because of their particular tax status or inability to raise capital.

The following is an example of tax leasing:

Corporation X: Buys solar energy equipment

- $million
- 10-year economic life

Cannot use tax benefits

Corporation Y: "Buys" the property, giving X

- $200,000 cash
- $800,000 note

Leases the property back to X for 9 years
Takes tax credits and depreciation deductions
Sells the property back to X for $1

7.2.4 Integration of Solar System Controls with Buildings Early solar research focused on components for residential domestic hot water (DHW) applications. The problem of integrating complex solar systems into non-residential HVAC systems did not come to light until the 1970s and still needs investigation and solutions. Unfortunately, little of the technology developed for controlling residential DHW systems carried over to the more complex needs of nonresidential solar systems.

The Department of Energy has contributed to the understanding and improvement of nonresidential solar system integration through a number of programs. The National Solar Heating and Cooling Program, initiated in 1974, included the Solar Heating and Cooling Commercial Demonstration Program and the National Solar Data Network. Funding through these programs resulted in the installation, evaluation, monitoring, and documentation of hundreds of solar systems in a variety of locations across the United States. The demonstration projects and data collection were cost-shared by DOE for both active and passive applications, and resulted in an unprecedented volume of case studies, data, and lessons learned for solar system designers, installers, manufacturers, and researchers. The Passive Nonresidential Experimental Program was started in 1979 to develop experimental, nonresidential buildings that use passive solar techniques to address heating, cooling, and lighting energy requirements.

The combined results of these efforts comprise both the raw material for future research and a series of concrete lessons learned that can facilitate improved operation of the gamut of solar systems applied to nonresidential buildings. However, it is important to note that solar technology, including its integration with existing HVAC practice, still requires considerable development and is far from accepted in the nonresidential building sector. The many systems resulting from the DOE programs mentioned represented the bulk of solar activity taking place at the time, and in most cases would not have been carried out without DOE support.

DOE-funded research frequently cites system complexity as a major difference between conventional and solar systems, both for active and passive nonresidential systems. There are a number of reasons for this complexity. Solar systems for nonresidential use typically involve a large number of operational modes for supplying building energy. Some of these modes call on the direct use of solar energy and the use of stored energy from auxiliary systems. The multiplicity of modes is complicated by the fact that heating, cooling, and hot water needs may occur simultaneously throughout a multizone building. This requires a complicated hierarchy of mode priorities beyond those typically encountered in conventional HVAC systems. Also, the variety of precise set points and differential temperature values required for optimal system operation make essential a clear understanding of solar concepts on the part of the control system designer.

The advent of integrated circuits and microprocessors for use in HVAC control fortunately has begun to meet the needs of nonresidential solar systems. The complexity required can be accommodated by currently available state of the art electronic controls and control components, as is demonstrated by the variety of custom control systems presented at the First Workshop on the Control of Solar Energy Systems for Heating and Cooling, sponsored by the Department of Energy and Boston University in 1978. Despite this advance, two problems still hinder the integration of solar controls and conventional HVAC controls:

1. Electromechanical and pneumatic controls are in wide use and better understood than integrated circuits throughout the HVAC industry. This may present a problem for solar retrofit applications. For new construction, major controls manufacturers have recently started concentrating on the newer electronic units, which should be more compatible with solar systems.

2. Control algorithms tend to be developed on a system-specific basis. There is a need for flexible, standardized algorithms for solar systems, especially those that can accommodate a variety of system types and adapt well to retrofit installations.

The problems of both control hardware and algorithm development were well addressed by Hayes, Winn, Hull, Johnson, Kent, Anderson, and others in 1978 at the First Workshop on Control of Solar Energy Systems for Heating and Cooling (AS/ISES, 1978). The preliminary research necessary for the widespread adoption of active solar systems has been done. A combination of consumer demand and private sector product development is now needed to increase the nonresidential use of these active systems.

Passive technology, in addition to being hampered by problems previously mentioned, also suffers from unique integration difficulties that still require considerable research and real system monitoring. These will be discussed in section 7.2.4.2.

7.2.4.1 Active Solar System Issues Vitro's analysis of projects monitored under the National Solar Data Program (Lodge and Kendall, 1984) produced the following ranked list of common causes of active solar system failure or performance degradation:

1. early start or late stop,
2. set point or time clock adjustments,
3. controller failure,
4. sensor failure, and
5. poor sensor location.

For the group monitored, these problems occurred twice as frequently as collector failures.

Two basic types of problems can be identified from the list: those that result from insufficient understanding of solar energy use and collection and those that result from hardware failures.

The first problem type is due to the differing premises underlying solar thermal technologies and conventional HVAC theory. The idea of dealing with a limited resource and the need to maximize collection efficiency is foreign to conventional methods of heating and cooling.

Areas of particular importance, as indicated frequently in system research and evaluation, are as follows:

1. Sensor placement must follow specific guidelines so that storage tank stratification can be used to maximize system performance.

2. Sensor placement should avoid possible influence of adjacent or accidental heat flows, especially thermosyphoning that can prevent freeze protection.

3. Pump controls need proper temperature differentials and run times ascribed to them to prevent system cycling. Proportional controls have been shown to improve morning, evening, and overcast day performance.

In addition, hardware failures stem from the environmental extremes encountered in solar energy collection. Sensor failures are often caused by high diurnal swings and collector stagnation temperatures. Controls, besides falling prey to custom algorithms and unconventional applications, are affected by on-site heat and humidity extremes.

7.2.4.2 Passive Solar System Issues Passive solar systems for nonresidential applications, unfortunately, do not permit the simple glazing-to-mass-ratio approach DOE developed for residential buildings. Integration is a complex issue, often involving passive heating, cooling, and daylighting strategies in what is now considered a crucial relationship with conventional HVAC systems.

The problem of controlling a hierarchy of different modes and systems is very similar in passive and active applications, with the exception that passive systems are even further removed from traditional HVAC components. Switches, fans, and motors are often replaced by occupant-controlled shades, vents, and insulating panels. As a result, control integration problems are twofold: those involving control systems and those involving building occupants.

An office building sponsored by a DOE program is an example of the effect of passive control integration on designers. The HVAC control system combines daylighting, direct gain, spray roof cooling, and active thermal storage with conventional split system heat pumps in each of 53 tenant suites. The resulting nine operating modes required a very high level of control system complexity and flexibility, and a significant increase in control-related costs. This cost increase was not caused by hardware needs, which were met with standard commercial controls, but by the number of different individuals involved in the installation of the controls. The jurisdiction and responsibility of the contractor, electrical and HVAC subcontractors, heat pump manufacturer, design team, and controls supplier were debated for nearly a year, resulting in a 41% increase in the installed controller price. Other projects experienced similar problems. The inherent complexity of passive/hybrid/conventional nonresidential systems requires that control system design, selection, and installation be given special attention.

The second problem affecting passive system control, one that is unique to passive solar applications, is the planned or unintentional response of occupants. User participation in system control is often desirable for the following reasons: these systems usually involve building elements in close proximity to users; occupant satisfaction with an interior environment increases when some control of heating, cooling, and lighting systems is possible; and comfort is affected by variables not easily measured or controlled conventionally (i.e., glare, radiant surface temperatures, etc.).

Even in passive systems that do not allow for user control, the proximity of solar features to users allows them to influence system performance significantly. Both Kantrowitz and Kroner found occupant impact to be a crucial factor in passive system performance (Kantrowitz, 1983; Kroner, 1983). Results are reflected in the DOE Nonresidential Experimental Buildings Program. Occupants typically used any means necessary to achieve comfort levels within their space, quite often to the detriment of passive performance. Kantrowitz's work indicates that users will, if so directed, properly control solar elements of spaces they regularly occupy, as long as this control satisfies their immediate comfort needs.

Both occupant and control issues concerning the operation of nonresidential passive systems require the attention of designers. To avoid performance difficulties the architect and engineer must work more closely than they would during conventional, nonsolar design.

7.2.5 Regulations

The development of active and passive technologies for use in buildings gave rise to the need for building codes and standards controlling solar applications. It is the responsibility of the architect and engineer to be in compliance with requirements; active and passive systems are sufficiently different from conventional systems and require reinvestigation of existing regulations, and often development of new regulations that are specifically directed to solar applications.

Codes and standards are developed to protect the public. They stem from the policing power of the government to regulate commerce and industry for the safety and general welfare of the populace. In today's society, numerous industry groups develop voluntary standards that supplement government regulations and aid industry growth through uniformity of requirements. These standards and guidelines are generally developed by the consensus process through negotiation among the principally affected parties.

An unusual aspect of the development of codes and standards concerning solar buildings and components is the basic motivation for their development. Historically, codes and standards have been developed to prevent major safety hazards or performance failures from jeopardizing life or general welfare. In codes and standards for solar buildings, however, the basic initiative of government-supported activities is to anticipate the regulatory process and thereby speed the introduction of this technology into general commercial use. Many of the research programs and efforts supported by the federal government were efforts to meet this need to expedite an otherwise long, tradition-bound process. As a result, research projects in safety, performance, durability, reliability, and even cost effectiveness were undertaken nearly concurrently with basic applications research in the solar criteria and performance specifications for solar buildings, systems, and components that were introduced into the more traditional codes and standards process with a solid basis of research knowledge.

Another aspect of the codes and standards efforts in solar technologies has been the unusual preponderance of attention given to design performance, durability, and reliability. This emphasis, again, was due to the intent of the government to accelerate the acceptance of the use of solar energy in normal commercial applications. It was felt that because of the newness and untried nature of this technology, additional guidance and control in the application of solar energy were warranted to reassure otherwise skeptical consumers, developers, manufacturers, architects, and engineers who were key to the widespread application of solar energy.

Regulations, codes, and standards have had a substantial impact on the architectural integration of solar energy systems, both active and passive. It is useful to examine these impacts in categories related to major types of regulations: fire, safety and environmental codes; solar codes; and building energy codes.

7.2.5.1 Fire, Safety, and Environmental Codes Many states and municipalities administer building codes that have provisions for solar installations. In many cases, these local codes are adopted from one of the major national codes: Basic/National Building Codes, Uniform Building Codes, Southern Standard Building Codes, and HUD Minimum Property Standards.

The effective design of solar energy systems in a building may be affected by provisions in these codes. Some key code provisions that impact solar designs are these:

1. requirements for fire-resistive enclosures around shafts or ducts that penetrate fire-rated floors or walls,

2. fire damper requirements for ducts that penetrate fire-resistive floors or walls,

3. flame-spread and smoke-developed limits for materials in air plenums,

4. fire resistance requirements for exposed construction materials,

5. application of structural materials and appearance requirements for roof-mounted signs to solar collectors,

6. sizing procedures for domestic hot water heaters that may result in greatly oversized water heating systems,

7. requirements for pressure and temperature relief devices that may not conform to the logic of solar system designs,

8. requirements for testing and rating pressure vessels in accordance with certain standards (usually ASME),

9. requirements for special locations for mechanical equipment utilizing ammonia refrigerant, such as some absorption cooling systems,

10. requirements for fire-resistive enclosures for fixed equipment,

11. required clearance around fired and unfired pressure vessels for inspection and maintenance, and

12. required procedures for disposing of waste materials that may be used in solar energy systems, such as toxic or hazardous heat transfer liquids.

These regulations were typically developed before the widespread application of active/passive systems. Designers and code officials had to interpret the intent of these requirements in the context of solar systems and attempt to provide a safe, dependable design. The individual organizations that develop codes worked with DOE to evaluate existing codes and, in some cases, to develop new provisions to facilitate solar applications.

7.2.5.2 Solar Codes Extensive work was begun in the mid-1970s in the Federal Solar Program to assess the potential impact that codes and standards might have on solar energy systems in buildings. The National Bureau of Standards, Center for Building Technology, took the leading laboratory role in these efforts and conducted extensive, multifaceted work on codes and standards. Several joint study projects were carved out with the major codes and standards organizations to determine the applicability and impact of the various code requirements on solar installations. This work ultimately led to the development of model solar codes at the federal level and in the private sector. The major federal codes are these:

1. HUD Minimum Property Standards Supplement, Solar Heating and Domestic Hot Water Systems 4930.2.

2. Performance Criteria for Solar Heating and Cooling Systems in Commercial Buildings TN 1187.

3. Performance Criteria for Solar Heating and Cooling Systems in Residential Buildings BSS 147.

These regulations provide a comprehensive, balanced set of requirements that have been extensively reviewed and modified. They have received review by professional and code organizations and through periods of public commentary.

In the private and local government sectors, a number of model solar codes have been developed:

1. Recommended Requirements to Code Officials for Solar Heating, Cooling and Hot Water Systems by BOCA (Building Officials & Code Administrators International, Inc.), ICBO (International Conference of Building Officials), SBCCI (Southern Building Code Congress International, Inc.), and NCSBCS (National Conference of States on Building Codes and Standards, Inc.).

2. Uniform Solar Energy Code—IAPMO.

3. County of Los Angeles Solar Energy Code—a good example of a local code.

In parallel efforts starting in the mid-1970s, numerous research projects were conducted by the national laboratories to develop standards and guide criteria to support the solar codes. At the National Bureau of Standards a number of areas were investigated, including these:

solar collector test methods,

solar thermal storage test methods,

solar domestic hot water heat test methods,

durability and reliability of collector cover plates,

durability and reliability of rubber seals,

durability and reliability of rubber hoses with various heat transfer fluids,

fire safety of heat transfer fluuids, and

performance measurement of active systems, passive systems and daylighting.

At Argonne National Laboratories, research work was carried out on the following: thermal storage, reliability and maintainability of solar energy systems and materials, and toxicity and other hazards of heat transfer fluids.

The Lawrence Berkeley Laboratory has focused research on other areas that have supported the development of codes and standards, principally daylighting performance and measurement, and building thermal mass performance.

Los Alamos National Laboratories in its extensive passive solar research program has provided data and information on passive heating and cooling that has been used in codes and standards development.

The Solar Energy Research Institute has conducted considerable research in support of codes and standards development. Notable among many areas are daylight measurement and passive systems performance.

The National Solar Data Network has provided a wealth of data useful in assessing code-related concerns in real buildings.

The work of government agencies has provided an extensive range of standards, guide criteria, and regulations that apply to federal programs. This work has fed into the private sector where major activity has also taken place in the development of standards.

These research efforts were beneficial to building designers since they established standardized procedures on which design calculations could be based and testing methods that could be specified to procure an industry-accepted level of performance. In addition to the national laboratories, the American Society of Heating, Refrigeration, and Air-Conditioning Engineers (ASHRAE), the American National Standards Institute (ANSI), and others developed specific requirements for testing of components and systems.

The codes and standards that were developed have several beneficial effects:

1. They have helped to set minimum performance levels for components and systems both for thermal performance and for durability and reliability. A system that complies with one of the federal standards will have a good prospect of performing well and being durable and reliable. For example, the requirements to withstand stagnation conditions will help ensure a long, productive life for solar collectors.

2. By setting reasonable and effective levels of safety performance, they reassure the consumer and thus foster the use of solar energy. An example of this is the double-wall heat exchanger requirements where toxic and/or nonpotable heat transfer fluids are employed.

3. By defining performance and quality levels, they have supported the effective administration of solar tax credits.

4. The test methods developed by NBS and ASHRAE have led to more uniform testing and reporting on solar collectors and DHW systems.

7.2.5.3 Building Energy Codes No discussion of the integration of solar energy systems into building design and the codes and standards that play a role in this would be complete without mentioning energy codes. Most energy codes exempt solar energy from the maximum allowable energy consumption budget. In many cases, this will require a designer to provide an analysis of the energy performance of the building incorporating the solar energy provisions. To assess adequately the solar energy contribution requires a thorough knowledge of the integrated action of the building and all its systems: architectural, mechanical, electrical, and so forth.

There are numerous energy conservation codes in effect and, in fact, practically every state has one of some level of effectiveness. Many base their codes on the ASHRAE Standard 90-75 or its updated version, 90A-1980. Other codes with nationwide applicability are the Basic/National Energy Conservation Code (BOCA) and the Code for Energy Conservation in New Building Construction (BOCA, ICBO, NCSBCS, SBCCI). The building Energy Performance Standards, though never put into law, have certainly fostered the concept of a comprehensive whole-building approach to energy design, which requires a thorough understanding of solar integration.

Solar System Regulations, Codes, and Guidelines

Argonne National Laboratory, 1980. *Interim Reliability and Materials Design Guidelines for Solar Domestic Hot Water Systems.*

ASHRAE, 1977. *Methods of Testing to Determine the Thermal Performance of Solar Collectors.*

ASHRAE, 1977. *Methods of Testing Thermal Storage Devices Based on Thermal Performance.*

ASHRAE, 1980. *Methods of Testing to Determine the Thermal Performance of Unglazed Flat-Plate Liquid-Type Solar Collectors.*

ASHRAE, 1981. *Methods of Testing Thermal Storage Devices with Electrical Input and Thermal Output Based on Thermal Performance.*

ASHRAE, 1981. *Methods of Testing to Determine the Thermal Performance of Solar Domestic Water Heating Systems.*

Building Officials and Code Administrators International, Inc. (BOCA), 1977. *Code for Energy Conservation in New Building Construction.*

Council of American Building Officials, 1980. *Recommended Requirements to Code Officials for Solar Heating, Cooling, and Hot Water Systems.*

County of Los Angeles, Department of County Engineer, 1978. *Solar Energy Code.*

References

Andersson, B., et al., 1984. *Energy Effects of Electric Lighting Control Alternatives in Response to Daylighting.* Berkeley, CA: Lawrence Berkeley Laboratory.

Appleton, J., 1975. *The Experience of Landscape.* New York: John Wiley & Sons.

AS/ISES, 1978. *Proceedings of the First Workshop on Control of Solar Energy Systems for Heating and Cooling,* E. F. Clark and F. deWinter, eds., Hyannis, MA, May 23–25, 1978, American Section of the International Solar Energy Society.

Balcomb, S. A., 1981. The impact of consumer/client issues on passive solar design. In *Proc. Sixth National Solar Conference.* Portland, OR, September 8–12, 1981. 6:419–422.

Banham, R., 1969. *The Architecture of the Well-Tempered Environment.* London: Architectural Press.

Fraker, H., April 1984. Formal speculations on thermal diagrams. In *Progressive Architecture,* pp. 104–108.

Givoni, B., 1969. *Man, Climate, and Architecture.* New York: Elsevier Publishing Company, Ltd.

Heerwagen, J. H., and R. Dean, 1984. Some reflections on psychological comfort and its application to energy conscious design. *Eighth National Passive Solar Conference Papers Preprint.* J. Hayes and D. Andrejko, eds., Santa Fe, NM, September 7–9, 1983, pp. 439–449.

International Association of Plumbing and Mechanical Engineers, 1976. *Uniform Solar Energy Code,* Los Angeles: International Association of Plumbing and Mechanical Engineers.

Johnson, W. S., and F. E. Pierce, 1980. Energy cost and analysis of commercial building shell characteristics and operating schedules. ORNL/CON-39. Oak Ridge, TN: Oak Ridge National Laboratory.

Kantrowitz, M., 1983. Occupant effects and interactions in passive solar commercial buildings. In *Proc. Eighth National Passive Solar Conference.* Santa Fe, NM, September 7–9, 1983, ASES, p. 433.

Kantrowitz, M., 1984. Report on occupancy evaluation from the passive solar commercial buildings program. In *Proc. of the 1984 Passive and Hybrid Solar Energy Update,* Washington, DC, September 5–7, 1984, p. 252.

Kroner, W. M., 1983. The impact of occupants on the performance of passive buildings. In *Proc. Eighth National Passive Solar Conference.* Santa Fe, NM, September 7–9, 1983, ASES, p. 445.

Lodge, T. L., and P. W. Kendall, 1984. *Component Report: Performance of Solar Collector Arrays and Collector Controllers in the National Solar Data Network.* Prepared for the Department of Energy, Silver Spring, MD: Vitro Corporation.

McLain, J. H., 1983. Size preferences and user reactions to direct gain and indirect gain configurations. *Eighth National Passive Solar Conference Papers Preprint,* J. Hayes and D. Andrejko, eds., Sata Fe, NM, September 7–9, 1983, pp. 461–466.

Olgyay, V. G., 1963. *Design with Climate: Bioclimatic Approach to Architectural Regionalism.* Princeton, NJ: Princeton University Press.

Ruegg, R. T., 1982. Acoustic benefits and costs of passive solar energy design. *Seventh National Passive Solar Conference Papers Preprint*, J. Hayes and C. B. Winn, eds., Knoxville, TN, August 30–September 1, 1982, pp. 589–594.

Sheet Metal and Air Conditioning Contractors' National Association. *Installation Standards.* Vienna, VA: Sheet Metal and Air Conditioning Contractors' National Association.

U.S. Department of Commerce, 1982. *Performance Criteria for Solar Heating and Cooling Systems in Commercial Buildings.*

U.S. Department of Commerce, 1984. *Performance Criteria for Solar Heating and Cooling Systems in Commercial Buildings.*

U.S. Department of Energy, March 1979a. *Reliability and Maintainability Evaluation of Solar Control Systems.*

U.S. Department of Energy, June 1979b. *Reliability and Material Performance of Solar Heating and Cooling Systems.*

U.S. Department of Energy, 1980. *Reliability and Maintainability Evaluation of Solar Collector and Manifold Interconnections.*

U.S. Department of Housing and Urban Development, 1977. *Minimum Property Standards Supplement.*

Wells, B. W. P., 1965. Subjective responses to the lighting installation in a modern office building and their design implications. *Building Science* 1:57–68.

Contributors

Bruce N. Anderson

Bruce Anderson has been involved with solar building design since 1972. Mr. Anderson is founder and President of Total Environmental Action, Inc., an interdisciplinary consulting firm in conservation and renewable energy. He has served as designer/consultant on dozens of solar buildings, and as principal investigator on numerous state and federal government research contracts. He was the cofounder and publisher of *Solar Age* magazine. Mr. Anderson has authored and co-authored the following books: *Solar Energy: Fundamental in Building Design*, *The Solar Home Book*, *Passive Solar Energy*, and *Passive Solar Design Handbook*, *vol. 1*. Mr. Anderson holds a Master of Architecture degree from the Massachusetts Institute of Technology.

Gregory E. Franta

Gregory Franta is President of Ensar Group, Inc., an international energy-design consulting firm with offices in Colorado and Maryland. As an architect and energy design consultant, Mr. Franta has helped design over 400 energy-efficient buildings. He has worked on projects in over thirty states and six foreign countries. He is involved with both commercial and residential buildings, specializing in passive solar heating and cooling, and daylighting.

Franta has coauthored and edited many technical publications including *Solar Design Workbook* and *Energy Design*.

Mr. Franta received a Master of Architecture degree specializing in Solar Technology from Arizona State University and a Bachelor of Architecture degree from the University of Colorado.

Harry T. Gordon

Harry T. Gordon, AIA, is a Principal in the Washington, DC, office of Burt Hill Kosar Rittelmann Associates, an architectural/engineering and energy research firm. He has extensive experience in the field of energy-conserving architectural design and solar system analysis and design, and has served as a consultant to both the public and private sectors. Mr. Gordon was instrumental in the Department of Energy's Passive Nonresidential Building Program which analyzed the design, cost, and performance of buildings using solar energy for heating, daylighting, and cooling. This resulted in the award-winning book, *Commercial Building Design: Integrating Climate, Comfort and Cost* (winner of the 1988 Progressive Architecture Research Award). He is a member of the board of directors of the American Solar Energy Society. Mr. Gordon received Bachelor of Architecture and Bachelor of Science degrees in building technology from Rensselaer Polytechnic Institute.

Major contributions to this chapter were made by John Holton, AIA; N. Scott Jones, AIA; Justin Estoque; Donald Anderson; and William Fisher, AIA.

Bion D. Howard

Bion Howard is currently Senior Energy Analyst for NAHB's National Research Center and is professionally affiliated with the National Research Center, the National Association of Home Builders, ASHRAE, SEIA, ASTM, ASES, and the Construction Specifications Institute.

His major accomplishments in solar energy research include extensive performance monitoring and modeling of passive solar residential buildings, and numerous publications on this and other research in the solar and energy conservation field. He has been a member of the ASHRAE Technical Committee for Solar Utilization for several years, chaired the PSIC Technical Committee for two years, and now chairs the Passive Solar and Energy Conservation Division of SEIA.

He was a member of the ASES Board of Directors, cochaired the *Building with the Sun* event at the 1985 ASES Conference, and authored the comparative report, *Performance of Passive Solar Space Heating Systems*.

Harrison Fraker, Dean of the College of Architecture and Landscape Architecture at the University of Minnesota, reviewed Mr. Howard's chapter and contributed his suggestions.

Douglas Kelbaugh

Doug Kelbaugh is Chairman of the Department of Architecture at the University of Washington. He previously taught architectural design at the University of Pennsylvania and the New Jersey Institute of Technology. He received Bachelor of Arts and Master of Architecture degrees from Princeton University and has been visiting critic at the University of North Carolina at Charlotte, University of Miami, and the Royal Danish Academy of Fine Arts, as well as guest speaker at over a dozen other schools of architecture in the United States and Europe. His passive solar home built in 1974 was the first in the United States to use a Trombe wall. His firm, Kelbaugh and Lee of Princeton, New Jersey, has won seventeen design awards in the last ten years. The firm's work, noted for its integration of aesthetic and energy concerns, has been published in over 100 periodicals and books. Its Roosevelt Solar Village won a national AIA Honor Award in 1985.

Edward Mazria

Edward Mazria has designed over three million square feet of building space in twenty-five years of architectural practice. He was Principal in Charge for design for the Mount Airy Library. Mr. Mazria holds a Bachelor of Architecture degree from Pratt Institute and a Master of Architecture degree from the University of New Mexico. He has taught architectural design, passive solar energy, planning, and programming methodology at the University of Oregon, University of Colorado, University of California at Los Angeles, and the University of New Mexico. As a principal in Passive Solar Associates he conducted a national seminar program for hundreds of architects, engineers, builders, owner-builders, and government employees throughout the country and abroad. In addition to architectural design and teaching, Mr. Mazria conducted extensive research on daylighting and solar energy, culminating in *The Passive Solar Energy Book*, published by Rodale Press, Inc. He is a member of the American Institute of Architects and holds a NCARB Certificate.

Donald Prowler

Don Prowler is an architect and Assistant Professor of Architecture at the University of Pennsylvania. He received a Bachelor of Arts degree in Art History from Princeton University—where he is currently a visiting assistant professor—and a Master of Architecture degree from the University of Pennsylvania in 1975. In his practice, teaching, and writing Mr. Prowler has consistently explored the relationship of technology and architecture. His activities have included cochairing the Second National Passive Solar Conference and editing its proceedings, receiving a Progressive Architecture award for research on architectural curriculum development, serving on a National Research Council Committee to review the Office of Conservation of the U.S. Department of Energy, and winning national and local design competitions. Most recently, Mr. Prowler has published the book, *Modest Mansions*, in which he examines basic residential design principles.

Layne Ridley

Ms. Ridley has been involved with the building industry and solar architecture for over a decade. During the five years she served as Executive Director of the Passive Solar Industries Council, she oversaw the creation and dissemination of scores of articles, newsletters, and other publications promoting intelligent passive solar design and construction. In conjunction with the Solar Energy Research Institute and the National Association of Home Builders, she also coordinated the development of PSIC's *Builder Guidelines*, the most sophisticated tool currently available for designing and constructing passive solar buildings. Most recently she authored *Bright Ideas*, a brief illustrated history of passive solar accomplishments over the last decade.

Author Index

Subject Index